Voices from Mutira

Change in the Lives of Rural Gikuyu Women, 1910–1995

second edition

Jean Davison
with the women of Mutira

BOULDER
LONDON

All photographs by Jean Davison
Maps, figures, and time line
by Jean Davison
and Lesli Brooks

Published in the United States of America in 1996 by
Lynne Rienner Publishers, Inc.
1800 30th Street, Boulder, Colorado 80301

and in the United Kingdom by
Lynne Rienner Publishers, Inc.
3 Henrietta Street, Covent Garden, London WC2E 8LU

Library of Congress Cataloging-in-Publication Data
Davison, Jean, 1937–
Voices from Mutira : change in the lives of rural Gikuyu Women, 1910–1995 / by Jean Davison. — 2nd ed.
p. cm.
"June 14, 1995."
Includes bibliographical references.
ISBN 1-55587-602-1 (pbk. : alk. paper)
1. Women, Kikuyu—Kenya—Kirinyaga District—Interviews. 2. Women, Kikuyu—Kenya—Kirinyaga District—Social conditions. 3. Rural women—Kenya—Kirinyaga District—Interviews. 4. Rural women—Kenya—Kirinyaga District—Social conditions. I. Title.
DT433.545.K55D38 1996
305.48'8963954067626—dc20 95-46622
CIP

British Cataloguing in Publication Data
A Cataloguing in Publication record for this book is available from the British Library.

Printed and bound in the United States of America

∞ The paper used in this publication meets the requirements of the American National Standard for Permanence of Paper for Printed Library Materials Z39.48-1984.

5 4 3 2

Contents

Preface to the Second Edition

More than ten years have passed since I first collected the life histories of women in Mutira Location, Kenya. Since that time I have visited Mutira roughly every third year, which has enabled me to track the continuing changes in the lives of each narrator. My visit in 1992 was eventful because the smallholders' tea strike was in process and the multiparty elections were due to take place at the end of December. Returning in 1994 gave me a chance to see how the results of each had affected the life narrators. I had two goals that year: to update the life histories to reflect changes in each woman's life in the past decade and to interview women who had participated in Kenya's liberation struggles for an article on women and nationalist struggles. I found that several of the women whom I had interviewed in 1983 were among those who were involved actively on behalf of the Mau Mau freedom fighters.

My thanks go to those who have helped with the preparation of this edition. David Northrup has used the text in courses, and his historical lens helped me better target the collection to the needs of historians. Peter Wang'oo and Margaret Wangeci Gatimu, both Gikuyu scholars, reviewed the manuscript for corrections in my use of their language. Susan Geiger's feminist perspective on women's life narratives pushed me to reevaluate my own work. Lynne Rienner, who helped launch *Voices* initially, has enthusiastically supported the project and has assisted at every turn. She is a pleasure of a publisher. Last but not least, Gia Hamilton shepherded the manuscript to its final form—no easy task. Her care is much appreciated.

Many people on two continents contributed to my work on change in the lives of rural Gikuyu women. First are two mentors, one American, the other Kenyan. Without the support of Shirley Brice Heath of the English Department at Stanford University to pursue the study of women's lives through retrospective accounts, it is doubtful the project would have begun. Without the determination and support of Stephen N. Mutunga of Kenyatta University, who took care of many technical details and later gave me the space to write, it is doubtful the work would have been completed. In addition, I would like to thank David Abernethy of the Political Science Department, Stanford University, for his helpful suggestions prior to my research and James L. Gibbs, Jr., of the Anthropology Department and Kennell Jackson of the History Department for their willingness to read the initial manuscript and for their valuable contributions as scholars of Africa.

Special acknowledgment goes to the unfailing generosity of the seven women whose narratives are recorded here. They spent many hours sharing their lives and voices with me—*nĩ wega muno muno* (many, many thanks). Erastus Mwai, then chief of Mutira Location, greatly assisted my entrance into the location and subsequent work. Janet Mithamo, Teresia Gĩciku Karimi, and Flora Karoki contributed to my orientation to the community and became valuable friends. The Muriũki family, with whom I stayed, were my extended family in the field and graciously shared with me their daily lives, observations, and humor. Three women's group leaders, Joyce Wamithu of *Uritu wa Gatwe,* Pricilla Njagi of *Winyerekia,* and Margaret Wagithi of *Utheri wa Kanitha,* welcomed me to their women's groups and provided valuable background on the activities of the groups. Finally, my research assistant, Joyce Karuana Kimanyi, spent many hours helping to transcribe the audio-taped life-history interviews. Without Karuana's assistance my research would have been a far greater task. I wish to thank the Stanford Center for International Studies and the Hewlett Foundation for making it financially possible for me to do the research in Kenya. In addition, to the Kenyan government, Kenya National Archives staff, Department of Adult Education, the Women's Bureau, and Maendeleo Ya Wanawake Organization for their hospitality and assistance—*asante sana.*

Jean Davison

Time Line of Major Events in the Narrators' Lives

	Wanjiku	Wamutira	Watoro	Wangeci	Wanoi	Nyambura	Wanja
1995						•Church wedding	•Inherits land
1990		•New house •Gets land		•Death			•New house •Gets shop
1985				•Joins adult ed. class	•Church wedding •TBA training	•4th son •3rd son •Knitting business	
1980	•Widowed		•Father's death	•Joins women's church group	•Adult ed. •Joins women's self-help group	•2nd son •Married •1st son	•Preschool teacher •Graduates secondary school
1975			•Joins Catholic church				•Secondary school, Mwea
1970				•Widowed		•Works as maid •Leaves school	
1965	•Husband returns from Voi	•Joins Anglican church •3rd wife arrives		•Church wedding	•Joins Catholic church	•Enters school •Baptized, Catholic church	•Confirmed, Anglican church
1960	•Returns home	•Daughter's death •Husband returns home	•Separates from husband	•Returns from Nairobi •Baptized, Anglican church	•Returns home	•Birth	•Primary school, Gatwe •Returns home
1955	•Interned	•Son's death •Husband takes 2nd wife	•Daughter's death •Released •Interned	•Moves to Nairobi			•Interned with her family
1950	•Liberation war •Husband to Voi to work •Salvation	•Returns home •1st child •Goes to Nairobi •Married	•Married	•Daughter born •Married	•Acts as Mau Mau scout •Interned •1st child •Married		•Birth
1945	•3rd son	•Irua •Mbuci/matũ		•Irua	•Becomes mid-wife •Irua •Ear piercing		
1940	•2nd son •1st son •Adopts Christianity	•Raised in headman's compound	•Irua •Matũ •Mbuci	•Mbuci/matũ •Father's death	•First year primary school		
1935	•Remarries •Daughter's death •Widowed				•Birth		
1930	•Daughter born •Married	•Birth	•Birth	•Birth			
1925	•Irua •Mbuci/matũ						
1920							
1915							
1910	•Birth						

1

Introduction: Change in Mutira Women's Lives

African women are negotiating increasingly complex changes, from subtle maneuvers to seismic shifts, that affect their personal lives. At times these changes are caused by externalities—fluctuations in the global market that impinge on the price of their export crops, for instance, or the fallout of policy prescriptions crafted by donor agencies to influence the direction and quality of "development." Women in Kenya's Mutira Location, far from the state's center in Nairobi, maintain a certain ambivalence about the government's ability to deliver development benefits that would improve their lives. Operating as groups or as individuals, they weigh various options, and some, notably through women's groups, are able to leverage resources beyond the state. It is within the context of districts, localities, and neighborhoods that rural Mutira women experience the greatest efficacy and are most effective in negotiating change.

The same women, however, periodically experience crises and transitions in their personal lives that demand their immediate attention and focused energy. During such times, changes occurring at other levels dim by comparison. What was true in 1983–1984, when these life narratives were first collected, still holds in 1995, as the following vignette from the field illustrates. It also positions me within the specific context of gathering rural Mutira women's life narratives.

Vignette from the Field, 1983

She came running down the track under the green canopy of banana trees, screaming at no one and everyone, her arms flailing, her eyes full of terror. At the time, with my rudimentary understanding of Kikuyu, I could decipher only part of what she was shouting, but the smell of fear needed no words. I stood still, all senses alert, and tried to quiet the instinct to flee. Having been in Mutira for only three days, I was wary of my reactions. Instead of vaulting, I found myself being carried along by a gathering crowd of peasants to a river, a river that moments earlier had swallowed the terror-stricken woman's husband.

A man, pewter gray in color, was stretched out on a grassy knoll above the riverbank, face up. He wore the mask of death. His four-year-old son stood over him looking bewildered. People gathered around them spoke in agitated tones, explaining that, while cleaning his wife's cooking pot after the midday meal, the man had slipped, fallen into the river, and drowned. The woman—one of many I would come to know in Mutira—was now a widow.

In a few short minutes her life had been transformed from one of relative security as a married woman to the insecurity of widowhood. The way she struggled and coped with this unforeseen event could alter her life course. Part of the transition meant learning new skills to ensure the survival of her family. The change also meant modifying her behavior to fit a new social category. Both were to become part of this life transition.

What was the conjugal context of this scene? What does it tell us about changing gender relations in Mutira? We must not lose track of who was washing the cooking pot. It could have been that the wife was preoccupied with cultivating one of her fields and did not plan to return home to cook the midday meal. Rather, she had left food from the previous evening in a pot for her husband to heat over the cooking fire. Or it could be that she had cooked the midday meal of *ugali* (maize meal cooked with water), but he was washing up.

The space in which the husband was washing the pot cannot be described as "private" or "domestic." He was washing the pot in a public river used by many people. The only private space in a rural Mutira home is the sleeping quarters or bedroom. That most domestic activities occur in public spaces occupied by both genders is contrary to early liberal feminist notions that identified women with a private sphere and men with public spheres (e.g., M. Rosaldo 1974; Sanday 1974). It became rapidly apparent that the public/male–private/female dichotomy had no place in rural Mutira.[1] Thus began my Mutira education.

The Collection's Purpose

The ways in which rural African women in one Kenyan location mediate change in their individual and collective lives is the major concern in this book. The collection examines the lives of seven women ranging in age from twenty-three to seventy-five years when their narratives were first collected. They were ten years older when their narratives were updated in 1994. They live in Mutira Location, Kirinyaga District, Kenya (see Map 1.1). From the time the oldest woman was born in 1910, on the eve of major European settlement, to the time the youngest woman married thirty

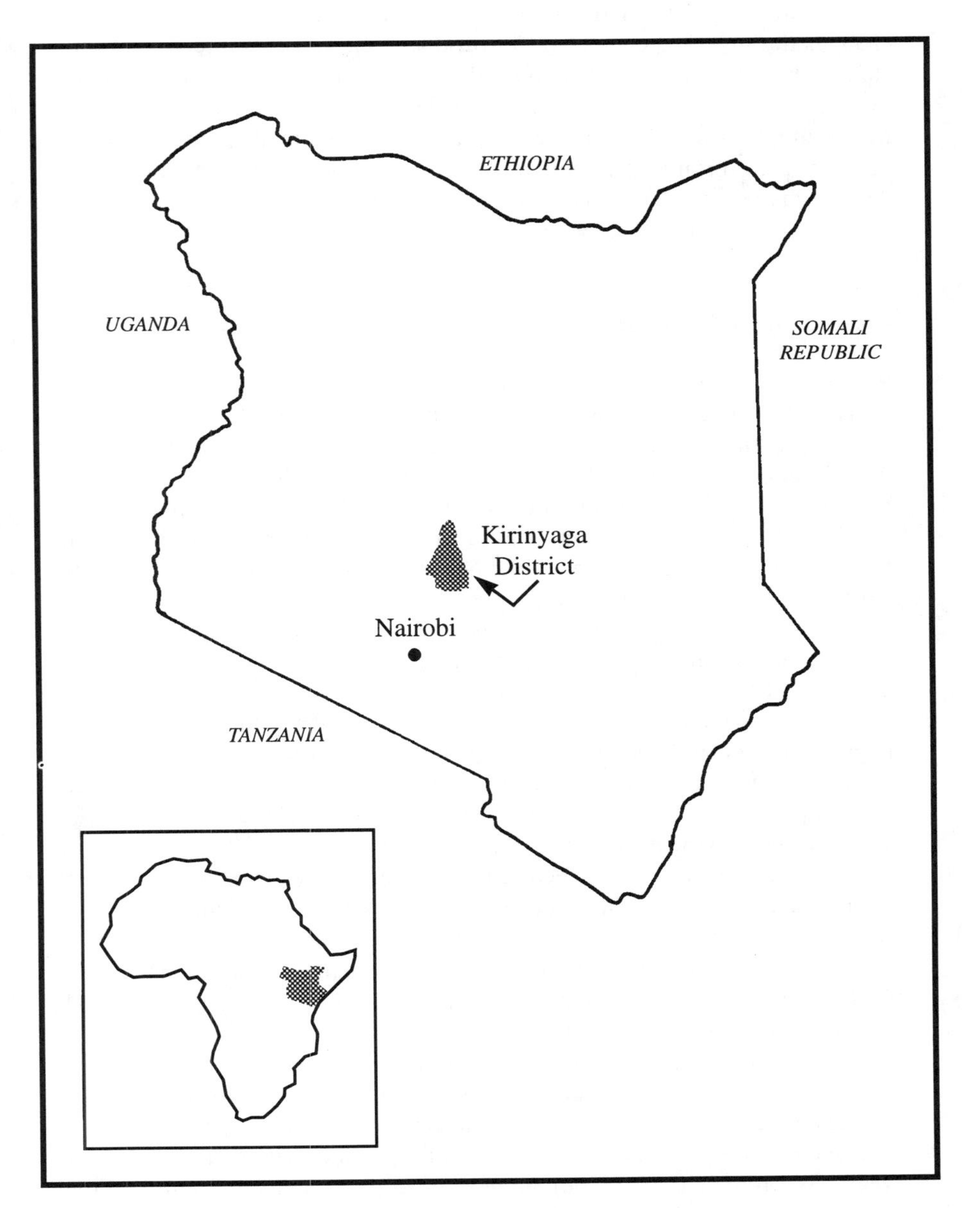

Map 1.1 Kenya, Showing Kirinyaga District

years after independence was a period of rapid social and economic transformation in this East African country. Tracking key social and historical changes through the perspectives of rural women was one objective of this study. The other was to learn about the transitions and transformations in the women's individual lives and how they responded to those changes. My assumption was that women actively participate in shaping the course of their lives through the decisions they make and the actions they take. Another assumption was that change and learning share a symbiotic relationship that is integral to people's lifelong development.

Perceptions of Change

Rapid advances in media technology force us to witness and learn about catastrophic events, such as drought and mass migrations due to civil wars, affecting entire populations in Africa. Yet the significance of such events in the daily lives of individuals is elusive. We see a Hutu or Tutsi woman vacantly holding a dying child in a refugee camp but do not learn about the survival strategies this woman employed to save her other children from hunger, disease, or ethnic genocide. Nor do we learn how she will change her life in the future to reflect her present experience.

Change as a multifaceted phenomenon acts as either an opportunity or a constraint depending on the significance a person attaches to a given situation. What constitutes a positive change for one person—for example, the introduction of a new farming method—may turn out to have a negative effect on another depending on the resources at the disposal of the two farmers. Economic differences between peasant farmers influence their opportunities for exploiting change (Boserup 1970; Due 1985; Guyer 1984; Moock 1986; Berry 1993; Bassett and Crummey 1993).

Macrolevel shifts affecting the lives of Gikuyu women result from historical and sociocultural forces often working in tandem. These are forces over which rural women have little or no control. At the same time, idiosyncratic changes occurring within the life span of a particular woman (a death in the family, relocation to a new place, the timing of biological changes) contribute to shaping her life.

Even though maturation, or biological growth, affects all individuals, the rate of physical change and its significance varies for individuals. For example, although the onset of menarche for Gikuyu girls occurs on average at 15.9 years of age, it can occur anywhere between 10.5 and 17 years (Worthman 1985:3). For some Gikuyu girls, menarche must follow normative sociocultural practices designed to mark the transition from childhood to adulthood, whereas for others it merely signifies a potential for reproduction. The social significance of this biological event varies greatly. What a girl learns in the process of the transition to adulthood stays with her for a lifetime.

Change and learning most often are linked in a mutually supportive pact. Learning new ideas leads to change. In turn, change prompts an individual to learn new skills and behaviors. The two, change and learning, enjoy a symbiotic relationship that becomes apparent in a life narrative.

Learning, in its broadest context, involves the acquisition of new knowledge, new attitudes, and skills, usually leading to a change in behavior. The acquisition of knowledge, as Hawkesworth (1989:549) reminds us, occurs within "the context of socialization and enculturation." The maturing adolescent, for instance, negotiates a complex bundle of lessons that includes new knowledge of her body and its reproductive potential, new skills expected of an adult woman in her society, and attitudes that usually are consistent with her particular age group. This bundle of lessons causes her behavior to change in a variety of ways that may or may not be congruent with the social context in which she lives. If the social context is rapidly changing—as it is in rural Kenya—the knowledge, skills, and attitudes she acquires from Gikuyu elders in the community may be dissonant with what she learns from schooling or her peers. Learning, to be relevant, must be consonant with new realities. It demands periodic shifts that provoke internal and external struggles.

Learning occurs in many places, more often outside of schools than inside them. Over the course of a life, a person is apt to learn only 25 percent of what she or he knows in a classroom setting (Cropley 1981). The rest occurs in the home, community, workplace, or through travel. As Gikuyu anthropologist Jomo Kenyatta reminds us in *Facing Mt. Kenya,* "education begins at the time of birth and ends with death" (1968 [1938]: 9). What knowledge did Mutira women acquire through indigenous means that helped prepare them for survival and change? What has been the impact of Western schooling on indigenous learning modes; on changing Gikuyu social formations?

Change affects individual Kenyan women differently, depending on the locality in which they live (rural or urban), and within that locality on their age, class, ethnicity or race, educational background, and personality. Class differences between the Mutira women in this collection are limited. Those who live at the top of ridges near Gatwe or Gathuthuma have access to slightly more land than those who live at lower elevations near Kagumo. Also, one of the women—Wanja—has more education than was the norm in her sample cohort or for the total sample of 101 women with which I began. The mean for the total sample was 3.7 years, but 60 percent of the women had never been to school. Wanja completed secondary school, which enabled her to secure a teaching job in Gatwe. This gave her an advantage that the other narrators do not have.

Six of the women are peasant farmers. Wanja combines teaching with farming. Other Mutira women with a similar level of education to Wanja's have jobs in teaching, nursing, or as government clerics.

The greatest diversity among the women comes from their age—that is, the age stage in which they find themselves. The older women are more conversant with changes that occurred in Gikuyu society because of the impact of colonialism, and again with independence in 1963. The younger women are more attuned to changes that have been taking place since independence. In personality, each woman is unique. Personal differences in aptitudes and interests have an effect on the ways women confront, resist, mediate, or embrace and utilize a variety of changes in their lives.

Organization of the Collection

I have, in this introductory chapter, two main objectives. The first is to review critical macrolevel changes in Kenya most affecting Mutira women over the last decade since the life histories were collected. The choice of which changes to focus on was influenced by my 1994 conversations with six of the narrators (one woman had died) and with other Mutira women who assisted in the initial research and who were keenly aware of changes affecting women in the location and district.

The second objective is more generic. First, I provide an expanded discussion of issues connected with person-centered ethnography as a life history methodology. Second, I discuss the use of life history as a genre and relate it to shifts that have occurred in life history production over the past decade with reference to African women's narratives.

Chapter 2 provides a profile of Mutira Location—the physical and geographical setting—and outlines social and historical changes that have occurred over the period of the women's combined life spans. The seven narratives follow, each with an introduction to provide a sketch of the narrator and to illuminate her particular relationship with me. Analysis of the life histories is left to the last chapter to allow the individual women to tell their stories, uninterrupted, before pulling together the threads of their lives for comparison.

Major Changes Affecting Mutira Women: 1984–1994

In reviewing the events of the last decade with Mutira women, three macrolevel changes impacting their lives stand out: (1) women's diminished political power at the national level; (2) the effects of structural adjustment on their productive lives, and (3) the effects of changes in attitudes toward sexuality and contraception on their reproductive lives.

Change in Women's Political Power

Since independence, new opportunities for education, better health care, new farming systems, and access to commodities previously unavailable have had a major impact on rural Kenyan women's lives. At the same time, changes in women's access to key decisionmaking arenas such as the national Parliament plummeted before making a comeback in the 1992 multiparty elections.

The United Nations Women's Decade Conference held in Nairobi in 1985 focused global media attention on Kenyan women's status on a number of fronts. The findings on women's political status were mixed. Even though a Women's Bureau had been established within the Ministry of Social Services, its ability to expand women's rights was limited to working mainly with women's groups. At the national level, few women were in key government positions. When Kenyan women, urban and rural, called for more women in national decisionmaking positions, President Daniel Arap Moi responded that God did not make a mistake in making man head of the household, and that even if women were appointed to high decisionmaking positions, they were still expected to be subordinate to their husbands at home (Ahlberg 1991:150). Women's representation at the national level was more symbolic than real. Some women, such as the environmental activist Wangari Mathai, chose to work outside the state apparatus. Her struggles with President Moi over preserving Uhuru Park in Nairobi drew international attention and are well known in Kenya. Without her efforts, a high-rise office complex would have filled the space long used as a people's park.

The degree to which women lost political ground in the 1980s is demonstrated by changes in their participation in Kenya's national legislative body. By 1991, Kenya had the lowest female legislative participation rate in Africa (see Table 1.1). Six women were members of the Kenyan Parliament in 1994 (3.2 percent of the total membership).[2]

Women's participation in the Parliament declined by half from 1974 to 1991 before it made a comeback in the 1992 elections (Table 1.2). The women who won seats in Parliament in December 1992 were mainly members of opposition parties rather than the Kenya African National Union (KANU), the ruling party.

Kenyan women's groups look to their sisters in Parliament to leverage support and funding for their development projects. Without a critical mass of women in Parliament, rural women in the mid-1980s were finding it increasingly difficult to sustain government support for their income-generating activities (see Davison 1985; Stampp 1986; Ahlberg 1991). Instead, they learned to tap other, nongovernmental resources. Whether having a critical mass of women Members of Parliament (MPs) will in actuality make a difference to rural women's lives remains to be seen; so far, Kenya's Parliament has had only token representation.

Table 1.1 Percentage of Women in National Parliaments for Selected Countries in Africa, 1991

Country	Percentage of Women in Parliament
Côte d'Ivoire	4.6
The Gambia	7.8
Kenya	1.1
Malawi	9.8
Mozambique	15.7
Rwanda	17.1
Senegal	12.5
Tanzania	11.0
Togo	3.9
Uganda	12.2
Zambia	5.1
Zimbabwe	12.0

Source: Inter-Parliamentary Union, 1991, Table II: 26.

Table 1.2 Women Representatives in Kenya's Parliament

Year	No. of Members	No. of Women Members	Percentage of Women
1974	172	6	3.5
1979	172	5	2.9
1983	172	3	1.7
1988	188	2	1.1
1993	188	6	3.2

Source: Inter-Parliamentary Union, 1991.

Equally disturbing to women's minimal participation in the Parliament is the transformation of Maendeleo ya Wanawake (Progress of Women) from an independent national women's organization to an arm of KANU.[3] Maendeleo ya Wanawake, after independence, functioned as a nongovernmental organization (NGO). However, in 1988 it was co-opted by KANU, the political party in power. The result is that Maendeleo ya

Wanawake no longer functions as an independent advocate of rural women's groups. It has become politicized by the state. Rural women, such as those in Mutira, are skeptical of the organization's motives. They have learned that the state can be an obstacle to change rather than an agent of change and empowerment.[4]

At another level, Kenyan politicians—largely male—depend on rural women to support them with votes and campaign activities, usually as "cheer leaders" (song and dance groups) for standing candidates. As Gikuyu scholar Beth Maina Ahlberg (1991:131) points out, "election campaign periods are especially critical for the exploitation of women's groups" throughout Kenya. Women's groups assisted male candidates in the 1983 elections when I was there and again in the 1992 elections. Candidates try to attract women's groups' support not only for their visual performance value but because in rural districts women outnumber men, and their votes are crucial. Promising support and inputs that may not be forthcoming in the future, politicians use the women's group fora to push their agendas and to control local social formations (Ahlberg 1991).

The disparity between men's and women's political power decreased somewhat in urban areas with municipal elections in 1992, but in rural Mutira women see few differences. The new political opposition parties in Central Province—the Democratic Party (DP) led by former Vice President Mwai Kibaki of Nyeri District, and FORD-A led by Kenneth Matiba of Murang'a District—were perceived by Mutira women with whom I spoke in August 1992 to offer a chance for political change. After the election, these women maintained that "many Mutira women" had supported the DP candidates. Nationwide, however, only 23 seats were won by the DP; the largest number of seats went to KANU (Ajulu 1993). Only 2 percent of voters in Central Province had voted for Moi (Ajulu 1993). Mutira women, including the life narrators with whom I spoke in 1994, were discouraged with the political process. Apathy had set in.

Structural Adjustment and Its Effects on Women's Production

In the last decade rural Mutira women have experienced escalating inflation coupled with slumping agricultural prices for the export crops they produce (tea and coffee). The buying power of the Kenya shilling dropped significantly before rallying in 1995. Export tea prices slid precipitiously after 1984, and coffee, whose global market price rose to an all-time high in 1986, suffered a setback thereafter. Although the latter half of the 1980s saw a modest economic recovery, macroeconomic imbalances continued, with Kenya's budget deficit reaching 5.6 percent of gross domestic product (GDP) by 1990/1991 (World Bank 1994:254). Real GDP growth was only 2.3 percent in 1991 but slid to 0.4 percent in 1992. Meanwhile the inflation rate accelerated from 20 percent in 1991 to 100 percent in the second quarter of 1993 (World Bank 1994:2).

In April 1992 the government of Kenya agreed with the International Monetary Fund (IMF) to reestablish a fiscally sound macroeconomic adjustment program, and in December 1993 a one-year extended Structural Adjustment Loan Facility was implemented (World Bank 1994).

Structural adjustment is not a term that has any meaning to rural Mutira women, but its social and economic effects are acutely felt. By way of illustration, not only were rural smallholders getting less for what they produced in the latter half of the 1980s and early 1990s, but the cost of essential commodities used by rural women had escalated since 1984. One of the narrators, Wanoi, related that whereas a loaf of bread had cost 7.50 Kenya shillings in rural Mutira in the mid-1980s, by 1994 it cost Ksh. 15.00, twice as much. In 1984 a loaf of bread in Nairobi cost roughly Ksh. 3.00, whereas by 1990 it had risen to Ksh. 5.77 (Kenya, Central Bureau of Statistics 1991:274). It is notable that whereas bread cost Ksh. 7.50 in Mutira in the mid-1980s, it cost less than half that in Nairobi, if Wanoi's memory is accurate. Notwithstanding, the difference between rural and urban prices is not inconsequential; transportation accounts for part of the high cost of commodities in rural areas.

Even though the inflation rate dropped to 55 percent in the third quarter of 1993, it increased again in the early part of 1994 when I revisited women in Mutira. They were most concerned about the downward spiral of their economic situation. "Things have gotten much worse economically," was the general consensus. One woman who produces tea explained, "The price of everything keeps going up, but we have not seen much increase in what we get paid for our tea."

For rural Mutira women structural adjustment translates to a reduced quality of living and increased anxiety over their economic future. As important as the macrolevel changes that affect their productive lives, however, are the changes that affect their reproductive lives.

Lessons Learned: Change in Sexuality and Reproduction

Attitudes toward sexuality and reproduction have undergone a dramatic change from the first quarter of the 1900s, when the oldest woman in this collection was going through *Irua*, the initiation ceremony marking the transition to adulthood. Knowledge and attitudes toward sexuality and reproduction have also shifted since the youngest women were going through biological maturation without the ceremony in the 1970s. A major factor influencing changes in sexual attitudes and behavior has been Kenya's family-planning campaign.

The Gikuyu historically depended upon communal, social responsibility to monitor sexuality and control reproduction (Cagnolo 1933; Kinoti 1983). The socially sanctioned practices through which sexuality was controlled, and information and skills about reproduction were transmitted from elders to the youngest generation of adults, varied. Practices that were critical to socialization in sexuality were: *Irua*, the extended initiation during which married women sang and danced *gitiiro* to teach young women about sexuality and responsible reproduction; *ngwiko*, a socially accepted practice whereby newly initiated youth of both sexes were allowed to sleep together and engage in sexual play and experimentation without intercourse under a strict code of behavior in a communally controlled environment designed to prohibit premarital pregnancy (Kenyatta 1968 [1938]; Lambert 1956; Ahlberg 1991); prenatal and postnatal sexual taboos that involved sexual abstinence on the part of a couple from the moment a pregnant woman felt life until she had completed breast-feeding a child—often two to three years (Worthman and Whiting 1987; Ahlberg 1991). Co-wives or lovers were expected to fulfill the sexual needs of a husband during the period of a wife's lactation.

All of the foregoing practices are described and defended by the older women narrators in this collection as integral to the Gikuyu way of life prior to missionary activities and "modernization."

The value that Gikuyu placed on communal responsibility for sexuality and reproduction began to be replaced in the 1970s and 1980s by an ethic that emphasized individual responsibility in sexual matters. A change in household formation contributed to the shift. The exigencies of smaller, single-family dwellings where a husband and wife shared the same house and same bed, instead of having separate houses within the same compound, made abstinence more difficult and the use of "technical solutions" for controlling fertility more appealing (Ahlberg 1991). In addition, husbands involved in circulatory migrant labor, who return home to their families once a week or once a month, expect their wives to meet their sexual needs regardless of a wife's reproductive cycle. This periodic separation has put additional sexual pressure on women as wives.

In addition to changes in housing arrangements and cyclical male labor emigration, the campaign of the state—orchestrated by Family Planning Association of Kenya (FPAK)—to overcome Kenya's escalating population growth in the late 1970s and 1980s (see Table 1.3) has resulted in a change in attitudes toward both sexuality and reproduction. Women (and men) have increasingly become dependent on technical devices (pills, coils, condoms, and tubal ligation) distributed by FPAK, rather than practices such as *ngwiko* and abstinence, to control fertility.

Contraceptive use among Kenya's citizenry increased from "under 20 percent" of the population in the mid-1980s (Ahlberg 1991:10)

Table 1.3 Population Growth Rate per Year, Kenya, 1979–1992

Year	Growth rate (%)
1979	3.8
1982	4.0
1984	3.6
1990	3.4
1992	3.0

Sources: Kenya, Central Bureau of Statistics, 1984; UNICEF 1990; World Bank 1994.

to 33 percent by 1992 (World Bank 1994:255). Significantly, Kirinyaga District, where Mutira is located, had a contraceptive use rate that exceeded the national average—52 percent in 1990—making it the district with the highest acceptance rate in Kenya at the time (*Daily Nation*, September 1990:4). To illustrate that the use of contraception has, indeed, begun to take hold, in 1984 when the life histories were first collected, a woman had on average 7.7 children during her childbearing years. By 1993 the fertility rate for Kenyan women had dropped to 5.4 children per woman (World Bank 1994:250).

FPAK's family-planning messages and active outreach to rural communities through locally trained community-based distributors (CBDs), who educate others in their communities about contraceptive methods and distribute contraceptives, has paid off. By way of illustration, Nyambura, the youngest narrator, who had refused the idea of using contraceptives in 1984 for religious reasons, by 1994 was using the pill.

With the introduction of contraceptives has come a new sexual morality, especially among young people. Although Gikuyu mores prevented unmarried girls from becoming pregnant forty years ago, such constraints no longer exist. The consequence in Mutira, as elsewhere (see Mbilinyi 1985 for Tanzania), is increased numbers of unmarried teenage mothers. As older Mutira women, who are the mothers of these teenage mothers, were beginning to realize in 1984, the new morality could increase their own burdens; it was a case of double jeopardy because they ended up raising their daughters' infant children in the daughter's absence. I visited several homes in 1994 where this was the case.

The previous sections have outlined major macrolevel changes impacting Mutira women's lives over the past decade. Most were directly impacted by the consequences of structural adjustment and were directly or indirectly affected by the changes in sexuality and family planning. They varied in their interest in national politics but were in general agreement that a political change was needed if the lives of rural women were to improve. Much more subtle are the shifts in their personal lives. Many of the life narrators had been affected by health problems over the last decade. But some managed to overcome these setbacks and made small gains in their lives. Two women became beneficiaries of a law passed in 1991 extending land inheritance rights to women.

In the following section, we consider the process through which the life narratives were collected and place the discussion within the context of subsequent issues raised in the 1980s concerning life history research and textual production.

Life Histories as Documents of Change

The Case for Life History Research

My interest in life history research was kindled oceans away from Africa. In New Zealand in 1979, where I was researching various aspects of change in Maori women's lives, I came across anthropologist Anne Salmond's engaging life history of an older Maori woman, *Amiria: The Life Story of a Maori Woman* (1975). I talked with Salmond about the methodology she had employed and became eager to try a collaborative life history approach. It was my conviction then that in addition to investigating the cultural category of "women" we needed to be listening to individual women's voices—especially those from cultures and societies different from our own. While in New Zealand I collected and recorded, in English, two brief life histories of older Maori women. The process taught me how to work with a life history informant from another culture: when and when not to ask questions, when and how to probe sensitively for responses beyond what I heard initially, and how best to encourage the narrator to take the lead. I determined then that what I wanted to do was to collect the life histories of Gikuyu women whom I had met in 1977 in Kenya and whom I had visited periodically since then. My continuing agenda was a cross-cultural comparison of change in women's lives (Davison 1980).

Between 1979 and 1983 when I left for Mutira, I managed to fight my way through the initial stages of a doctoral program that privileged quantitative research in order to be allowed to pursue the kind of qualitative, person-centered research I felt was critical to documenting changes in individual as well as collective women's lives.

In terms of methodology, I decided that the Gikuyu women whose life histories were to be collected should not be those whom I had previously met. Instead I planned to interview a sample of no less than a hundred women from which I would select the final life history participants.

The initial sample interviewed gave me a sociocultural profile of the women, including their clan affiliation, educational background, marital and maternal status, their religion and affiliation with women's groups. As age status is a major defining social factor in Gikuyu culture (Kenyatta 1968 [1938]; Middleton 1953; Lambert 1956; Mathu 1971; Muriuki 1974), I divided the women into age cohorts of ten years (women in their twenties, thirties, etc.), selecting the life narrators from three age cohorts (see Appendix, Table 1). Having a profile of each age cohort gave me some notion of how representative a life narrator was in relation to her cohort group and to the sample as a whole. Collecting several women's life narratives representing different age stages would enable me to track historically the way Gikuyu social norms had changed over time and to elicit women's perceptions and analyses of these changes. I was especially curious about the impact of formal schooling on these norms.

In carrying out my research and in the final writing of the text I was keenly aware of my own "positionality"—including my gender, age, race, and ideological orientation as an anthropologist/multicultural feminist (see Said 1989:207; Mbilinyi 1992:56; Opie 1993:55–56).

Two approaches were pursued in collecting the life histories—the primary one using ethnographic methods and the secondary one using archival methods. I see the two as complementary. The primary research method I used in 1983–1984 was referred to then as "person-centered ethnography" (Langness and Frank 1981). I believe it still has currency. Its techniques are known to feminist scholars who in the 1980s also began to question the validity of what had formerly been considered objective research and to replace it with subjective accounts that deconstructed women and their lives (see Whitehead and Conaway 1986; Geiger 1986; Davison 1986; Heilbrun 1988; Personal Narratives Group 1989).

Person-Centered Ethnography

The process of ethnography has intrigued me since the 1970s; it forces the person undertaking it to give up "the comforts of home" in mind and body. Ethnographic research in a rural setting such as Mutira Location involves giving up electricity, running water, and a toilet seat for an extended period of time—for me a year and a half. It also means adjusting to a different diet and learning new ways of cooking (also see Jackson 1986). It demands that we learn the language, and if possible the nonverbal forms of communication, of the particular group in which we plan to live and work so that we do not have to depend on an intermediary such as an interpreter. In my case it took me over a year to learn the dialect of Kikuyu spoken in Mutira Location before I got there and another three months in the field before I began to feel comfortable with it. I had no choice. Very few older women spoke English or Kiswahili, Kenya's national language. Another requirement of fieldwork in a rural Gikuyu community is adjusting to the changing rhythms of the agricultural cycle, the community's cultural rituals (especially rites of passage), and its multiple relational networks. For me, adjustment meant flowing with whatever occurred and learning from it. It also meant opening my eyes and keeping my mouth shut in many instances to observe fully what was taking place—to let it seep in. Ethnographic research in rural Mutira required patience and stamina; for instance, I had to learn to balance a container of water on my head or shoulder so that by the time I arrived at the top of a ridge from a stream below there was minimal loss of water. It required remembering my positionality and obligations.

Often when writing up the results of an ethnographic experience, however, the significance of everyday activities that we became a part of and their social meaning for the actors are lost in attempts to generalize about a particular group. Talking with an individual while collecting a life narrative reveals how that person interprets the events and activities that punctuate her or his life. Discourses illuminate the process. O'Tuathail and Agnew (1992:192–193) argue that discourses are best thought of as "sets of socio-cultural resources used by people in the construction of meaning about their world and their activities." The actor, then, is the focus.

At the time I began my work in 1982 few feminist scholars had written about cross-cultural, person-centered research. However, sociologist Ken Plummer's notions of interactionism resonated with the intersubjectivity I hoped to achieve through my research. He argued that "the cornerstones of interactionist thought embody a profound distaste for abstraction, reification, and absolutes; the humanly constructed, and hence ambiguous and emergent, meaning is their root concern" (1983:52–53). Plummer's deconstructionist stance was like a light in the dark. It had relevance for my work in Mutira. Since that time, a critical mass of feminists has emerged who similarly value work that gets at the concrete dailiness of people's lives—particularly women's lives—sifting the threads and interpreting the patterns (Geiger 1986; Personal Narratives Group 1989; Gluck and Patai 1991; Mbilinyi 1992; Abu-Lughod 1993; Stanley 1992, 1994). In my case, Gikuyu women's specific experiences and discourses were at the heart of the inquiry.

The development of a life as subjectively experienced involves periodically the construction and deconstruction of meaning as our worldviews shift with new knowledge, circumstances, and accumulative experience. The transitions and sometimes transformations that occur along the way are not without struggle, ambivalence, and uncertainty, as the life histories in this collection illustrate. At the same time lives-as-lived reveal how individuals create meaning out of change and contribute to their own learning in the process.

People who have not had the privilege of learning to read and write, and whose economic or geographical circumstances prevent them from acquiring audiovisual or electronic communications equipment, depend to a large extent on oral means of communication. The majority of rural women in Mutira fit this category. They are not literate nor do they have access to communications equipment other than, occasionally, a radio. Given that Gikuyu women (and men) in rural areas depend most on oral communication, a methodology that makes use of ongoing, discursive interviews was required.

Ethnographic methods privilege oral information-gathering techniques and at the same time place an individual within a specific sociocultural context. Person-centered ethnography is suited to collecting the life histories of nonliterate individuals. It allows us an opportunity to hear the voices of those who cannot write but who have opinions and ideas that we need to hear.

My research techniques involved lengthy interviews with each life history narrator, which were audiotaped with their permission and then, at the end of each day, transcribed and translated by the light of a dusky kerosene lantern into English—a time-consuming operation. I also "tracked" each woman on the day I interviewed her, following her in her rounds, participating in her daily activities and the various interactive networks she shared in order to get a feel for the rhythm—the unfolding variety as well as the routineness—emblematic of her particular life. Cross-interviews with relatives and acquaintances helped me to verify and provide further context for particular aspects of each woman's narrative. The taped transcriptions became the basis for the written narrative account—the life history.

Life History Production: Issues of Genre

Writing in 1945, Kluckhohn (pp. 81–82) observed that life history as a textual genre is difficult to define: "The lumping of 'biographical' and 'autobiographical' documents is dictated by the circumstance that it is often a highly arbitrary decision as to which category is the appropriate one." Kluckhohn contended that often what results is more biography than life history in an autobiographical sense.

The ongoing debate in anthropology over where life histories belong was resumed in the latter part of the 1970s and 1980s. Renato Rosaldo, with the publication of *The Story of Tukbaw: "They Listen as He Orates"* (1976), maintained that life history and the case study, like autobiography and biography, preselect their data into a meaningful whole and as such are separate literary genres. Crapanzano, who collected the life history of a Morroccan outcast (1980), agrees with Rosaldo. However, he makes a distinction between the case history and biography, on the one hand, and life history and autobiography, on the other. He suggests that as texts the first two bear the "impress of a narrator," who may analyze and evaluate the material, whereas the latter two present the informant from his or her own perspective (Crapanzano 1980:8). In actuality, life history serves both purposes.

The life history that takes shape within an ethnographic context is an oral account of a living person's life told by that person to someone, often from a different culture, who records it. Collecting the narrative becomes a collaborative effort negotiated by two actors—the elicitor and the narrator. Each comes to the project with a set of assumptions about the other that may or may not turn out to be accurate. Differences in age, cultural orientation, race or ethnicity, class, and marital status feed into these assumptions. Likewise, each has an agenda that helps to shape the narrative. In addition, the narrator has the advantage of being able to withhold or proffer information about her life depending on the relationship that develops between the two individuals. The elicitor has the responsibility to craft the transcribed, translated text into a form that is rendered meaningful to a reading audience outside the culture of the narrator.

Life history as a literary genre straddles autobiography and biography. Where a life history is recorded by an ethnographer or historian, and the transcribed text adheres to the informant's oral narrative, it approximates autobiography. However, if the elicitor rearranges or deletes material found in the original transcribed text in order to clarify meaning for an external reading audience, the impress of a second person other than the original narrator is felt. If the original narrator has a chance to hear her narrative read, she may further edit it. The document or text that results I refer to as *collography* to indicate that it derives from a collaborative effort between elicitor and narrator.

Life Histories of African Women

Life history research and production in Africa has escalated over the past decade. In particular, historians and social scientists have been sensitive to the invisibility of women in the literature. For this reason, much of the research that has taken place in Africa over the past two decades has been centered on "bringing women in." The last decade also has seen a shift in class orientation; increasingly life histories focus on peasant voices rather than on kings, leaders, and chiefs.

Prior to the mid-1980s scholars collecting life histories often failed to explain how their informants were chosen or how the data were collected. Exceptions are Crapanzano's life history of a Morroccan outcast published in 1980, and Shostak's portrait of a !Kung woman published the following year. More-recent life histories have attempted to overcome this omission so that we are better able to determine whether the issue of representiveness matters or not.

Prior to the 1980s a number of African life histories had appeared (see, e.g., Gollock 1928; Perham 1936; Sachs 1937; Winter 1965; Barrett and Njama 1966; Barrett and Muchai 1973; Kuper 1978). However, only a handful of those produced prior to the 1980s focused on women. Mary Smith's *Baba of Karo: A Woman of the Muslim Hausa,* originally published in 1954, is one of the earliest. Smith's work is pertinent to mine because she collected the account of one individual woman's life rather than attempting to paint with a broad brushstroke an aggregate picture of all women's lives in Hausa society. In a period generally characterized by androcentric ethnographic accounts of African societies that give little weight to individual actors, *Baba of Karo* provides a solitary light.

In the 1960s more women's narratives began to emerge. Among them were Laurentin's sketches of women in the Central African Republic (1963), Andreski's *Old Wives Tales* (1970), and in East Africa, Waciuma's small autobiography, *Daughter of Mumbi* (1969), one of the first autobiographies produced by an African woman. Waciuma's life narrative proved helpful because it documents one Gikuyu woman's perspectives on what it meant to be a Christianized "mission Gikuyu" (one educated in a mission) as well as describing her socialization into the Gikuyu way of life.

An increasing number of African scholars were writing about women in their societies during the 1970s and 1980s (see, e.g., Bolande 1977; Mutemba 1977; Muchena 1979; Obbo 1980; Oppong 1983; Chieza 1983; Kariuki 1985; Afonja 1986; Amadiume 1987; Gaidzanwa 1985; 1988). However, very few included life histories as part of their studies. In most cases, surveys and focused interviews were used. A similar preference for surveys rather than person-centered ethnography characterized ethnographic studies of women in African societies during the same period (see, e.g., Abbott 1974; Caplan 1975; Mullings 1976; Obbo 1980; Poewe 1981; Guyer 1984; Moore 1986; Oboler 1985; Skjønsberg 1989). Norwegian sociologist Skjønsberg was one of the few social scientists to include life history data. She collected short life narratives of both women and men in the Chewa village of Kefa in eastern Zambia, who shared their opinions about ongoing changes in the historical development of the village.

A similar inclusion of mini–life histories was used in a study of change in a southern Gikuyu village in conjunction with a cross-cultural demographic study in *Village Women: Their Changing Lives and Fertility—Kenya, Mexico and the Philippines* (American Association for the Advancement of Science [AAAS] 1977). The life history vignettes of Kiaguri village's government-appointed chiefs and their wives encompassed a period of eighty years, between 1896 and 1976. They demonstrate how Gikuyu elite females and males differed in their perceptions of change in the same village.

Resonating with the growing interest of historians and anthropologists in life narratives of Africans was the work of psychologist Sarah LeVine, who made a comparative study of the lives of six Gusii women in Kenya (1979). LeVine's collection, although more psychological case studies than life histories, helped me understand how ordinary women in one rural location perceived themselves and how they viewed change in their daily lives. Unlike the women in the AAAS study of Kiaguri (1977), none were the wives of chiefs. All were married, economically poor, and in their thirties or forties. Although LeVine's selection of women was confined to those she knew and with whom she had rapport, she assures us that they were representative of other Gusii women of their age at the time. She concentrated on their roles as wives, mothers, and daughters-in-law, eliciting each woman's perceptions of these roles in Gusii society. Given the variety of marital circumstances and personalities, no two women had quite the same perceptions. LeVine's work prompted me to include several women within the same age group in order to illustrate differences between them.

Shostak's *Nisa: The Life and Words of a !Kung Woman* (1981) pushed my thinking about life history research a step further by bringing together elements of ethnographic text as context with the life narrative of one woman, Nisa, a !Kung woman in her fifties. Nisa proved to be a gifted storyteller. She may or may not have been representative of other !Kung women in her age group. Similar to *Baba of Karo* three decades earlier, Nisa was singled out as the sole narrator. Her story provides an insider's view of the various age stages through which she passed in !Kung society and her feelings about the transitions. As age grading and rites of passage historically were critical aspects of Gikuyu life, Shostak's approach with Nisa gave me a model to consider in working with older Gikuyu women.

Equally important to my research was Shostak's self-awareness in the text. Her introductory comments tell us about her relationship with Nisa and how she came to select her. She also describes her working relations with the older woman and what she learned from these encounters. In short, *Nisa* cut new ground by bringing the elicitor into the text in a more explicit way.

Geiger's review of life history research methods and texts in the mid-1980s (1986) reflects a ground swell of interest that was surfacing in women's discourses and women's life histories among feminist scholars. Concurrently, two groups of feminist scholars emerged that singled out women's personal narratives as a legitimate enterprise for study. One was the Personal Narratives Group centered at the University of Minnesota and the other was the Women's Research and Documentation Project (WRDP) housed at the University of Dar es Salaam. Here I concentrate on the WRDP group, as it is based in Tanzania, a neighbor of Kenya, and because it produced a collection of seven life histories of African women. The women narrators in the WRDP collection represent various niches in Tanzanian society including a peasant, bargirl, trader, cleaner, and community leader (Ngaiza and Koda 1991). The collection addresses moral and ethical issues concerned with anonymity, authorship, and the impact of participation in other women's lives (Mbilinyi 1992:66). In their introduction to the collection, Ngaiza and Koda (1991:5) reveal their own positionality:

> Life histories are embedded in the social relations of class and gender which dominate women's perceptions of the course of their lives, to them the most important points of reverence may be their relationships with their husbands, their children or kin. . . . In telling their stories the women reproduce their own images of themselves.

Ngaiza and Koda's comments remind us that essentializing African cultures and African gender relations can be dangerous. We need to be alert to such tendencies in the production of women's life narratives.

The late 1980s saw a burgeoning of life history research, some better than others. Romero's *Life Histories of African Women* (1988) draws on accounts of women from diverse cultures in Africa. The women vary greatly in circumstances, from a highly educated woman in an urban setting to impoverished women in both urban and rural settings. Mirza and Strobel's edited collection *Three Swahili Women: Life Histories from Mombasa, Kenya* (1989) centered on the women's experiences of slavery—either as owners of slaves or as slaves themselves. The narratives were first collected by Strobel in the early 1970s in conjunction with her historical work on the East Coast slave trade. Strobel collaborated with a Swahili scholar, Sarah Mirza, on the translation and interpretation of the earlier taped narratives. The three women exemplify some of the class and ethnic diversity of Swahili society, according to Strobel (Mirza and Strobel 1989:3). They were selected because they occupied different positions within Mombasa's hierarchical social structure. They also were selected because they were "approachable conversationalists" (1989:3). Strobel makes no claims for representativeness; rather, she concentrates on diversity within a complex society.

In contrast to Romero (1988) and Mirza and Strobel (1989), who gloss over any problems they may have encountered in soliciting life histories, Mbilinyi is explicit about the dilemma in which she found herself when she set about to collect the life history of Kalindile, an older woman in Rungwe village in the southern highlands of Tanzania (see Kalindile and Mbilinyi 1991). She perceived the project to be a collaborative one between herself and Kalindile, but found herself labeling as "reactionary" Kalindile's ambivalence about the male-dominated liberation struggle and the older woman's desire to see her society restored to what it had been, presumably in "precolonial times" (Mbilinyi 1992:39). Mbilinyi's interpretation of Kalindile's world tended to essentialize what "should be" rather than what was—in terms of Kalindile's reality. Having come face to face with her own positionality, Mbilinyi developed a more sensitive listening ear and learned not to prejudge Kalindile's opinions and perceptions. Mbilinyi's work is closer to my own work in viewing life history production and interpretation as being a collaborative effort, one that encompasses the struggles and feelings of both the elicitor and the narrator.

In sum, African women's narratives provide a unique opportunity to grasp the concrete dailiness of their lives in the process of change. Person-centered ethnography, for me, provided the means. Chapter 2 outlines the context in which the research took place.

Notes

1. The public/private gendered dichotomy has been challenged by an increasing number of feminist scholars, beginning with Sudarkasa (1976) and Afonja (1980). In the 1980s the critique gained momentum (see Jaggar 1983; Afonja 1986; Amadiume 1987; Davison 1988a; Gaidzanwa 1988). In the 1990s, in the wake of postmodernism, it generally has been discredited for its "totalizing" aspects (see Phillips 1992; Jaggar and Rothenberg 1993; Collins 1993; Flax 1992; Nicholson 1994).

2. In late 1995, in response to public pressure to have more women members of Parliament, President Moi appointed an additional woman to Parliament, bringing the total number up to seven.

3. For a study of Maendeleo ya Wanawake, see Whipper (1975/76). Also see Ahlberg (1991) for problems of women's self-help groups, and Feldman (1984) for a feminist critique of Kenyan women's groups.

4. After the 1992 multiparty elections, Mandeleo Ya Wanawake detached itself from KANU, though its leadership was still aligned with the party in 1994.

2

Kenya and the Gikuyu: Social and Historical Contexts

Kenya is described by the United Nations Development Programme as a less developed country. In the late 1980s and early 1990s the incidence of poverty in Kenya increased to around 45 percent of the population in rural areas and 30 percent in urban areas (World Bank 1994:256). Of the total population of nearly 28 million, 10.4 percent were estimated to be living in absolute poverty in 1991 (UNDP 1994:135). The depth of poverty also had intensified.

Only 50 percent of Kenya's population in 1991 had access to safe water, and 14.5 percent were without access to sanitation (UNDP 1994: 135). The number of doctors in 1990 was just 3,357, or 14/100,000 citizens (Kenya, Central Bureau of Statistics 1991:195). The infant mortality rate in 1992 was 67/1,000 live births, and maternal mortality rate was 170/100,000 births (UNICEF 1994). Although 82 percent of adult (15 years and over) males are literate, only 60 percent of adult females are literate. The mean number of years of schooling for adults 25 years and over is 3.1 years for men and only 1.3 years for women (UNDP 1994:135).

Even though the number of children enrolled in primary school increased from 98,869 in 1986 to 106,572 in 1990 with nearly equal numbers of boys and girls enrolled, the percentage of those who entered the first year of secondary school as a percentage of those who successfully completed the previous eight years dropped from 49.4 percent in 1987 to 46.3 percent in 1990 (Kenya, Central Bureau of Statistics 1991:186). The number of girls as a percentage of boys enrolled is 70 percent at the secondary level. The alternative to secondary school is to farm or herd cattle at home or seek employment. Reduced economic growth in the latter part of the 1980s, however, translated to a lower number of job opportunities. Out of 400,000 new entrants to the Kenyan labor force between 1986 and 1990, only 90,000 (22.5 percent) gained employment (World Bank 1994:256). Kenya's unemployment rate has escalated in the last decade. With far fewer chances for employment than their male counterparts, female school leavers tend to remain in the rural areas to farm. Eighty-five percent of Kenya's women continue to live in rural areas. Among them are the women of Mutira.

We concentrate here on the setting in which Mutira is located in Central Province, the changing sociocultural context, and the historical framework in which the women's life narratives are situated.

The Setting: Mutira Location

Mutira Location was selected as a research site from a number of possibilities in Kenya for two reasons. First, the location's temperate climate made it an ideal working site. Second, my previous contact with two families in Mutira on earlier visits to the location in 1977 and 1980 facilitated reentry into the community in 1983.

Kirinyaga District is the smallest district in Central Province. Formerly, it was part of Embu District, but in 1963 the new Kenyan government redefined a number of former colonial districts to reflect a more equal distribution of population. Kirinyaga was created with its district headquarters at Kerugoya. Lying on the eastern edge of Central Province, Kirinyaga is bounded on the east and south by Embu District, on the west by Murang'a and Nyeri districts, and to the north by the Mount Kenya Forest. It is located between 1° and .08° south of the equator. The southern part of the district contains the rice-growing lowlands of Mwea, whereas at the higher elevations coffee and tea are grown. Maize, beans, potatoes, and bananas are staple crops of the majority of Gikuyu in the district.

Kirinyaga is divided into three administrative divisions—Gichugu, Ndia, and Mwea—with a total of ten locations. Each location is administrated by a chief, with assistant chiefs appointed by the central government for sublocations in each location.

The population of the district in 1990 was 447,951 with the primary ethnic group being the Gikuyu (Kenya, Central Bureau of Statistics 1991:2). According to population figures for 1990, there are more females than males in all age groups in the rural areas (outside Kerugoya). It is probable that the war for liberation in the 1950s and the more recent urban migration of younger males in search of employment have contributed to the discrepancy. In Ndia Division, where Mutira Location is situated, there were 62,781 females to 57,603 males in 1981 (Kirinyaga District 1982: 15). The average population density for the district in 1990 was 312 people per square kilometer (Kenya, Central Bureau of Statistics 1991).

The district is agriculturally productive because of its rich volcanic soil, a sufficient water supply, and favorable climate. The volcanic soil is conducive to the growing of coffee and tea. There are normally two seasons for rain—*mbura ya njahi* (the pigeon pea rains or Long Rains) that

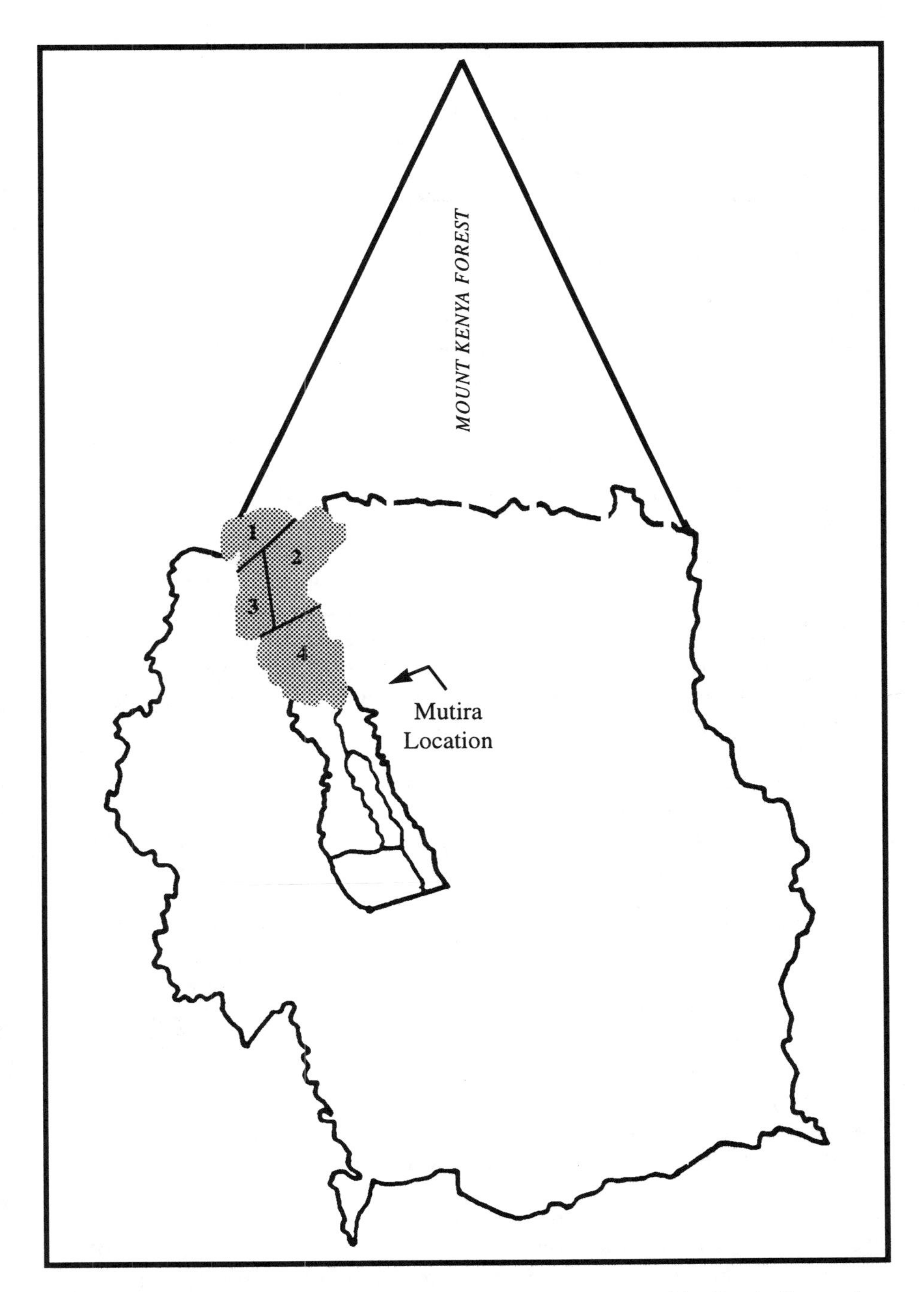

Map 2.1 Kirinyaga District, Showing Mutira Location (shading indicates the four northern sublocations: 1. Kaguyu, 2. Kabari, 3. Kagumo, 4. Kirunda)

fall mainly at night between March and June, and *mbura ya mwere* (the millet rains or Short Rains) that fall between mid-October and early December. However, there is great variation in rainfall between years; in 1984 there were no Long Rains, whereas by 1994 the rains were heavy.

Even though Kirinyaga District generally has a favorable environment for agriculture, farming is limited to small-scale production. The Agricultural Census of Large Farms, 1981–1982 (Kenya, Central Bureau of Statistics 1984) shows no large farms (over twenty acres, or 8.1 hectares) in Kirinyaga District in contrast to other districts in Central Province. In a sample of thirty households in Mutira in 1985, I found no household with more than eight acres of land (Davison 1988b).

In Ndia Division there are over thirty-five tea-buying centers and one of Kenya's largest and oldest tea-processing factories at Kangaita. Tea production has increased over the last decade, and in late 1993 a new tea factory was opened at Kiamaina. Most producers in Mutira Location own less than seven acres of tea. They harvest the crop year round.

It takes a minimum of three years before a tea bush can be harvested, so the cultivation of tea is a long-term investment. Periodically, the tea bushes must be pruned back to encourage new growth. Pickers select the best quality tea (two new leaves and a bud) and transport the leaves in large baskets to local weighing stations where they are weighed and sorted according to three grades—two leaves and a bud brings the highest price. An experienced adult picks up to sixty kilograms (132 pounds) in a six-hour period. In 1983 a picker received 80 cents—less than a shilling—per kilo. The average amount earned in a day was Ksh. 40.00. (US $3.00). By 1992 a picker received Ksh. 1.50–2.50 per kilo.

In August 1992 when I visited Mutira, smallholders were striking—refusing to pick their tea—because they realized only Ksh. 2.50 per kilo, while the final auction price for export tea was Ksh. 28.00 per kilogram. Women wondered who was pocketing the difference and blamed the problem on the management of the Kenya Tea Development Authority (KTDA, a parastatal) and the state. In addition there was a bottleneck in the processing of tea leaves, as the outdated equipment in the Kangaita factory was not keeping up with smallholder producers' output. The producers/pickers refused to pick tea over a three-month period (between May and July 1992), which left the once even carpets of green tea looking scruffy and neglected. The conflict between growers and KTDA was resolved in August 1992 with growers earning between Ksh. 4.00 and Ksh. 5.00 per kilogram. The pickers went back to work. However, there was a great backlog at local weighing stations. The way the smallholder producers/pickers perceived the problem was that KTDA was punishing smallholders for the strike by making the pickers wait nearly all night for their tea to be weighed, sorted, and collected for transport to a tea factory.

By 1994 when I returned to Mutira the tea fields once again were even carpets of emerald green. Producers were getting roughly Ksh. 4.50 per kilo. Women maintained that the opening of the new factory at Kiamaina in late 1993 had helped to solve the processing bottleneck that was in evidence in 1992.

To get some understanding of the shift in tea prices over the decade, we should realize that growers earned Ksh. 2,184 per one hundred kilograms of tea in 1983 with an increase to Ksh. 5,184 in 1984, a good year (Kenya, Central Bureau of Statistics 1991, Table 74:97). By 1987, however, they earned Ksh. 2,037 below what they earned in 1983. In 1990 the producer price was stabilizing at Ksh. 3,521 per hundred kilograms (Kenya, Central Bureau of Statistics 1991:97).

Mutira Location also has four coffee cooperatives, each with its own factory. Similar to tea, coffee is a long-term investment from the time the saplings are planted to the harvesting of the first crop. The branches of the tree must be regularly trimmed so that lateral shoots and suckers are cut away, allowing only the main branches to grow and assuring the best grade berries. Because the trees are planted farther apart than tea bushes, they tend to collect weeds more readily. Women spend a good deal of time weeding around the base of the trees with a machete and hoe. The yield for coffee is higher per kilo than that for tea (Ksh. 1.50, in contrast to Ksh. 0.80 for tea in 1983), but coffee requires more inputs in terms of fertilizer and copper fungicide to prevent coffee berry disease *(Collectoruhum coffeanum).*

Coffee production has fallen in Kirinyaga District since 1987. Whereas the overall producer price had been Ksh. 3,844 per one hundred kilograms of coffee in 1984 and had risen to a high of Ksh. 5,020 for the same amount in 1986, by 1987 the price had dropped to Ksh. 3,662 (Kenya, Central Bureau of Statistics 1991, Table 74:97). In 1990, after some growth in 1988 and 1989, the producer price again fell to only Ksh. 3,636 per hundred kilograms—less than it had been in 1984. By the end of 1994 the price for coffee berries in Mutira had improved, with producers earning Ksh. 60 per kilo, according to Mutira women interviewed.[1]

Because it was impossible to get around by foot to every one of the eight sublocations in Mutira Location, four in the north were chosen based upon representativeness of economic activity (in one, mainly coffee is grown; in another, mainly tea; and in two, a mix of coffee and tea) and accessibility. The sublocations included were Kirunda, Kagumo, Kaguyu, and Kabari, with elevations ranging from 5,400 to 6,500 feet. Kaguyu and Kabari border the Mount Kenya Forest and were the site of heavy fighting during the liberation struggle in the 1950s. A broad trench still exists that local Gikuyu were forced to dig to prevent Mau Mau guerrilla fighters in the forest from entering the internment villages to obtain food and recruit followers. In addition, local people (including children) have accidentally stumbled across active grenades left by the colonial army at the edge of the forest, sometimes with disastrous results. The legacy of the guerrilla war for liberation is still a part of the people's lives. The majority who either fought on the side of the Land and Freedom Army (labeled "Mau Mau") or supported their efforts remain bitter toward the minority of Gikuyu who became Home Guards (those trained by the British to police the internment villages) or who remained loyal to the colonial government.

The research site that included the four sublocations forms a triangle cornered by three small market centers—Gathuthuma and Gatwe in the north and Kamuiru in the south. In addition, a larger market is located at Kagumo. The southern end of the site (at the lowest elevation) consists of fairly flat land where coffee is the principal cash crop. Just north of Kagumo is a mixed area where both coffee and tea are grown. At the highest and coolest elevations, tea is the cash crop. North of Kagumo are steep ridges, running north and south, separated by streams or rivers.

Historically, the ridges were occupied by different Gikuyu *mbari* (patrilineages). Since the early 1960s, the land has been subdivided by male *mbari* members who have legal title. The entire area was formerly part of the Embu Reserve under British colonial administration. The southern end at Kamuiru was taken over by the British during the Emergency (1952–1960) for an internment village and is now subdivided into separate, individually owned parcels. Although the Gikuyu living on the ridges have historical roots in the location, many of those living at lower elevations around Kagumo were formerly squatters who were given small parcels of land previously held by the colonial government in the immediate postindependence period.

Kagumo is one of the oldest continually inhabited Gikuyu villages in the area. Today it is a growing market center. I spent about half of each week between September 1983 and March 1984 living in Kagumo. The other half of the week and from March onward I lived in the homestead of a Gikuyu family located in Kabari Sublocation, which gave me easy access to most of the life history narrators, the majority of whom lived at the northern end of the location.

The Sociocultural Context: The Northern Gikuyu

Before describing the Gikuyu, a word needs to be said about the spelling of the name of this major ethnic group in Kenya that accounts for 20 percent of Kenya's total population. The Gikuyu refer to themselves as *Agĩkũyũ,* the plural form, and *Mũgĩkũyũ,* the singular. For this reason it is more accurate to refer to the group as Gikuyu, following the lead of

Gikuyu author Ngugi wa Thiong'o (1967, 1977), than Kikuyu, which was the way early Europeans spelled it (e.g, Hobley 1910; Routledge and Routledge 1910). Kikuyu refers to the language spoken by the Gikuyu.

The Gikuyu are linguistically related to other Bantu-speaking groups in central Kenya (including the Kamba, Embu, Mbere, Tharaka, and Meru), who share common historical roots that date back to a prototype population known as the Thagicu. Migrating from the north, the Thagicu settled in the Mount Kenya region sometime between the twelfth and fourteenth centuries (Muriuki 1974). As splinter groups formed, it appears from archeological evidence that one group migrated south and settled on the southwestern slopes of Kirinyaga (Mount Kenya).

Subsequent Bantu migrations from the northeast, followed by periods of settlement, intermarriage, and further splintering, characterize the history of the Thagicu in the fifteenth and sixteenth centuries. It is from one of the splinter groups that settled at the convergence of the Thagana (Tana) and Thika rivers that Gikuyu trace their descent (Muriuki 1974). From the settlement at Ithanga, subgroups migrated in several directions, some north to Nyeri, others northeast to Kirinyaga, and some south to Murang'a over the next two centuries. Those who migrated still further south toward Kiambu in the eighteenth century came into contact with a hunting people they called the Aathi, from whom they acquired land in exchange for goats and with whom they intermarried (Fisher 1954; Kershaw 1975/1976; Muriuki 1974; Leakey 1977).

Similar migrations followed. The Gikuyu began to identify themselves as distinct groups identified with particular areas. The result was the emergence of clans, each of which traced descent back to a particular ancestress. The number of clans varies somewhat with informants (Fisher 1954; Middleton 1953), but the number usually given is nine.[2] Two clans may have originated through contact with neighboring Kamba: the Acera and Agaciku. Although Gikuyu trace their descent from one of the nine clans, their oral tradition relates the existence of male and female progenitors—Gikuyu and Mumbi—from whom the nine clans arose. They are believed to be the mother and father of the nine clan ancestresses.

Ambler (1988) argues that the ethnic divisions that were first recorded by European visitors to Kenya in the nineteenth century were more the artifacts of the visitors than any acknowledged recognition of ethnic identity on the part of the people who lived in communities in the Mount Kenya region who may have had competing or contradictory claims. What were most familiar were the family, lineage, and locality. "Individuals and lineages established their links to others within the same ethnic population through membership in widely dispersed clans, which traced their histories, genealogically, to a place and time of common genesis" (Ambler 1988:33). Clan affiliations that linked local lineages together may have cut across language boundaries. To argue for or against a developing sense of ethnic identity for nineteenth-century Gikuyu is fruitless. We simply do not know whether they experienced a sense of ethnic identity. What we have to go on is the historical records of travelers and oral accounts that were passed down from one generation to the next. The rest is conjecture. I accept lineage and clan ideology as a basis for practices that served to bond certain groups of Gikuyu into a shared sense of community. I also recognize that differences in dialect developed that serve to distinguish Gikuyu groups by region and locale.

Northern Gikuyu groups settled on the steep slopes of Kirinyaga, whereas southern Gikuyu groups, migrating south toward Kiambu, settled around the Chania River according to oral history (Leakey 1977; Muriuki 1974). Over time, the regional dialects and local traditions that developed made it easier for colonial anthropologists to distinguish the two groups. It was the need to consolidate the identities of indigenous people for purposes of indirect rule that stimulated the search for geographically identified "tribes" under colonial capitalism. The next two sections on Gikuyu economy and social formations provide reference points for understanding the changing cultural context in which the life narrators are embedded.

Gikuyu Economy

Formerly hunter-gatherers, the Gikuyu over time adopted horticultural practices, beginning with the cultivation of cocoyams, sweet potatoes, bananas, and millet. The cultivation of crops was segregated by gender: men cultivated yams and bananas; women, sweet potatoes and millet. Women also gathered a variety of wild spinachlike greens, tubers such as arrowroot (taro), and berries. Sugarcane was grown and honey collected from men's hives in the forest for the production of beer (*njohi*). Maize was introduced early in the nineteenth century and has become a major staple crop (Hoorweg and Niemeyer 1980). When it serves as a food crop it is cultivated by women, but when it is sold as a commodity it tends to be grown by men. In addition, European potatoes, cassava, and rice have been added to the food repertoire. Legumes include dwarf beans, cowpeas, pigeon peas, kidney beans, lentils, and garden peas.

In addition, Gikuyu today grow cabbage, tomatoes, onions, carrots, kale, and swiss chard. A great variety of fruits exists, known by the generic term *matunda*. In addition to bananas, they include passion fruit, mangos, papaya, loquats, plums, pineapple, oranges, and avocado pears.

The staple dish of most rural Gikuyu is *githeri*—maize kernels and kidney beans boiled together for several hours. Once cooked, the dish may be preserved in a cool place for up to three days without refrigeration. To give variety, pigeon peas, carrots, potatoes, onions, or kale are often added. Although the generic term for food is *irio*, the Gikuyu have a favorite dish, *irio cia Agĩkũyũ* (literally, Gikuyu food), that they serve to visitors; it consists of maize kernels, potatoes, garden peas, and beans mashed together. In addition, older Gikuyu enjoy millet porridge, particularly when it is allowed to ferment.

Meat of goats and sheep are roasted, often at the end of a ceremony. The animals historically were used for sacrificial purposes to seal an agreement, as a means of restoring health to a community, or to honor someone on a special occasion. Usually the animal sacrificed was a ram that was kept indoors in a special place in a woman's house, was fed sweet potato vines, and was allowed to fatten for slaughtering.

Goats and sheep also were used as a medium of exchange to acquire property and as bridewealth (*rũracio*). Kershaw (1975/1976) notes for the southern Gikuyu (Kiambu) that in the nineteenth century Gikuyu from Murang'a acquired land from the Aathi (Ndorobo) through a series of payments of sheep or goats. Cattle—both Zebu and imported European—were used similarly, but the Gikuyu did not keep large herds. Gikuyu who can afford them now keep a few cattle mainly for milking. The milk is boiled with tea leaves as a hot drink.

In rural areas meat is served only on special occasions to celebrate a ceremony such as *Irua* (circumcision) or to welcome a special visitor. In short, many Gikuyu are largely vegetarian.

Cash-value crops such as tea and coffee were not grown by the Gikuyu until the 1940s, when the colonial government first allowed Africans to cultivate them (Leo 1984). Up until the 1940s, the only cash crop Africans were free to grow in any quantity was maize, because it was needed to feed African laborers working on European plantations. Strichter (1975/76:59) indicates that by 1947, there were 4,749 Gikuyu/Embu/Meru women employed in agricultural labor, out of a total of 5,606 for this group, which was 49.4 percent of the total female labor force at that time. However, Mutira women living within the reserve were less likely to be employed because most had access to land, as the narrators and other women confirmed.

Colonial administrators and farmers feared that, in contrast to the production of maize, coffee and tea might compete with settler production of the same crops (Leys 1975). In Mutira Location, however, people did not cultivate either cash crop until 1959 or 1960. First, during the 1950s, the large majority of Gikuyu in Mutira were either fighting with the Land and Freedom Army (the Mau Mau) in the nearby forest or they were interned in villages set up by the colonial government under its emergency powers to prevent collaboration with Mau Mau.[3] Second, the majority were largely unaware of a change in colonial government policies allowing them to cultivate cash crops. While they were interned or fighting for liberation, in 1954 the colonial government instituted a land and agricultural reform package known as the Swynnerton Plan (named for then assistant director of agriculture R.J.M. Swynnerton) designed to encourage Africans who accepted land consolidation and entitlement to grow export crops. It was not until the end of the Emergency that people in Mutira began to plant tea or coffee, now their major cash crops.

In addition to growing tea and coffee for export, Gikuyu living in the Mwea Irrigation Settlement Scheme, set up in the 1950s, grow rice for sale in Kenya and for export, mainly to Japan. Other northern Gikuyu cultivate pyrethrum, which is exported and processed abroad, then sent back to Kenya for local sale. Marketing boards, a colonial invention of the 1940s, operate as parastatals of the state. They impinge on the daily lives of rural Gikuyu farmers by controlling the marketing and distribution of most cash-value crops.

Gikuyu Social Formations

Culturally, the northern and southern Gikuyu share the same social and political practices, modified over time by interchange with the Rift Valley Maasai and later with the Europeans. This section describes key institutions and practices that Gikuyu identify as significant aspects of their culture that are undergoing change.

Mariika: The significance of age sets. The concept of *mariika* was central to Gikuyu society. The term refers to age sets (*riika* is the singular). *Mariika* provide a means of keeping track of generations, related directly to the year in which a particular group (both male and female) was circumcised. The circumcision group (generation) was given a name that identified it with a particular event or characteristic of the group. Lambert (1956:20) notes that in one location in Nyeri, those circumcised in 1893 were given the name *Nuthi* (jigger fleas) because the abominable insects were unusually prevalent that year. Another age set might be called *Ngigi* (locusts). Later age sets in Nyeri (names varied according to location) came to be associated with the arrival of Europeans, notably *Chiringi* (with the introduction of the shilling in 1923) and *Ndege,* the Kiswahili word for bird that also means airplane (Lambert 1956:21).

Ambler (1988:23) argues that "corporate age sets provided an alternative to lineage affiliation, balancing the power of elders in community politics." I argue that the age set, or *riika,* was not perceived as an alternative to lineage affiliation, but rather as complementary to lineage—another dimension of Gikuyu social formation.

Members of a particular *riika,* circumcised at the same time, were given a rank in the age groupings. The rank defined the behavior of individual members within a *riika* and their behavior toward members of other age sets, both younger and older. The older members of a particular *riika* became, the more respect the *riika* was accorded. The concept of *riika* is recognized and respected by older people in rural Mutira.

Mariika acted as an agent of gender-specific social control whereby members monitored the behavior of their own *riika*. For example, during *ngwiko*, when the newly initiated were allowed to sleep together, young circumcised males of the same *riika* monitored one another's sexual behavior to ensure that one of their members did not go beyond the limits of Gikuyu propriety. Kinoti (1983) insists that a major purpose of men's *mariika* was to maintain the age set's honor. A similar concern for honor was evident among women of the same *riika* who took steps to protect their fellow members from male harassment during dances and celebrations. One older woman in Mutira described how young women used to hide long wooden cooking spoons (*muiko*) down the backs of their tunics to beat a young man if he began sexually harassing one of their *riika* mates during an event. "The girl would scream for help and we would run and beat on him with our spoons," she testified.

Older people in Mutira, both male and female, relate that a strong bond forms between members of a *riika* during *Irua* and continues as a form of mutual social aid throughout the life span. However, younger Gikuyu, usually circumcised in hospitals today, have little affinity for the concept of *mariika*. In place of *Irua*, today's young Gikuyu seek peer bonds through school classes. Moreover, as the life histories illustrate, the strict social separation between the sexes once prevalent among rural Gikuyu is breaking down as young people of both sexes come into contact with one another in primary school classrooms, on the playground, and through church activities.

Rites of passage and age stages. In the past, the transition from one life stage to another was marked by rites of passage, which play a central role in the life histories of the older women. Each stage was given a special name for both males and females. The terms used by southern and northern Gikuyu vary according to location, but the meaning is the same. Among the Gichugu and Ndia Gikuyu in Mutira Location the terms for female stages until recently were

gakenge	newborn (applies to both sexes)
kaana	infant (applies to both sexes)
karigũ	a small girl
kirigũ	a big, uncircumcised girl
mũirĩtu	a grown, circumcised girl

mũhiki	a bride with young children
wamũng'ei	a woman with three or more children, one of whom is circumcised
mũtũmia	a woman with several children who have been circumcised
muongia (also *kiheti*)	an old woman past menopause

Each of these stages was marked by a particular ceremony—the generic term is *mambura*. A *kaana* became a *karigũ* once she had completed *mambura ma twana*—ceremony of the children—and had been removed from her mother's bed to a bed of her own or with other children. A *karigũ* became a *kirigũ* with ear-piercing; a *kirigũ* became a *mũirĩtu* through the ritual of *Irua*. This initiation ceremony, which at one time lasted several months (Kenyatta 1968 [1938]) combined a course in Gikuyu history and customs with lessons in sexuality and skills for adulthood. The peak physical experience of *Irua* was circumcision, which tested a young person's physical stamina and willingness to endure pain while symbolically eradicating gender ambiguities associated with early stages of childhood. An initiated adult gained social respect and was recognized for her/his reproductive potential—the power to procreate in a culture that valued wealth-in-people.

Marriage was not a single event, but a series of substages that brought together two clans and two extended families. Of utmost importance was *rũracio*, or bridewealth: the number of herd animals, usually goats and cattle, that the groom gave to the bride's family to compensate for the loss of her services to her natal family and to establish the parentage of future children (C. Clark 1971; Mathu 1971). Formal negotiations were held between adult males of the bride's clan and family and those of the groom to establish the amount. Usually, the payment was rendered through a series of installments over time. Currently, *rũracio* often includes a payment of Kenya shillings, determined by the amount of formal education a family has invested in its daughter. A *mũhiki* refers to a woman who has left her father's homestead to become a bride in her husband's father's homestead, if he remains in the paternal home, or in a separate homestead over which her husband has control.

A ceremony called *nyumithio*, which was linked to the initiation of a woman's first child, allowed a woman to be called *wamung'ei*. During *nyumithio*, as we learn from the oldest woman, a woman received *kirira*, or special secret knowledge, from the elders (older women). After several children had been circumcised, she became a *mũtũmia* and was eligible for membership in the *kiama*—council of elders—which was composed of both men and women in Mutira Location.

Old people were referred to by the general term *andũ akũrũ*, but a very old woman who had "lost most of her teeth" and was past menopause was known as *muongia*. Accorded great respect, she was allowed to take an active role in sacrificial ceremonies. Hobley (1938) relates that old women were also feared because they had the power to bring evil or bad luck, especially if encountered in a group. Consequently, the respect may have been partly a result of fear. Old people (of both sexes) nearing death were treated with great deference and attention for fear they might inflict *kirumi*—a curse put upon a living person or their property by the dying person (Hobley 1938).

Over time, the distinct age groups for females have merged into four groups: *kairĩtu*, which refers to any uncircumcised girl; *mũirĩtu*, referring to a circumcised, unmarried girl; *mũhiki*, a young bride with young children; and *mũtũmia*, which refers to any woman who has had several children. A nearly parallel sequence of age stages exists for males: *kahiĩ* (boy); *mwanake* (circumcised young man); and *mũthuri* (any married man with children regardless of age). Old people are still referred to as *andũ akũru*.

The Gikuyu family can be envisioned as circular, rather than linear as in Western cultures. Each new generation replaces its grandparents, who are then free to become ancestors. That such a belief still exists among older Gikuyu is indicated in the way many women in Mutira answered the question, "For whom were you named?" Quite often the answer was, "For my father's mother" or "my mother's mother." When asked why, the response was usually, "Because it was me who gave birth to my father (or mother)." The imperative of replacing four grandparents and trying until success is achieved explains why Gikuyu until recently sought to have a minimum of four children (Herzog 1971).

Changing gender roles. Formerly, both men and women shared the agricultural work load except when men were at war. Men usually cleared the land, helped to prepare it for cultivation, and cultivated yams and bananas; women cultivated most other crops; and both sexes helped with the harvest. Women produced, processed, and had control over the distribution of most food crops. From the parcels of land she was allocated by her husband at marriage—often as many as seven or eight in different areas—a wife was expected to raise enough food to feed her husband, children, and any visitors. Women in polygynous marriages in which the relationship between co-wives was favorable often shared cultivation, food processing, and preparation tasks. In homes in which the relationship was not good, each wife cultivated her own parcel with the help of her children and prepared her family's food. A similar pattern in polygynous households exists today. In addition, a custom known as *ngwatio* (whereby women formed groups to help one another collectively with agricultural tasks such as hoeing and weeding on a rotating basis) still persists.

In Kirinyaga District, an increasing number of men work in towns and in the capital city of Nairobi, leaving their wives and mothers with the major burden of cultivation and food processing (Davison 1985). In addition, women whose husbands are often absent, or who are widowed, must perform the bulk of tasks associated with cash crop production. Formerly, children contributed substantially to agricultural production, but with the introduction of formal schooling that source of labor has been drastically reduced. Further, schooling has meant an added financial burden, because it necessitates earning cash for school fees and uniforms. Cash crops provide the predominant source of income for school fees and commodities like sugar, kerosene, and clothing that cannot be made at home. In short, Gikuyu peasants have become dependent on a money economy that, in turn, requires the growing of cash crops that are dependent upon the fluctuations of a world market economy.

Men continue to control most political and ceremonial aspects of Gikuyu society, except those in which the orientation is strictly female, as in female circumcision ceremonies or, more recently, in women's self-help group activities. Men, particularly in public, tend to dominate—-though a woman's submissive position decreases with age. Male heads of homesteads usually have the final say in matters concerning land use and the homestead. Nonetheless, the peripatetic habits of many adult males and an increased rate of absenteeism means that often women in a homestead are left with the responsibility of making decisions normatively recognized as belonging to men.

Though Gikuyu women in groups are assertive, their behavior as individuals depends upon their age and status. Husbands—at least in public—demand respect. Wife beating as a means of controlling married women is still condoned among some Gikuyu. Obedience and respect for elders, highly valued, extend to male-female relationships. There is often a five- to ten-year age difference between a husband and his first wife (and more with subsequent wives). Consequently, a wife's position is one of public deference to her husband, though in private she may have greater leeway. Age rank applies as well to co-wives. First wives have primary authority over additional wives, who are usually younger and less experienced in homestead tasks and family matters. Younger women defer to older women. Yet, within constraints of age and sex, individual women demonstrate that they have the ability to control certain aspects of their lives and to mediate change.

Related to the role and position of women is that of children. Children are highly regarded by the Gikuyu and are included in all aspects of life, whether it is a circumcision or a clan meeting. Child care is the responsibility of the entire extended family, not just the mother. Though the father is absent much of the time, when he is at home he shows great affection for small children in particular. Children are in close contact with their mothers' bodies for the first year and are held often by various members of the family. From then on, older siblings are responsible for much of the child care, and grandmothers are as important as mothers once a child is weaned.

Motherhood is not an end in itself. A woman's productive role does not terminate once her reproductive one commences but instead takes on new meaning. Sociologist Nancy Chodorow's (1978:4) observation that historically in the United States "a woman carried out her childcare responsibilities along with a wide range of other productive work" still holds for rural Gikuyu women. At the same time, children determine a woman's social status to a great extent. A woman is usually identified with the name of her firstborn child. For example, a woman whose first child is named Wawira is Nyina-wa-Wawira, or Mother-of-Wawira. The more children a woman has, the more prosperous she is considered. Mothers who have raised many children are highly regarded by both sexes.

It was my role as a mother of children that allowed me to gain an acceptable position in Mutira Location. I was known not by my name but by the name of my firstborn child—Nyina-wa-Stepheni. In addition, it was my position as a mother that gave me access to certain information that I otherwise might have been denied.

Changes in spatial arrangements. The Kirinyaga Gikuyu currently live in homesteads (*micii*, singular *mũcii*) located adjacent to their fields. Spread widely over the steep ridges of Mount Kenya, from a distance the homesteads resemble clusters of brown mushrooms protruding from a green patchwork of maize, tea, and coffee. Each *mũcii* is enclosed by a hedge or log fence with a single entrance. Ideally, it contains the paternal head of family, his wives or wife, their unmarried children, often his married sons, and sometimes single male or female relatives. The Gikuyu historically were polygynous, but with the influence of Christianity and Western education, the trend has been toward monogamy. If a man chooses to marry more than one wife, theoretically he must provide *rũracio*, or bridewealth, and a separate house for each within the homestead. In practice, whether or not *rũracio* is actually transferred depends upon the integrity of the man marrying and the circumstances of the man's family, as we shall see in two of the life histories.

The Gikuyu living pattern is undergoing change. Until recently, the male head of a homestead lived separately in his own large *thingira*, or man's house, at the rear of the compound, with houses for each wife and her children extending in a semicircle on either side of the *thingira* toward the entrance. Behind each house were egg-shaped granaries woven from sticks and elevated slightly above ground. In front of the houses, which faced toward the center of the homestead, was an open, pounded earth yard called the *nja*, where many of the family activities such as food processing, laundry, and feeding of small herd animals took place during the daytime. Unmarried, circumcised sons moved out of their father's *thingira*, where they had lived from about age six, and built their own smaller bachelor houses, called *kithunu*, where they lived until they married. Upon the birth of a first child, a married son built a house for his wife and her future children. Until that time, she lived with his mother, learning from her what duties she would be expected to perform in the new homestead. With the increased cost of building materials, today some husbands are building single-family houses that contain separate sleeping rooms for husband and wife or wives. However, a single house is unusual in cases of polygynous marriage, as wives prefer to have their own houses to avoid conflict.

The Historical Context

The first edition of *Voices From Mutira* was prefaced by quotes from two colonial actors—one male, the other female. Together they reflected the way Europeans living in Kenya at the midpoint of colonial occupation perceived Gikuyu women. One was from the Danish writer Isak Dinesen, whose racialist stereotypes of Gikuyu people in *Out of Africa* (1937) degraded them as "children" or as crafty workers; she viewed them as "her" Gikuyu. The other quotation was taken from C.W. Hobley, a colonial administrator who perceived himself, perhaps, to be an amateur ethnographer. His use of the term *savage tribe* in describing the Gikuyu and his assumptions about the position and roles of Gikuyu women, in particular, are emblematic of the ethnocentricity that permeated the colonial establishment and the androcentricity that characterized European males in the first half of the twentieth century and still lingers in some quarters. Though these pejorative colonial voices are absent from this edition, we cannot talk about Gikuyu-colonial relations without being sharply aware of the discrepancies in the way most colonials viewed the Gikuyu and the way individual Gikuyu women, such as those in this volume, view themselves. Nor can we listen to the women's retrospective accounts without gaining some understanding of how demeaning a process imperialism is—economically, socially, and psychologically. These life histories validate the importance of history from below.

The Early Twentieth Century: Land and Droughts

At the time the oldest life narrator, Wanjiku, was born (around 1910) groups of British settlers, encouraged by promises of land, spread northward like so many greedy fingers from the small colonial trading post of Nairobi in southern Kenya. The Gikuyu of Kiambu and those further north in Fort Hall and Nyeri districts were directly in the path of the land-hungry settlers. Many Gikuyu suddenly found land they assumed to be theirs expropriated for "Crown use" by a colonial government they thought was only temporary. Some, forced into landlessness, became squatters or laborers on settler plantations. Others fled north and eastward into reserves set aside by the early 1930s for "native" use. Of necessity, however, most were forced to adjust—their spears were no match for British arms. Gikuyu in Mutira Location began to experience crowding at the lower elevations as the amount of land at their disposal within the "native reserve" dwindled. Increased population within the prescribed confines of a reserve prevented the practice of shifting cultivation and led to conflicts over land. At the lower elevations, intensive land use soon led to soil depletion and erosion of the ridges. Notwithstanding, women in Mutira prior to the 1950s were able to cultivate small plots in several ecological niches. Wanjiku notes, "Before Mau Mau [she means the Emergency], we used to cultivate in different places—that way we could harvest at different times."

Production was limited to food crops for family members and visitors. In contrast to Kiaguri village farther south, little of their produce was sold to colonial occupiers. Extra amounts might be exchanged for other items, such as goats, in local markets. Wanjiku describes learning to count as being important "so that one could count the equivalent thing for trading in the market." Although food was usually plentiful, Wanjiku was able to remember one year—historically recorded by British observers as 1918—when no rain fell.

As we learn from the Kiaguri informants, a serious drought occurred in 1896 (American Association for the Advancement of Science 1977). It took many lives. People had known droughts before and they would know them again. The Mutira Gikuyu labeled the drought that occurred in 1918 the "Hunger of Kimotho," for a local chief appointed by the colonial government—the implication being that a chief appointed by the British was not able to feed his people. Wanjiku was about eight years old at the time. Other droughts occurred in the 1930s and 1940s, when the women in their fifties were children and Wanjiku was a *mũtũmia* with two young sons.

In particular, a drought in 1941 affected both settlers and Africans. To the Gikuyu, it was known as *Ng'aragu ya Njugu* (Hunger of the Storks) for the large Maribou storks who destroyed grain crops. Yet Wanjiku does not mention this drought, possibly because she was less affected than Gikuyu living in drier regions. At the time, she was living in her husband's home on the edge of the Mount Kenya Forest, at an elevation where mountain mists provide a certain amount of moisture during most months. Drought is cyclical and its effects are felt differentially, depending upon local ecology and climate. This was certainly the case with the drought that occurred in 1984; those living in the lower, drier regions such as Mwea were far more affected than those living at higher elevations such as Mutira.

A drought is a phenomenon that people may anticipate but cannot control in Africa. A plague of locusts, similarly, may destroy an entire year's supply of maize or millet. But if little or no land exists on which to grow food, the problem becomes intensified. Beginning in the 1920s, Gikuyu began to lose patience with the continual land grab taking place around them, with the institutionalization of indirect rule through British-appointed "chiefs" where none had existed, and with the imposition of a "hut tax" on each family to be paid in cash, through newly appointed chiefs. Their political opposition to these colonial measures began to grow and take shape in the form of a movement led in the 1920s by Harry Thuku, who was arrested and detained by the colonial state in the late 1920s. His incarceration led to a mass outpouring of sympathy and a mass demonstration in Nairobi, led by Gikuyu women. This early activism by women put the colonial state on notice at a time when other issues central to women also were taking shape. Missionaries played a key role in those issues.

The Controversy over Female Circumcision

The arrival and intensity of increased numbers of European and American missionaries in the early 1920s in Kenya had profound consequences for the Gikuyu. Particularly affected was the institution of *Irua*. As early as 1906, the Church Missionary Society (CMS), sponsored by the Church of Scotland, had become an instrument for the initial attack on Gikuyu cultural practices such as animal sacrifice (declared "pagan"), nonburial of the dead (considered "primitive"), and female circumcision connected with *Irua* (deemed primitive and barbaric). By the 1920s, missionaries had made notable progress in terminating practices of animal sacrifice and nonburial of the dead (Clough 1990:139). What remained to be conquered was female circumcision—and, often, the "provocative, immoral" dances and songs that accompanied it. It is notable, however, that male circumcision, which also involved a surgical procedure lacking the hygenic standards of Western medicine, was not singled out for abolition. Moreover, both sexes participated in the "provocative dancing and singing," yet the Protestant male missionaries chose to focus on the female aspects of *Irua* as most needing attention and curtailment.

The various Christian denominations that had carved out territorial spheres of influence in central Kenya were not in accord on the issue of female circumcision. For example, whereas the Gospel Missionary Society

(GMS) and the African Inland Mission (AIM) opposed the ritual surgery, the CMS was divided over the issue of gradual or immediate termination of the practice. The Catholic missionaries were opposed to making female circumcision an issue at all, preferring to monitor its practice within the walls of their missions rather than outlaw it (Clough 1990; Ahlberg 1991).

Wanjiku was probably circumcised around 1924 or 1925 at about the age of fourteen. Her retrospective account of *Irua* gives no indication that she was aware of any controversy brewing over female circumcision. Yet clitoridectomy became an issue that attracted the colonial government's attention the following year, largely through the concerted efforts of missionary medical personnel.

In 1926, the colonial government, under pressure from Church of Scotland and US AIM missionary leaders, began a campaign to outlaw female circumcision (including surgery on the labia minora and clitoridectomy) among the Gikuyu in Central Province (see Sangren 1982; Clough 1990). Opposition to outlawing the practice came from some Gikuyu Christians, who could not see the Biblical rationale for terminating such a culturally critical practice, and from most non-Christians. They were supported in defending the cultural practice by the Kikuyu Central Association (KCA), which began to link the controvery over female circumcision to land alienation as just one more example of colonial hegemony. Nonetheless, the missionary activists were able to pressure the colonial state to use the native councils, whose members were Gikuyu male elders, as a vehicle for controlling the practice.

Native councils were encouraged to pass resolutions reducing the severity of the operation (particularly the removal and suturing of the labia minora and half of the labia majora). They also were directed to regulate the performance of clitoridectomy by female circumcisers to ensure that sterile conditions were met. Female circumcisers, who also were midwives, were to be issued permits by the councils stipulating under what conditions the operation might be performed. At the prospect of trying to police female circumcisers, council elders balked. In a resolution passed by the Fort Hall Local Native Council (1927), it was noted that male members attending a *baraza* (outdoor public meeting) in May of that year refused to commit local female circumcisers to regulations imposed by the colonial state (Kenya National Archives 1927a).

A heated debate emerged within the councils, and factions developed between the few mission-educated Gikuyu who favored abandoning the practice or altering its severity and the many who advocated continuing the practice of clitoridectomy as an essential part of the Gikuyu way of life. The Nyeri Native Council, meeting on March 9, 1927, expressed the feelings of many Gikuyu that despite the Chief Native Commissioner's dissatisfaction with the practice, "it is the custom of the Kikuyu people to circumcise girls, and the vast majority are in favour of the continuance of this rite" (Kenya National Archives 1927b:49).

The controversy continued over the next several years, with most Gikuyu stubbornly refusing to succumb to the wishes of a foreign government. In addition, many Gikuyu left the European mission churches to start their own Gikuyu Christian churches in order to maintain cultural practices they felt were essential to the Gikuyu way of life, including clitoridectomy and polygyny.

By 1930, the controversy over clitoridectomy led a colonial district commissioner in Fort Hall (now Murang'a) to write to the provincial commissioner in Nyeri,

> In the present state of native opinion, I think the less talked about the operation of clitoridectomy the better. Natives are sick to death of the subject, so is everyone else. Nothing but harm can result from constantly raising the question, and no matter how many resolutions are passed, they could never be enforced [Kenya National Archives 1930:23].

By 1934, in the minds of Kirinyaga Gikuyu and those of neighboring Embu (then lumped together in Embu District) the colonial directive to outlaw clitoridectomy had become identified with covert measures for controlling population and land. A request was made that year by the Embu district commissioner to the provincial commissioner for Central Intelligence Division (CID) assistance "to combat the disaffected native propaganda campaign in Embu District averring that Europeans are trying to depopulate the land by preventing the circumcision of women" (Kenya National Archives 1934:28). Because female circumcision was considered to be a necessary prerequisite to marriage (see Kenyatta 1968 [1938]), Gikuyu believed that the government was trying to control population growth in the reserve so it could claim "unused" land.

Though the controversy raged among Gikuyu elders, both male and female, it does not seem to have reached young women like Wanjiku in Mutira Location who were participating in *Irua* during the 1920s. Clitoridectomy was the accepted practice; a girl did not question the wisdom of the elders. Nor did Wanjiku envision any alternative to achieving adult status.

Wanjiku believed, like most of her people, that one must "buy maturity with pain." Maturity, in a society that had no extended period of adolescence, meant an abrupt break with childhood and the assumption of an adult role with its accompanying responsibilities and privileges. One of the signs of a mature adult was her/his ability to endure pain with stoicism. By demonstrating her ability to withstand pain during *Irua*, a woman demonstrated to others that she was ready to accept the pain that accompanied childbirth. Moreover, Wanjiku points out that participating in *Irua*, in addition to providing socially acceptable physical maturity, equally provided the means for a social transition to adulthood.

Even though some mission Gikuyu began to give up female circumcision in the 1930s and 1940s, other Gikuyu held onto the practice as central to the Gikuyu way of life—a symbol of what it meant to "be Gikuyu" for a people struggling against colonial domination and repression.

World War II: The Impact on Gikuyu Nationalism

In the 1940s, Kenya's neighbors to the north became embroiled in World War II, but for the older women in Mutira the war seemed remote. Although Gikuyu males, as British subjects, participated in the war, people in Mutira knew little about their experiences until men returned home with stories they told their age mates and sons. Wanjiku's husband was not involved. The only reference she made to World War II is when I asked her how she knew that her conversion to Christianity was in 1948 and she explained that it was three years after the end of the "Italian War." Yet those who had fought in the battles of northern Africa learned new and useful skills, particularly how to make weapons. For those who were to become strategists of the liberation front, likewise there were lessons. That Gikuyu men should fight other people's wars for liberation while their own people became increasingly oppressed by colonial occupiers rankled the former warriors. But for women in Mutira, war was a distant spectacle that had little reality.

Mau Mau, Women, and the Struggle for Independence

Gikuyu women in the Kirinyaga area were cognizant of the unequal treatment they received under colonial capitalism, and there were isolated protests against British colonial regulations that particularly impacted them. For example, women in Ndia Division had been forced by British-appointed chiefs to dig terraces and plant grass as part of a soil conservation measure in the 1930s. But by 1938 they had had enough; they rebelled against the measure. Pulling up the grass they had been forced to plant, they marched with it to the colonial headquarters in Nairobi (Kenya National Archives 1938:14; Lambert 1956:100; Rosberg and Nottingham 1966:178). Older women in Mutira remembered hearing about the event.

When war came to Mutira at the beginning of the 1950s, Wanjiku, as a mother left with three growing sons by a husband working far away, found her life very much changed. The lessons of World War II had come home to roost as Kenyans began demanding a role in government and control of their land. Young Gikuyu men without land took to the forests to form a Land and Freedom Army dedicated to liberation. The Mau Mau

Rebellion against British occupation erupted in 1952. The following year, Gikuyu in Kirinyaga, including Wanjiku and her children, were forced into fortified villages, leaving their cultivated fields and homesteads open to pillage.

As new Christian converts, Wanjiku and her husband had enrolled their sons in a missionary school, but a State of Emergency made school attendance dangerous. Wanjiku's sons attended sporadically. Long days of forced labor and nights of fear became a daily pattern for many Mutira women. "A lot of times we would hear the airplanes coming to kill the Mau Mau fighters in the nearby forest. Then we became frightened," testifies Wanjiku.

At the time I began collecting the life histories in 1983–1984, little had been written about women's roles in the liberation struggle. A decade later, that has changed. A rapidly growing literature by Kenyan and non-Kenyan women has emerged on the subject, including Likimani's fictional account (1985), Kanogo's work on squatters and their role in the liberation struggle (1987), Stamp's piece on women's role in liberation in southern Gikuyu (1986), and Presley's research on Kiambu women activists (1992) among others.

Personal accounts of men's roles in the struggle existed (e.g., Barrett and Njama 1966; Barrett and Muchai 1973; Wachanga 1975; Kinyatti 1987). What was missing were women's personal accounts. Likimani's *Passbook Number F.47927: Women and Mau Mau in Kenya* (1985) is a composite picture of several women, whom Likimani knew personally, who had participated in Mau Mau in various ways and who shared with her their stories. Yet none of the women were involved as guerrilla fighters. Rather, they were part of the "silent support wing" that Presley refers to in her study. Whereas Kanogo (1987) traces the way Gikuyu squatters of both sexes became part of the underground liberation struggle, Presley (1992) concentrates on women in Kiambu. She draws on the personal histories of several women actively involved in the struggle both in terms of working with KCA as early as the 1920s and later as scouts and food providers in support of Mau Mau during the 1950s. She argues that women were not passive supporters but played active roles as committed nationalists to the struggle. However, her account singles out women activists rather than the general adult female population to make her case. In the life narratives in this collection women's attitudes toward Mau Mau vary from ambivalence to fear to hero worship. Most women had relatives who were involved in the struggle—some on both sides. Others, such as Wanoi, were actively involved themselves. Though differentially involved in the nationalist struggle in its Mutira form, all of the woman suffered dislocation.

In the 1950s the large majority of Gikuyu in Mutira were either fighting with the Land and Freedom Army in the nearby forest or they were interned in villages set up by the colonial state under its emergency powers to prevent collaboration with Mau Mau (Kenya National Archives 1953). By the latter part of 1951, Mau Mau activities in Embu District were giving the district commissioner cause for concern, and by 1953 "villagization" was well under way with seventy-one internment villages constructed by mid-1954 (Kenya National Archives 1951; 1954:9–10). In addition, detention camps had been set up at Kerugoya, Embu, and Ndoma, and a total of 831 men had been detained. There is no indication in the Embu records of women being detained, though people in Mutira related that women were also detained (Kenya National Archives 1954:10; interview with F. Karoki, Gatwe, May 1984).

Two of the women narrators in their fifties were married to men employed by British colonials in Nairobi during the 1950s. Both women were forced to leave Mutira at the beginning of the Emergency to join their husbands in Nairobi. In one case, the woman traveled at great risk because the colonial government had put up roadblocks and she had to travel in secrecy to reach her destination.

The three women who remained in Mutira were interned with their families in the fortified villages during the height of the fighting in the location. Wanjiku, the oldest, was never sure whether she was going to be beaten by Home Guards or Mau Mau, so she kept to herself and prayed for liberation and the end of war. Another woman's husband became a Home Guard for the British, much to her consternation. She has bitter memories of his brutality during the digging of the trench. The third woman's husband was supportive of the Mau Mau freedom fighters, as were other members of her family who served with the Land and Freedom Army. She became committed to the nationalist struggle and served as a scout for the forest fighters.

Part of women's being interned, beginning in 1953 in Mutira, was not only being forced to leave their homes, but leaving their homesteads (including cows, goats, and sheep) and cultivated fields open to pillage. According to Emergency Regulations enacted by the Emergency War Council in 1953, provincial commissioners were empowered to "require the removal and disposal, or the destruction, of crops or any specified crop," as well as seizure of animals to feed the British troops (Kenya National Archives 1953). Mutira women spoke bitterly of the way British troops and, especially, Home Guards had destroyed their crops, taken valuable property, including herd animals and household items, and left the women with little to sustain their families. For these women, life was bleak with much of each day devoted to forced construction of a fifteen-foot-deep trench skirting the forest to prevent Mau Mau guerillas from contact with the people.

Spatially, the internment villages were the antithesis of the Gikuyu settlement pattern, the latter consisting of scattered homesteads dispersed over the steep ridges of Mutira. In contrast, the internment villages were modeled after the British village, with square mud and wattle houses with little land between them. The villages were extremely crowded and had inadequate water and sanitation facilities for the number of people. A whole village was surrounded by a high barbed-wire fence to confine the people and control their access to Mau Mau guerrilla fighters.

It was not until shortly before independence, when the people were released from the villages, that Wanjiku, the oldest woman, and her husband, who was away working in Voi at the time of the Emergency, were reunited. He found his hardworking wife had already cleared the ridges below the homestead for the cultivation of tea and coffee—a decision she made on her own, unaware that her economic future would be determined by an international market far beyond her control.

Freedom, Independence, and Hopes for a Future

Wanjiku perceives Kenya's liberation from colonial rule as the beginning of her own freedom from the heavy responsibilities and hardships she endured during the 1940s and 1950s. Schooling became easier to obtain, and everyone rushed to enroll their children. The hope was that educated children would return the investment by becoming wage earners who would later support their parents in old age.

Though Wanjiku embraces the idea of schooling, the kind of education children now receive challenges the Gikuyu way of life and makes new demands, in her view. Wanjiku sees the life she knew as a child slipping away. Schooling is partially responsible. Once schooled, young people disappear from the rural areas. They no longer respect their elders, and social distance between *mariika* disintegrates. Wanjiku's life best reflects the changes that have occurred within Gikuyu society during the twentieth century because, of the seven narrators, she has lived the longest.

The Life Narrators

The life narrators were chosen from three different age categories—old age, mid-life, and young adult. Among the women in their seventies from the original sample of 101 women there were few differences. The oldest woman, selected from fifteen possible candidates, is typical of her peers. She is a widow. She has never been to school and remains illiterate. Wanjiku lived with three grown sons, their wives, and fifteen grandchildren in a homestead on a ridge adjacent to where I lived in 1983–1984. In 1994 only the youngest son and his family remained in the family compound.

She is an Anglican convert to Christianity. She cultivated maize and beans and occasionally assisted other family members in picking tea in 1984. By 1994 she was too old to do much work. During my first stay in Mutira, she was largely responsible for the care of three small infants, the children of two daughters-in-law and a granddaughter.

Four women in their early fifties were chosen from twenty in this group in the initial sample. Here there was more variability. Two life history informants—Wamutira and Watoro—were selected because they represented spouses in polygynous marriages. Wamutira is the first of three wives, Watoro the second of three wives. In Watoro's case, she had separated from her husband. Of the two women who represented those in monogamous marriages, the husband of one had died. Wangeci was a widow. The other woman, Wanoi, was chosen because of her profession: she was in 1983–1984 one of the few traditional midwives (known as Traditional Birth Attendants, or TBAs) in Mutira Location. Three of the women in this cohort had never attended school. Wanoi, who attended for one day, ran away and never returned. Later, as an adult, however, she joined a literacy class so that she could write her name and keep birth records.

All four women were Christian converts—two Anglican and two Catholic. Three of the women had children who had died. One did not. All are full-time farmers and relatively poor. Watoro, the poorest, did not have sufficient income from coffee cultivation to buy a cow, whereas Wangeci, the widow, had enough income in 1984 from selling tea leaves to purchase cement to construct floors in her house and a well in her compound.

My original intent was to select only one woman in her twenties, but I discovered enough variation with regard to education and marital status among the sixteen women in their twenties in the original sample that I decided to include two women in this group to reflect the differences. One woman, Nyambura, represents the majority of her peers who have completed several years of primary schooling (the mean number of years of school attendance for this age group was 6.4 years).[4] The other represents the minority of women in her age group who have attained a secondary-school education. Nyambura is married with four children. The other woman, Wanja, is a single mother with three children. One is Catholic, the other Protestant. Nyambura is a full-time farmer, whereas Wanja, who has a secondary-school diploma, is a nursery school teacher, shopowner, and part-time farmer.

Economic status was not directly determined through the sample survey of 101 women, but I indirectly assessed it through observations of housing and homesteads. Most women in the sample were at the low end of the economic scale; that is, they lived in mud and wattle houses with thatched or corrugated iron roofs, no electricity or running water, and no sanitation facilities other than a pit latrine. For most women, earning income for their children's school fees was a constant problem. In all cases, women raised and processed the majority of their family's food, but they used cash payments from tea or coffee production to pay school fees, buy school uniforms and books, and purchase commodities such as sugar, cooking fat, kerosene, and clothing.

Once I made the selection of life history narrators, I approached each one to elicit her cooperation, explaining that the oral narrative would be audiotaped with her permission and would eventually be translated into a written text. All of the women agreed to participate and were interviewed for one to two hours on a weekly basis over a period of nine months in 1984 with follow-up visits in 1985, and in 1994 over a period of several weeks. The interviews were transcribed and translated at night. Notes on one week's interview with a woman became a springboard for the next week's session. As time progressed and a rapport was established, the women became more open in sharing the intimate details of their lives. At many of the interviews, my research assistant was present. She was not allowed to participate at others because she was an "uncircumcised girl who has not yet given birth" in 1984. In particular she was excluded from sessions having to do with *Irua* and childbirth. A decade later Karuana was a mother with two young children. She accompanied me on many of the interviews in 1994, helping with translations where needed, as my Kikuyu had become rusty.

At the end of 1984, each woman was given a gift of her choice to compensate for her time over the year. One woman chose a battery-operated radio, another a pedal-operated sewing machine. Most chose dresses. I was fortunate in beginning the interviews during the dry, postharvest season (December–February), when women's agricultural tasks were at a minimum. Once the planting season began, women were more occupied. During that season I compensated their time additionally by contributing my labor to their fields after each session.

On returning to Mutira in 1989, I saw five of the women briefly. They expressed surprise to see that I had returned and welcomed me warmly. When I again returned in August 1992, I learned that one of the women in her early fifties—Wangeci—had died of an illness with complications. She had told me, "God has chosen me to share this with you." She was one of my best teachers, with a sense of humor that delighted me. I was saddened. I visited most of the other women, who had much to tell about the tea strike then in progress and about the upcoming multiparty elections. By the time I returned in 1994 to update their stories, the women were beginning to say, "See—she keeps returning. She doesn't forget us."

The narratives of the women follow this chapter, beginning with the oldest woman, in her eighties, and ending with the two youngest, now in their thirties. Although none of the women objected to having her real name used in the written text, I have chosen not to use the names by which the women are known in their communities. Instead, common Gikuyu names for women are used, and, where necessary, names of husbands and children have been changed to protect their anonymity. For the most part, the women's stories are presented as they were told to me, with minor changes in sentence structure where it seemed appropriate for clarity. Where stories and riddles became redundant across the narratives, I deleted some and retained others. Each narrative begins with a brief introduction describing the woman, my relationship with her, and changes in her life over the past decade.

Notes

1. The price that a small producer gets for coffee berries varies greatly, depending how much is taken out by the local cooperative, KCPU (Kenya Coffee Producers Union), the state, and local councils where a producer grows his or her coffee. One producer may be earning only Ksh. 20.00 per kilo whereas another earns as much as Ksh. 60.00. The national price for dried bean also fluctuates enormously by year. In October, 1995 the price was US$114 per 50-kilogram bag, whereas the previous year at the same time it had been twice this amount (Kenya *Economic Review,* October 1995).

2. Gikuyu traditionally did not communicate amounts beyond nine to others because they believed it might bring death to people and animals if they were enumerated completely.

3. The 1954 Handing Over Report for Embu District (which included Mutira Location at the time) indicates that, by the latter part of 1951, "Mau Mau activities" were giving the colonial government cause for concern. By 1953, villagization was well under way, with seventy-one internment villages constructed by the following year. In addition, detention camps had been set up at Kerugoya, Embu, and Ndoma, and a total of 831 men had been detained by July 1954 (Kenya National Archives, 1954:10).

4. See the appendix for tables showing marital status, education, and participation in women's groups among the six different age groups in the original sample of 101 women in Mutira.

Wanjiku

3

Wanjiku: The Life of a Traditional Woman

Wanjiku, the oldest woman in the group of life history narrators, has the distinction of being born prior to the period of major British colonial penetration in Mutira Location. Born sometime in the year 1910, she has a vantage point from which to view the changes that are occurring in the Gikuyu way of life. She critically assesses those changes; some are "good"—for example, the coming of Christianity, which brought with it an alternative to "traditional" medical practices. Others are "bad" such as the breakdown of *mariika* (age groups).

Chosen in 1984 for her representativeness of women in their seventies, Wanjiku was then and, in 1994, still is a widow. She lives in a homestead, formerly headed by her husband, with the youngest of her grown sons and his family, who provide her major economic support. Formerly, her second-born son also lived in the homestead, but in 1989 he moved his family across the road to the other side of the ridge, where he built a new, larger, timber house. Because the homestead is only one ridge away from where I stayed, Wanjiku was easily accessible. In addition, she is related through marriage to the family with whom I stayed, which meant I saw her on many occasions.

Wanjiku is the oldest of three adult women living on the ridge; the other women are her sons' wives. She stays with the youngest son. Fourteen grandchildren ranging in age from small children to young adults enliven the two compounds on the ridge. Wanjiku has a special attachment to her youngest son's wife, who fetches her mother-in-law's water and firewood, shares the cooking, and picks what Wanjiku perceives to be "my tea." In return, the older woman takes care of her daughter-in-law's youngest son, not yet in school, when her daughter-in-law is away cultivating or picking tea. Thus, a comfortable reciprocity exists between the two women.

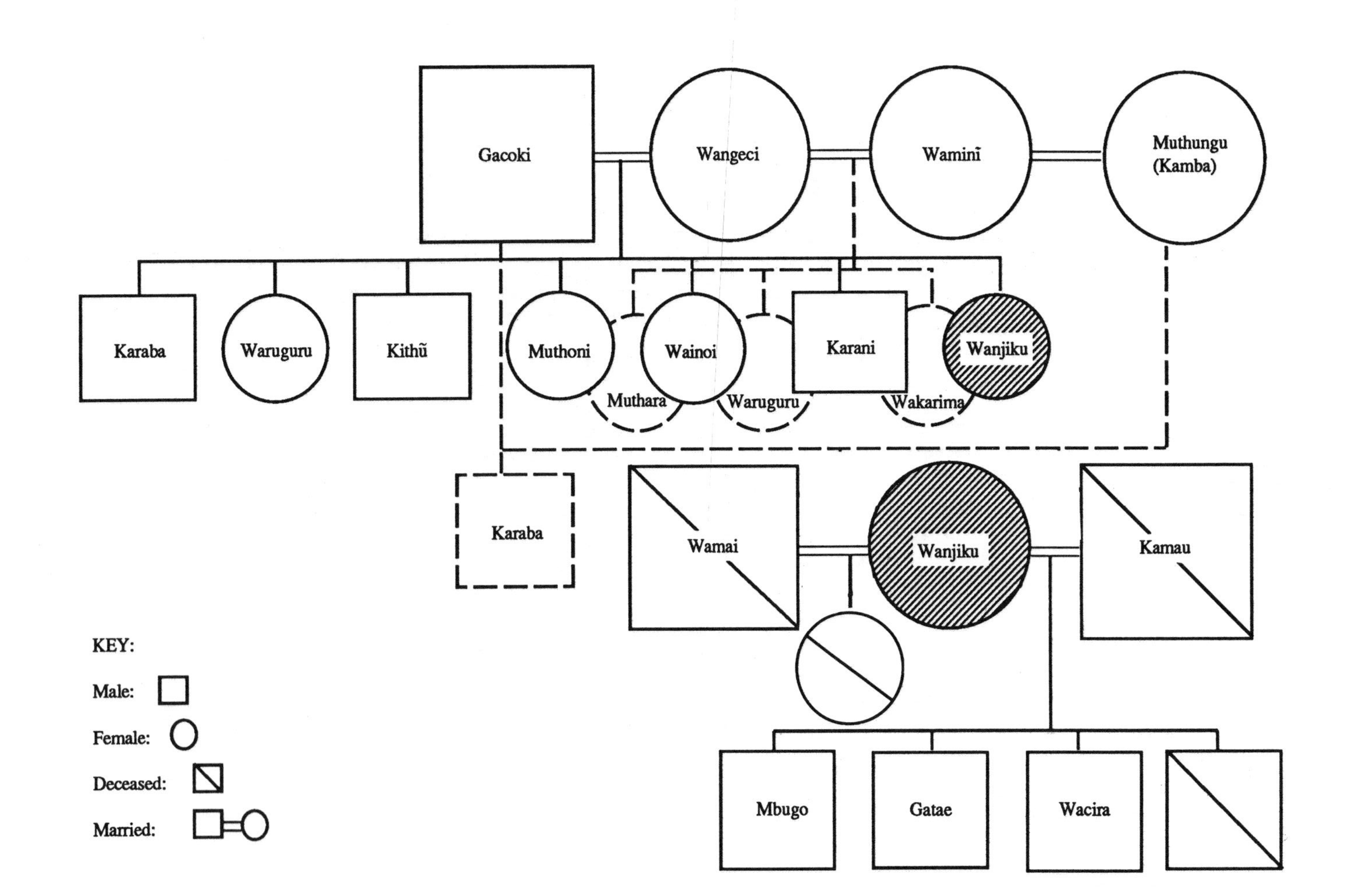

Gacoki
Wangeci
Waminĩ
Muthungu
(Kamba)
Karaba
Waruguru
Kithũ
Muthoni
Wainoi
Karani
Wanjiku
Muthara
Waruguru
Wakarima
Karaba
Wamai
Wanjiku
Kamau
Mbugo
Gatae
Wacira
KEY:
Male:
Female:
Deceased:
Married:

By 1992, the youngest son had built a new three-bedroom timber house with a cement floor and glass pane windows in the homestead. Wanjiku, however, continues to stay in her older mud and wattle house, tending the cooking fire she and her daughter-in-law once shared. The children go between the two houses, often helping their grandmother, who is nearly blind now.

A heavyset woman, Wanjiku has become very lame and gets around with difficulty with the aid of a carved walking stick. She also suffers from arthritis. These physical disabilities have frustrated her efforts to participate in many farming activities—a frustration she openly acknowledged in 1984. By 1994, her disabilities confined her to the homestead and her cooking fire. She views her major usefulness in life as completed and accepts that death may come in the near future. She has no fear of death, accepting it as an inevitable part of life.

When we first began working together in 1983–1984, Wanjiku could not separate her own life experiences from those of all Gikuyu—she is firmly rooted in her cultural community. However, gradually, as she came to know me and we shared the care of her grandchildren, personal feelings began to enter her story. The fifth interview was a turning point. When we began to discuss *Irua*, I observed her becoming uncomfortable as she sought anonymity in generalizations. I suspected that the presence of my research assistant—then a young, uncircumcised girl—was making it difficult for her to talk freely. When I asked her if this were so, she seemed relieved and acknowledged that it was. She explained, "You are a grown woman with children—a *mũtũmia*—so I can tell you these things, but I cannot share this *kirira* (secret knowledge) with a young girl." Her observation posed a problem in terms of the ultimate reading audience, and I explained that young, uncircumcised women might eventually be reading her story. This did not seem to make much difference to her because, she explained, "They are of a different culture, and what they read will be in a different language. I cannot share this *kirira* with a *mũtũmia* from this place because she is too young to know such things." It was as if she understood that in going outside the immediate cultural community and in the process of translation to English, the spoken word would lose some of its power. And so it does. The written, translated text can never capture the complete texture, nuance of meaning, and physical expression that are implicit in the initial telling of the narrative in Kikuyu. What is told here is mediated by the writer in the process of translation and transcription—a process necessary to render the narrative comprehensible to an audience from a very different set of cultural communities.

For the remainder of the sessions related to the experiences of adult women—*Irua,* marriage, childbirth—I worked with Wanjiku alone. She was then far more relaxed and much more open with her recollections, but whenever a woman of a younger *riika* appeared, Wanjiku would shoo her away playfully, explaining that she was giving Nyina-wa-Stepheni *kirira.*

As the months went by, Wanjiku and I established an intimacy born of shared experiences—childbirth, children's diseases, and death. During 1984, we spent one morning a week together, caring for three babies in the compound whose mothers were away working in their *mashamba* (fields). The mornings gave me a chance both to observe Wanjiku in her role as a grandmother and to observe the behavior of the growing infants. Moreover, Wanjiku often contributed anecdotes about her life that did not enter the more formal sessions, but that she allowed me later to include in the final account of her life.

Through many shared hours, Wanjiku came to trust me and "adopted" me as her special apprentice, sharing willingly the Gikuyu *kirira* she chose to tell me and those events of her life she could remember. At times, her voice was touched with a sense of urgency, as if she might not get the chance again to share the critical aspects of her culture. At other times, she displayed a sense of humor, musing over life's ironies.

When I asked Wanjiku, as we shared a cup of tea in 1994, what had been the greatest change in her life in the last decade, she related that the increasing pain of arthritis and not being able to see made her feel helpless and dependent on others. As a woman who had once independently planted tea in her husband's absence and who had been the matriarch of the family since her husband's death, not being able to share in the activities of tea production or to provide for herself materially left her feeling desolate. She expressed that she had lived beyond her time. On a happier note, though, she also observed that her sons were doing well because each had built a new home for his family. She is proud of her sons' achievements. Wisdom and humor characterize *Cũcũ's* (a respectful term meaning "grandmother") narrative. This, then, is her story.

—J.D.

I am called Wanjiku. I am the second-to-last-born of my mother, Wangeci. I was named for the sister-to-my-father. I was born at Kiaritha. My father was called Gacoki. He was a big, black man. He did not have a temper, for he never beat my mother. He and my mother, who was his first wife, had eight children. Waminĩ and Mũthungu, his other two wives, each had three children that I can remember. Mũthungu, the third wife, was not Mũgĩkũyũ [a Gikuyu]. She was a Kamba [Bantu-speaking group to the south of Kirinyaga District].

There were many children growing up together in my father's compound. We would all eat together. The food—even a cob of green maize—was put together on one tray basket, and the child who did not want to eat from the same tray was forced to. We would sit together around the tray and share amongst ourselves. One year, when I was about Njoki's size [an eight-year-old granddaughter], we did not have much to eat because no rains fell. People called it *Ng'aragu ya Kimotho,* the Hunger of Kimotho. Kimotho was an important elder in Kirinyaga at the time (1918). We were very hungry. Even our cows died. But the next year the rains returned.

My older sisters—Waruguru, Muthoni, and Wainoi—took care of me when my mother was working in the *shamba* or cooking. As soon as I was walking, my sisters gave me a small gourd and I would go with them to the stream to fetch water. Later, I learned how to collect firewood with a *mũkwa* [tumpline] and how to fetch green vegetables and carry them home in a *kiondo* [basket]. When I was young I was never beaten by my mother, because I was an obedient child. I was quiet, too—a child who did not disturb others.

My mother, who was a jolly woman, taught me how to use a digging stick for cultivating and later on I learned to use a *kibanga* [machete]. But even after I was married, I found that the *kibanga* can be dangerous if used without care. You see this scar on my leg? My husband's mother hurt me with a *kibanga* when we were cultivating close together, so it taught me not to go near anybody with a *kibanga* My mother used to tell me which ones I was related to when we went visiting. She would say, "If you see so-and-so, that is your *cũcũ* [grandmother] and that one you see there is your uncle. He is a relative and this one here is a clansmate." To know the members of our clan—Ũceera—was important then. That way one knew who could be called upon for a circumcision or wedding. We even helped each other at harvest time.

When I was growing up, there were terms given to girls for the stages they went through—from the time they were small until they matured to become women and then became old. The first was *karigũ,* which means a small girl. Then came *kirigũ,* which was for a big, uncircumcised girl like Njeri [her ten-year-old granddaughter]. After a girl was circumcised, she became a *mũirĩtu.* When she got married and had young children she was known as *mũhiki.* A woman with three or more children, one of whom had gone through circumcision, was called *wamũng'ei.* The woman who had three or more children circumcised was known as *mũtũmia. Muongia* refers to an old woman like me who has no teeth and can no longer give birth. These are the terms that were used when I was a child, but *karigũ* and *kirigũ* are not used now and even considered abusive. *Mũirĩtu* is used for any girl child before she gets married and has children. *Mũhiki* is still used to mean a bride and *mũtũmia* refers to all married women with children. Sometimes *muongia* is used for very old women, but not so often as it was used when I was a child growing up.

The first change that occurred in my life was when I was taken from my mother's bed—at about four or five years of age. There was a ceremony called *mambura ma twana* [children's ceremony] at that time. It came soon after I was weaned. How were we weaned? Our mother refused to let us suck anymore. A child would cry for a few days and then get used to it. When the mother wanted to get another child [resume sexual relations], a goat would be slaughtered by a *mũndũ mugo* [medicine man]. A strip of goat's skin called *rũkoro* was cut and put across the chest of the child. The slaughtering of the goat was to purify the child. At the same time, two women shaved the heads of the mother and child to make them clean. Then the mother and father, together with the *mũndũ mugo* and the two women ate the roasted meat of the goat. From this time, a child could not sleep in her mother's bed. She would have her own bed made of a soft skin or sleep with the older children.

When I was a child growing up, we wore a goatskin. It used to be gathered and tied at one shoulder. When I realized that I was a girl is when I was given a *mwengu* [goatskin skirt with pointed flaps in front and back, usually decorated with beads].

As children we were taught how to count. We were told to collect sticks. Then we would count one to five and tie a bundle of five sticks together. We counted bundles of five sticks until we got to the number needed. Another way a young child was taught to count was by using the fingers. It was important to learn because of selling or buying goats. One needed to be able to count well so that one could count the equivalent thing for trading in the market.

We also learned to measure length using *ndigi* [string]. When building a house, a stick was placed in the ground where the fireplace was to be at the center of the house and strings of the same length were tied to the stick pointing out in all directions. Then other sticks were tied at the opposite end of each string and put in the ground to mark where the outside wall of the house would be. It was just like today's tape measure.

So you see, even though we didn't have written numbers, we still could keep track of things and knew how to measure.

How did we exercise our brains as children? We were taught stories and riddles as we sat near the fireplace at night, waiting for the food to cook. The person with a riddle would say, *"Gwata ndai"* ["Catch a riddle"]. The person playing replied, *"Ndogwata"* ["I am ready"]. Are you ready? Here are some for you:

Ndarekia mũkoni haha watwarairuruma Mbere.	I dropped a banana stem here, and its noise was heard at Embu [a distant place].
[Answer:] *Gĩkuo kia mũndũ mugo.*	The death of a medicine man.
Ciariranira.	They cry at each other.
[Answer:] *Thara mũrima ũria noyu ũngi.*	Napier grass on both banks of a river.
Kanya gatune rware.	A red pot in the field.
[Answer:] *Thathĩ wamũhiki.*	Red soil smeared over a bride.

One used to "give cows" [metaphorically] to the person asking the riddle if he/she did not know the answer. It was not actually cows but just saying that cows would be given—that way one could get a lot of cows verbally if one knew the answers to new riddles that the other person didn't know. Often children were taught the answers to riddles by their parents in the same way children today are taught the answer to a math problem in school. A child was taught riddles so that when she went to tell them to other children, she would have a lot of cows and would win—just like when a child nowadays gets many good marks in school, she is given a number [rank] to show where she stands in the class. The one teaching riddles was happy with the child who had a good memory for the answers.

Some stories made us think, too. The boys were told stories by their fathers and grandfathers and the girls were told stories by their mothers and grandmother near the cooking fire. I remember one that was told by my grandmother about two big men created by *Ngai* [God].

Once there was a man called Mwaramwaka and another called Mũriakamiri. Mwaramwaka would sleep for the whole year. Mũriakamiri was a very strong man who was never defeated by anybody—he would even kill wild animals.

One day, Mũriakamiri thought of going to look for somebody who was as strong as he was. He ended up at Mwaramwaka's place. He met this one still asleep, for the year was not yet over. I tell you, Mwaramwaka had a lot of cows and when Mũriakamiri reached the place where they were kept, he started eating Mwaramwaka's cows. The servants went to call Mwaramwaka, but they had trouble waking him. Finally he woke, and went out to meet a man the size of a giant eating his cows. Mwaramwaka went to Mũriakamiri and told him to start eating the cows from one end and he would start from the other end. So they ate the cows and met in the middle and started to fight. They fought and fought and Mwaramwaka was defeated. Mũriakamiri took the very large bag that he never left behind when he went hunting and opened it. Inside were all the animals he had ever killed—an elephant, buffalo, lion, gazelle, and rabbit. Now he put Mwaramwaka on top of all these animals, closed it and went on his way.

Soon Mũriakamiri started feeling thirsty and when he reached a lake he went to take some water. Just then, a bird came and told him not to take water there for the place was dangerous. Mũriakamiri despised the bird for threatening him and bent down to take water from the lake. Suddenly, there emerged a water snake with nine heads, and it came toward him. Mũriakamiri started killing the snake by hitting it on the heads. But the ninth head jumped away and disappeared to tell the other snakes what was happening.

Now, Mũriakamiri picked up his bag, slung it on his back, and went on his way. But *Ngai*, the Creator, saw all that he had done with the strength *Ngai* had given him. *Ngai* regretted it and so he removed the strength from Mũriakamiri. All of a sudden, Mũriakamiri felt the bag grow very heavy. So he put it down. And when he did this, it opened up and all the animals he'd ever caught came out and ran away. Then *Ngai* told Mũriakamiri to go too. Now Mũriakamiri was weak. He realized that he had no strength to kill any longer.

This story taught us children to grow up fearing the power of *Ngai.* It taught us to use our strength in useful ways and not to abuse others with it. If we went to fight somebody and overpowered him, we learned we might be killed too. Most of the stories we heard had a lesson in one way or another.

Whereas stories and riddles were usually told at night, a proverb could come anytime. These were wise sayings that were a way of counseling us. For example, we were told, *"Rũrigi rweta giriria mũndũ mũkwa"* ["A string makes one wait for a rope"]. This means that first one uses a string to carry things before she buys a *mũkwa* [carrying rope]. We were also told, *"Gũkĩriria kũretagira mũndũ bainda"* ["Patience brings one rewards"]. As a girl got older, her mother might say, *"Wendo mũnene wĩ thina"* ["A lot of love has problems"], meaning that what you love so much today may destroy you tomorrow. We had songs that taught moral lessons, too. I remember one that came after the missionaries began to start churches and schools. It tells people to forget the old ways, like drinking *njohi* [native beer], and be baptized. Even nowadays, we begin songs for weddings and church ceremonies that give advice about wise behaviors.

* * *

When I was a child about the size of Njeri, my mother began teaching me about how I should behave around men. If I was sitting badly, with my legs spread apart, she would tell me that this is not the way a woman sits. I was told that moving about with boys is bad because when the time reaches for circumcision [actually clitoridectomy, though all women refer to it as "circumcision"], the blood during the cutting would go back into the stomach. Whenever I left cooking utensils scattered all around, she would come and tell me that a woman does not do this. If I talked rudely, I was told, "A woman does not talk this way."

When I got a little older, about fourteen, my ears were pierced—meaning that I had bought a new stage of maturity with the holes in my ears. First, I got the upper rim of the ears pierced—that is called *mbuci.* Then, after those healed, the lower lobes were cut and wooden sticks were put in. This is called *gũtura matũ.* Then, when I showed the first signs of growing breasts—before I had my first menstruation—preparations were made for *Irua* [circumcision].

It was the Agĩkũyũ tradition for one to undergo circumcision in order to be termed a grown person. At that time, one bought this stage with pain. The parents would see the girl was growing breasts. Other people might notice, too, and they would point it out to the parents and say, "You should not let your daughter stay a *kirigũ.*"

By "buying maturity with pain," I mean that the pain of the old days and the pain of nowadays are different. First, I felt pain having *mbuci* done. Then later, I felt pain when *matũ* were cut. But these were less than the pain of *Irua.* With *Irua,* I was cut deeply with a *kienji* [broad-bladed knife used for the operation]. It was like being slaughtered. The wounds were covered with castor oil, and *ithangu ria ithakwa* (a very soft, light green leaf with a texture like velvet) was used to cover the wound.

I began going to circumcision ceremonies even as a child so I had seen what happened. It was the old women and my mother, though, who told me that to go for *Irua* is a good thing. The old people wanted me to go before I began menstruating because if a girl had *mambura ma mũtũmia* [menstruation] before being circumcised it was a bad omen, and the parents would lose the first goats of *rũracio* [bridewealth] when a girl was married. My mothers prepared me by telling me what would happen during *Irua,* and the parents informed the relatives and neighbors that on such-and-such a day, Wanjiku would be circumcised.

On the morning of *Irua,* those of us who were candidates were taken to the river by women of our clans. The women and the candidates would dip into the river and start washing each other. Then the women smeared mud all over me and after it was washed off, I was carried on the back of a woman of my clan who was married with only one child up to my mother's house. There, I was dressed for *Irua.* We were dressed with beads made of seeds and gourd tops which were strung across the chest. We wore a skirt made of reeds and seed beads called a *thira.* Those going to watch, though, wore ordinary clothes.

The women accompanying us to the field where we were to be circumcised blew on flutes made out of bamboo. They danced and sang special songs for the occasion. Once at the field, they sang and danced even more, waving clubs in the air.

Ĩi, ĩi, ĩi—ni mwana,	Yes, yes, yes—it is the child,
Nĩ mwana	It is the child
Watuma ngauma ngau nyũmba njuke kĩbaro.	Who has made me come from home to this field.

Then they sang:

Ĩi, ni mburi.	Yes, it is the goat.[1]
Ĩi, ni mburi ya Wanjiku.	Yes, it is Wanjiku's goat.
Ĩi, Wanjiku ndure itangi cunika.	Yes, Wanjiku, bleed so the goat can't be snatched away from you.

There were five of us circumcised together that time—Thegoiya, Wakonyo, Wakũthii, Muthoni, and me. Many people came to the field to watch us. Everybody who was able to walk was there—even small children. They were surrounding us in a big circle. We went to the center and spread out our *mathangu* [leaves] on the ground where we would be circumcised. When I sat down, my supporter—my mother's mother who was chosen by my mother—stood behind me like this [she demonstrates how she was held so her legs were spread apart]. Another woman was holding my hands. The circumciser, who was an old experienced woman, was in front of me, cutting and hewing away meat from my body. I felt so much pain and I screamed very loud. After the cutting, the circumciser put castor oil on the wounds—oil that my mother had brought in a container especially for my circumcision. Then an *ithangu* [leaf] was tied over that place. So, you hear, that is buying maturity with pain. I give you this *kirira* because you are my friend and you will understand.

After I had been circumcised, I walked home very slowly because of the bleeding. If I felt faint, water was poured over my head. Many people of my clan were accompanying me, singing and dancing. When I got home, all I wanted to do was go to bed. I just went in and slept, but other people—the visitors—went on dancing and eating because the clan women had done a lot of cooking—things like *irio*, porridge, and beer. I was later given good food to eat, and my parents slaughtered a goat for me.

After *Irua*, there was a whole month of being washed and having oil put on the wounds and *ithangu* changed until the wounds healed. So now, if you were to see me there, where the meat was stripped off, you would find it very hard [scar tissue].

Anybody who has not felt the pain of *Irua* cannot abuse me. If an uncircumcised girl abused me, we would fight. The girls nowadays do not know such pain. The ones who went through *Irua* together, we have felt pain together—that shows body maturity. We are of the same *riika*. We cannot abuse each other. We are known by our *riika* name—that, and the pain we shared, kept us together from that day.

From *Irua* I learned what it meant to be grown-up, with more brains. This is because after circumcision, I began to listen to my mother's advice that moving about with men could easily make me become pregnant once I began menstruating. Also from *Irua*, I learned what it means to be pure Mũgĩkũyũ—to have earned the stage of maturity when, being a circumcised person, one no longer moves about with those not yet circumcised.

These things I am telling you, Nyina-wa-Stepheni, make my lips fearful to think of the way things have changed. Now, a girl misses something by not going through *Irua*—she does not know when she is talking nonsense in front of a grown person. Part of *Irua* was learning how to behave around the elders and how to act with different age groups. Nowadays, because there is no transition to adulthood, people go talking to anybody. And when a girl goes to school, she is warned by the teachers not to say to any girl, "You are not circumcised" [as a taunt]. In school, they do not want to know which girls are circumcised and which are not.

If a girl gives birth today, she starts moving with those who have not done so yet. In the old times, that would not happen. A woman who had had a child would not talk with one who hadn't, telling her the secrets of childbirth. But today, *hiaya*, a woman who has had a child talks and talks about it. That is when her friend knows she has gone through another stage and is no longer of her age group.

There are no *mariika* nowadays as in our time. Then, we who were of the same *riika* could do anything. We would share our secrets. We would agree to sit down with our legs apart so that we could see who in our *riika* was loose in sleeping with men. There was an old woman, like me, who would take all the girls together and inspect them to see who was having sex.

*Riika*mates used to help each other and straightened each other's behaviors if they saw one of the group doing things that were wrong. How did we help each other? If a girl was caught by a man who tried to have sexual relations by force with her, she would scream for help and the other girls of her *riika* would run and pull the man off, beating him. That happened once to me with a man who wanted to marry me. When he tried to carry me off, I screamed and my agemates rescued me. Also, we would help each other with work in the *shamba,* rotating to each girl's place, and at the end of our work the girl whose *shamba* we cultivated fed the rest of us. We called this *ngwatio.* Even after we got married we helped each other. If one gave birth, the rest would go to see her, carrying millet porridge, bananas, and even firewood. Today, we still have *itega* [custom of bringing gifts to a new mother] after a woman gives birth.

In those days, you would not find any girl who was a *mũkoma ndi* [one who was impregnated and gave birth before she was married]. At that time, a girl feared to become pregnant while still living at her father's home as she knew she would never marry as a first wife. The difference now is that if a girl gets pregnant, she will be married as a first wife or she can go back home to live. If she wants to continue her schooling, she can leave the child at home with her mother and go back to school. Now a girl may get married even though she is not circumcised, but back then, if a girl refused, it was considered a bad omen and she never could marry. It was the missionaries who found that circumcision was meaningless. The girls who went to church refused to go for *Irua* and so others began to follow. But it was brought up again during Mau Mau—then the tradition was followed to show one's loyalty to Gikuyu traditions. When we got *Uhuru* [Independence], things changed even more—after that it was not practiced so much here anymore. Now, the government has banned it for girls. A girl no longer has to buy maturity the way we did.

* * *

After Irua, I was counseled to wait for my first menstruation and to notify my mother immediately when it came. When I first saw blood, I went to my mother and she cautioned me to stay in the house until the days were over. Then my mother gave me water, and I washed and she started telling me to be careful around men when going to dances because I could easily become pregnant. By this she meant that when I went to dance ceremonies with men or visited a man's place, I should not let him touch my clothes. If a man tried to touch my clothes—to undo them—I told him it was bad, and he would not go any further because young men had also been counseled by older men on their behavior. If a man raped a girl and she became pregnant, he had to marry her and no one else. The relatives of the girl made sure it happened.

When we went to dance ceremonies was usually at night. We'd hear somebody playing a flute, and we knew there was a dance. We'd dance *mũgoiyo* [a dance held on a night when there was no moon and the *njahi*, or beans, had been planted]. A circle of fires was made, and the dancers encircled them. Men stood with their backs to the fires, each holding his partner who stood with her feet on his. The two bounced up and down slowly in time to the music. [The same dance among Gikuyu is described in Hobley 1910.] We'd also dance *mweretho* [a young people's dance in which each man would toss his female partner in the air while she shook her body. It was erotic and considered distasteful to British colonial senses.] *Mweretho* was later forbidden by the missionaries. Then *ndumo* came at the end of the year after the harvest. *Ndumo* was danced by the girls naked—I have danced it many times. We would gather in the field and dance all night. We wore beads around the neck and a little reed skirt, but the rest of the body was naked.

It was at one of the dance ceremonies that I met Wamai, who became my first husband. We were of the same village—Wamai and me—but from different clans. We both came from *Itũra ria mbari ya Nguna* [village of the Nguna people]. His clan was Unjiru, mine Ũceera. Wamai was a man whom we called *kiumbi*. It means one who is attractive to girls. He is also a good dancer, can talk well, and laughs a lot. Girls would go and visit him for the night at his *kithunu* [unmarried man's house]. We liked a young man with such characteristics.

When Wamai first started showing an interest in me, he came near the granary at our home and blew his nose. I went out to see who it was. We talked. He said we ought to cultivate together. Yes, men and women often cultivated together. Men liked to cultivate yams and bananas, but they would help with the millet and sorghum. They did not like cultivating sweet potatoes—that is a woman's crop.

Wamai visited several times this way, blowing his nose, and then one time he told me he wanted tobacco—you know, the kind you pinch in the nose [snuff]. I went to my father and asked for tobacco and told him who I was giving it to. I would not have asked if I had not liked Wamai—a girl had her own mind. So my father gave me tobacco and I took it to Wamai. Love started from there.[2]

Wamai took the tobacco to his father and told him it was from the daughter of Gacoki called Wanjiku. When a young man informs his father who the tobacco comes from, the father begins to check to discover if there has ever been a relationship in the past that would prevent the marriage. For example, where the mother comes from—if there has been any bad feelings with these people, that would prevent the marriage. Or if the man is a clanmate who has not been seen in the area for so long that one's parents don't know you are of the same clan, then you will be told not to marry. Another thing, if it is the Ũmboi Clan and Ũnjiru Clan—they are clans that do not marry with each other because of past relationships that were not good between them. It is the same with the Ũithekabuno and Ũnjiru, because long ago the Ũithekabuno would carry oaths against other clans and no girl would marry into such a clan. But in our case, it was found that there were no bad relationships between my clan and his.

Wamai's father told him to tell his mother to brew beer—the local beer made from sugarcane that we call *njohi*—and to take it to our place to give my father in exchange for the tobacco. The giving of beer is called *gũthokia.* A man carries the beer in a very large gourd to the father of the woman to be married. With *gũthokia,* Wamai's parents and mine became *athoni,* meaning that as their children were marrying they will be joined as parents.

When Wamai and his brother brought the beer, I took it to my father and he asked, "Wanjiku, have you given us this beer?" I said, "Yes, Father—it comes from the father of Wamai." Then I began to make sour porridge for Wamai and his friends to show the community that we had become friends.

After some time, the arrangements began for *rũracio.* Now the elders of both our families met to decide how many goats and cows Wamai should give to my father. Women were there, too. They had brought the beer and prepared the food for the occasion. After a lot of talk on both sides, the men settled on the amount. Wamai began to bring the cows and goats that had been agreed upon, but not all at the same time—just a few at a time as he got them. Then my father told him it was time to *gũthinjiro.* This meant that Wamai brought another goat to my father's place that was slaughtered as a sacrifice and eaten by all who were there so that people would know that now I belonged to Wamai—I would only marry him.

My mother and my other mothers counseled me about being a good wife. They told me, "Now that you are going to Wamai's home, do not go there with *ng'aa*—empty feelings. There are some women who marry and do not give the people in her husband's home food and do not listen to their advice—those ones talk *ng'aa.* It means that such a woman will not show respect for the man's family. I was told to give respect to any woman or man I met at Wamai's by talking nicely to them. I should be hardworking and hospitable. If I cooked food, I was told to give it to all the children I saw and to the husband's parents. My mother warned me that if people discovered I had *ng'aa* and did not care for other people there, the *rũracio* might be taken back because it showed that I was one who could not be ruled [controlled]. My mother said to me, "Now that you are going to your husband's place, you are no longer in my hands, but under your husband's care and rule. Respect him and do as he wants—whether it is washing his clothes or heating water over the cooking fire for his bath. Go and be a good woman."

Then one day, Wamai came and removed me from my father's place and took me to his home. He came alone, because there was no need for anybody else to help him take me as I loved him and had agreed to go. It is only those women who refused to go after the *rũracio* had been paid that were taken by force to the man's place. But even though I wanted to go, I felt sad about leaving my home that day because I realized that I was separating from my family.

Once I went to live at Wamai's, I became a member of his clan and from that time I have remained Unjiru. When I first came here, I stayed in Wamai's mother's house until my husband built a house for me and I was officially put into it. During the time when I was staying with the mother, I was observing how she was cooking food and taking care of her house. She also gave me *kirira.* She would tell me how a married woman should behave toward her husband and the moral codes of our people that only elders know.

Finally, the day reached for me to *kumanda*—to get some raw vegetables from the *shamba* and cook them in the new house, which meant that now I would live with my husband. A goat was slaughtered by my husband's father and a piece of its skin was tied around my ankle. Before I went to *kumanda,* I removed the dress I had on and put on a woman's dress made out of a skin. I tied a *mũkwa* around my waist as a sign that now a woman will be installed in her own house. Then my husband's mother took me by the hand and led me to the *shamba.* She got some yams and put them in a basket, collected bunches of bananas and sugarcane, then took me back to the new house. Now Wamai and I could live together in the house. Up to that time he had been continuing to live in his *kithunu.*

I found that marrying was a big change—learning about sex and my husband's habits once I moved to the new house. I had been advised to be obedient to my husband and his parents—now I was experiencing what it meant. I was cooking for Wamai and heating water for his bath. And after staying together that way for awhile, I found I was pregnant.

I knew I was pregnant when I missed two periods and then began to feel changes. I did not feel well and could see my body changing. After about nine months, I was ready to give birth. I was in my house and my husband's mother and my own mother were there. They told me to sit on a stool and then to hold my breath and push hard. Then the child just came out. It was my husband's mother who caught the baby and washed her over a broken piece of cooking pot. Then she cut the umbilical cord. My mother pushed on my sides and stomach to make the afterbirth come out. Then they washed me.

After the umbilical cord was cut, those two women cried, "*Ariririti, ariririti, ariririti, ariririti*—whom have you called the child?" And I answered, "Wambui," which is the name of my husband's mother. The first girl is always named for the husband's mother, the first boy for the husband's father. If the child had been a boy, the women would have called "*ariririti*" five times instead of four to tell people in the compound that it was a boy.

I stayed for about one month without working, just taking care of the baby. All that time, my husband's mother was cooking for me, fetching water, and washing me. She taught me how to wash the child in a broken cooking pot and how to care for her. My own mother brought food to me from home. My husband slaughtered a goat so I could take the soup to get strong again.

After I had my first child, I felt different because I was no longer a girl. One cannot be a girl after she has felt the pain of childbirth. That is why Agĩkũyũ girls are told that they do not know the pain one feels when the ear of the child cuts a woman's body as the child pushes its way out. A woman who has given birth is different from somebody like Karuana [my research assistant], because now that woman knows two things—how to get pregnant and how to give birth. She has a new kind of knowledge. But long ago we would never share this knowledge with a woman who had not had a child. It was considered *thiri* [secret]. That is why I cannot share these things with Karuana.

* * *

The baby was not even one year [old] when my husband died. When one loses somebody like one's husband through death, she experiences a lot of changes and differences. Like me, I was married to Wamai who later died and left me with only one child. Then after a short while, the child died too. The husband's parents refused to let me go back home to my parents' place.

Yes, I saw Wamai die. What happened is that one day he went to the marketplace and he was given a piece of cooked meat that might have been poisoned. When he came home, Wamai was seriously sick. His father told him to sleep at his mother's house because I had a child. He slept that day, but with a lot of stomach pains. The following day, it was recommended that *kubibo* should be done. *Kubibo* means that if one got sick, there were people who used to be called to come and make cuts using a *kienji* on the sick person's body and then that one would suck out the sick one's blood and spit it out. No, the person who did the cuts and sucking was not a *mũndũ mugo*. It was just an ordinary person who knew how to practice *kubibo* on other people. Though *kubibo* was practiced on Wamai, he never recovered. He died the following day, and I was there to see him.

I felt a lot of pain and cried to see him dead, thinking that now he was leaving me all alone. My friend, I was really shocked. For a time, I was feeling lonely and found myself with no energy to do anything. And then, soon after, the child died, too. Now my thoughts were always sad and my heart missed happiness. First the husband and then my first child —I thought life was grim for me. I wanted to return to my father's home, but my husband's parents would not allow it. They continued to treat me well. They were not eager to see me gone. At times, I felt like going, and when I went home, then my husband's parents would come and take me back. So I finally decided to stay here as I had been given some land at their *shamba* where I could cultivate. They told me that I should never marry elsewhere because they liked me so much.

I stayed there for about three years without marrying. At the time, Wamai had a younger brother close to my age. He was an uncircumcised boy when his brother died, though he was big. His name was Kamau. He had been very happy when Wamai married me and I came to stay at their place. He even helped his brother bring the beer to my parents before we married. And when I arrived here, he was always helping me to dig in my *shamba.* That boy loved me, but he kept his love for me in his heart. Other boys used to tease him after Wamai died and tell him that if they were him, they would have gotten circumcised so as to marry me. The father also liked me, and so to make sure that no other man talked to me we would go to cultivate together with Kamau in the same *shamba.*

Kamau was not younger than me. Girls used to grow and mature faster than boys. You see, my age and his were the same, but I got circumcised earlier so as not to begin menstruating before *Irua.* Finally, when Kamau got circumcised, then we were able to marry. But I knew he liked me even before that because once when I returned home after Wamai died, Kamau came for me at my parents' home and told me that I had to go back, and if I didn't, he would never marry another. With Wamai, we got married in the Agĩkũyũ tradition. But with Kamau, we married traditionally when I moved into a house with him, then later we went to church and he put this ring you can see on my finger. When we married, Kamau did not have to take *rũracio* to my parents because his brother had taken most of it by then. He was only asked to take the few goats that had not been taken. It was common in those times for a man to marry his brother's widow. And you can read in the Bible where it says that one can take his brother's wife if the brother happens to die.

Wamai and Kamau were similar in character. Wamai never mistreated me nor beat me and neither did Kamau. Even up to the time Kamau died last May, he had never beaten me. He loved me so much. With Kamau, I had three sons. We would have four, but one, born after Wacira, died when he was not yet one year. So there were two of my children who died—the first born and the last born.

* * *

It was at the beginning of the Italian war [World War II] when Kamau and I became Christians, but it was in 1948 that I became saved. You know, in the church there are Christians, and then there are those Christians who have been saved. The saved ones do not take tobacco [snuff] nor drink. And they don't abuse anybody. Christians just go to church, but they may spend the rest of Sunday abusing people at home. Some drink beer, others gossip or take tobacco. But the one who is saved can't do any of these things. When I became saved—that was the most important change in my life.

How did I come to be saved? It was when the *mũndũ mugo* was unable to heal the swelling that was here below my ear where you see this scar—that is when I decided to go to God for His healing. What happened is that my face started to swell so that I could only look to the side and not straight ahead. After my face and neck swelled, it turned into a large, pus-filled wound that hurt a lot.

The *mũndũ mugo* came to cleanse me of the bad omen that had befallen me to cause the sore. He dug a hole in the ground and put a folded banana leaf—curved like a container—into the hole. Then he poured water into the banana leaf. He put *muthaiga*—a chalklike powder that was his medicine—into the water. Now he dipped a bunch of leaves into the water mixture and sprinkled it over me saying, *"Rũmuka. Rũmuka, wariga. Cio wanariga mũndũ mugo, una mwoni wa mbũgu."* ["Get well. Get well, you who is not known. The one who is medicine man, the one who sees *mbũgũ* (objects such as stones and bones used by the medicine man in divination) has washed away all the bad omen."] When the *mũndũ mugo* did all he could, and the wound did not heal, and it had cost a lot of cows to have his ceremony, I decided that *ũgo* [a medicine man's healing ceremony] was not important. All during the years when I was having my three sons, I had stayed suffering with that wound. But in 1948, I began praying to God for his healing, and the wound healed—that's when I got saved.

At the time, I joined the Mother's Union [Anglican women's support group]. It was a group that vowed never again to carry out old Agĩkũyũ customs and to end those things that would not please God—like taking beer and abusing one another. If one of the women in our group got sick, we would help her by going to her *shamba* and cultivating it, fetching firewood and water and anything else that people in her homestead were missing. It was a group of women that helped each other.

I felt happier in my heart when I became saved, knowing that now I was not on bad terms with anybody and that even if I died now, I would gain afterlife. I know that even now when I am old and unable to walk well, God is waiting for me to come. Anytime He comes for me, I am ready to go and rest with Him. I know that one day I will die, for nobody remains on this earth forever.

* * *

It was about four years before Mau Mau [the rebellion against the British in 1952] that I was saved. When Mau Mau came, it changed things very much for our people here. When I first heard about Mau Mau, I was staying together with my children in a house at Kabare. Mbugo, the first-born, was about John's age [a grandson, aged fourteen], Gatae was a little younger, and Wacira was the size of Karimi [grandson, aged five]. The one who followed Wacira had died by then. My husband was away working in the railway station at Voi then. He was the one who swept the station and kept it clean. So I was alone with the children. During emergency time [1952–1960], one was not allowed to move from place to place. We had to stay in one of the villages that the government had assigned us to. Nobody wanted to go—we were forced to stay in a village. When going to the toilet or to the river for water, we were taken by Home Guards carrying their guns [Home Guards were Africans appointed by the colonial government as local police]. A lot of times we would hear the airplanes coming to kill the Mau Mau fighters in the nearby forest. Then we became frightened.

While living in the villages, we had to dig a big trench up here [at the edge of Mount Kenya Forest] to keep Mau Mau fighters out of the villages. We would wake very early in the morning, before the cock crowed and the trumpet sounded. It was still dark. The British soldiers came round telling people to open up their houses and come out. If you were met asleep, you could be killed. Then we would start walking all the way from Kiaritha up to the place where the trench was being dug and arrive after sunrise. We were each given a portion of the trench to work on. Then we would dig with our *jembe* [hoes] all day, removing the soil until the hole became deep. If we started to drag behind working, we were beaten. Later, the trench was filled with bamboo sticks, sharpened at each end, to keep the Mau Mau fighters from crossing, but some came across anyway. Nobody knew where or how they used to cross to get to the villages for food. It's like if a human being is closed in a house, he/she will find all means possible to get out.

After we were released from digging the trench at the end of the day, we would go to the *shamba* and cultivate just a little portion—that was supposed to be enough for our food. There was a curfew and beginning at three o'clock we were forced into our houses and the doors were shut. Later, we were taken to the toilet and river for water, then back to our houses. We were like prisoners.

I never took the Mau Mau Oath because on the night when the freedom fighters removed people from their houses for the Oath, they happened to skip my house and I kept quiet. The good thing about Mau Mau was that they never killed anybody who didn't reveal them [to the British]. If you had seen Mau Mau but didn't reveal them, they'd leave you alone. They did not use my house because I had not taken the Oath—those who had not taken it were called "lice" or "bedbug" and were avoided.

So me, I only prayed to God that He would protect me and my children as my husband was away. At times, we would be met by white soldiers carrying very long guns. They would come and ask us in Kiswahili,

"Wapi Mau Mau?" [Where are the Mau Mau?] We would say, "We don't know," and they would just pass on and not ask again for awhile.

During Mau Mau, if I was seen with you [a white person], I would be beaten and killed and my house would be burned down by Mau Mau supporters. And you, being white, would be killed, too. Those times were bad. People were living in between fear of Mau Mau and fear of the Home Guards. Both were our enemies. The Home Guards supported the British and the Mau Mau were on the side of the Agĩkũyũ. If you made a mistake with the Home Guards, you would die. If you made a mistake with the Mau Mau you would die, too.

During that time, my children were going to a school run by Anglican missionaries at Karaini. But the attendance was poor because people were sad and afraid. The students were always afraid of Mau Mau coming and burning down the school and beating or killing people there. They never burnt Karaini, but they went there once. So going to school was hard then.

The day that we got our independence [December 12, 1963], we started shouting *"Uhuru na Umofa"* ["Freedom and Unity"], and the news traveled fast from one person to the next. There was an agreement amongst us that nobody would go to sleep, and we spent the whole night before dancing and singing, "Munyao, raise the flag on Mount Kenya" [Munyao was a Kamba who climbed the mountain to plant the first Kenyan national flag on the summit]. We were so happy because we would never be ruled by foreigners again. It also meant the end of the beatings we were experiencing during the Emergency.

After *Uhuru,* when all the roads were cleared [of British roadblocks], my husband came home from Voi. He found us here, having cleared the forest. Before Mau Mau we used to cultivate in different places—that way we could harvest at different times. We might plant maize and beans down near Karaini first, then up here later—that way we had food for eating and food for storage. During Mau Mau, some of the *mashamba* were taken by the British, and so we had to come back here and clear more of the forest. We began to plant tea and coffee on the hillsides. Some people at Embu had begun planting coffee before Mau Mau, but here we did not start until after *Uhuru.* The tea and coffee factories gave us seedlings to plant, and government officials came and showed us how to cultivate them. Later, we paid back the factories for the seedlings out of the first harvest.

I decided to try both tea and coffee, but tea grows better up here. Once I learned how to pick coffee and tea from the officials, I taught my sons how to do it. Now it is my sons and their wives who are responsible for the cultivation. Coffee only has to be harvested twice—in late May and

November—but with tea you have to pick it all year round. We get more shillings for coffee but tea is easier to grow. Why? Because it does not need spraying with pesticides the way coffee does. There is a disease that can destroy coffee if one is not careful.

* * *

After *Uhuru,* my sons went back to their schooling. The oldest one—the one who stays at Kagumo Teacher's College—he has gone up through Form Six and has even gone abroad. The other two finished Form Four [secondary level]. One works in the coffee factory as an inspector and the other was just appointed an assistant chief.

How is schooling different nowadays from when my sons went to school? The level of schooling my sons acquired was the highest one could go then. But today, people are not satisfied with four years of secondary school—that has become the lowest level of schooling that people want to achieve, because a good job requires more schooling now. But people today—those with a Form Four education—do not want to stay in rural areas like this. They want to work in a town. Also, we who are older can have trouble from children who attend school because sometimes they can abuse somebody who is not schooled—even an older person like a parent! Long ago, when I was growing up, nobody dared to abuse somebody in an older *riika.* Today, you can see boys and girls of different age groups mixing and even joking with one another. The importance of *mariika* in Agĩkũyũ tradition has disappeared with schooling.

There is no use taking a boy to school nowadays and leaving a girl behind, because girls who have been to school are more helpful to the family than boys who've been to school. Why? Girls help their brothers and sisters acquire the things they need—even school fees—with the money they earn from a good job after completing school, but a boy may move to the city and forget about his family.

When Kamau was working at Voi and I used to receive letters from him, I wished then I had gone to school so I could read the letters without anybody reading them for me. But just because we couldn't read, didn't mean we didn't think. Before there were schools, we thought a lot, but in different ways. When a person was sick, the *mũndũ mugo* had to think out the cause of the disease and make a cure. When one saw she was pregnant, she used to tie knots on a string from the day she had sexual relations to the day she gave birth to keep track of time. When counting cows or goats, men used sticks to represent their property so they could keep track of the number of animals. Young children had the responsibility of keeping track of all the cows and goats when they went herding, and sometimes the father would test them to make sure they knew which were his from those of the neighbors. We exercised our minds with riddles and songs. The one solving a riddle had to have knowledge of Agĩkũyũ customs and the surroundings [environment]. Unless you know our traditions and the way we live, you cannot solve the riddles. So we had a different way of thinking that did not use books. Sometimes, I experiment by thinking—I see what and how others do something like building a new house and I remember how they did it, then come back here and try to do the same from what I can remember. That way I am able to learn new things.

* * *

A long time ago, if the first child of a woman was mature and ready to go for *Irua,* the father and mother would be shaved [hair from their heads] while all the elders were sitting in a circle. Then the two parents would be given *kirira* by older people, and a goat would be slaughtered and eaten for the occasion. It was the *mambura* [ceremony] called *nyumithio.* It means the oldest child is removed from the house of the parents—*kumithio*—and must build his own house if he is a boy. Or if it is a girl, it means that soon she will leave her father's home to be married somewhere else. After *nyumithio,* the mother's head was shaved completely to show that she is now at a new stage of life—an elder with a grown child—*wamũng'ei.* She put *mikwa* [large ear plugs] in her earlobes. The man put metal rings in his. At *nyumithio,* no woman whose first child was not circumcised was allowed to attend. They wouldn't come because they knew that they wouldn't be given anything to eat at the ceremony. It was a ceremony only for older women.

When Mbugo went for *Irua,* he was taken to a hospital for the operation. When he came back, I stayed with him at home, cooking *ugali* [hardened maize meal porridge] until he healed. By that time, I was a Christian, so I didn't have my head shaved or go through *nyumithio* as other women did. I was already a member of the *kiama* [elders' council], too. Usually men and women whose first child had been circumcised could join the *kiama.* Yes, the *kiama* was for both men and women here. There never was a council for just men or just women alone. But all the members of a *kiama* had to be of the same clan. Nobody outside the clan was ever given *kirira.* The role of the *kiama* was to initiate new elders and to decide on punishment for wrongdoers. If somebody stole a goat, he would be tied up with rope and put in a beehive [located in a large hollow log] and rolled down a hill with burning banana leaves stuffed into the beehive to make the bees angry. The decision would be made by [members of the clan who were] the *kiama.*

Usually, men and women whose first child had undergone circumcision could join the *kiama*. If a woman went to seek *kirira* from the elders, she would be given it. She would go to an older woman who belonged to the council for *kirira*. She would do as the older woman advised, a goat would be slaughtered, and then the elder woman would initiate her while all the other elder women were seated around them. The woman being initiated had not reached menopause, but had had her first child circumcised. But the one initiating her had to be past menopause.

I was a member of the *kiama* of my husband's clan, but I joined earlier than most women. The reason is that I was initiated by my husband's mother after I was married there. She gave me *kirira*, then later initiated me. She never tested my knowledge as is done nowadays in secondary school or university. I was given all the Agĩkũyũ knowledge required and we just learned it. If we became a member of the council, it was assumed we knew it. So I became a member of the *kiama* from that time.

I went through menopause a long time ago—before Mbugo was married. I never felt any headaches or anything you are telling me of [headaches, sweats, hot flashes, depression were described]. It's only that I noticed menstruation had stopped. It was not a big change for me. Long ago, I was happy because I was young and healthy and had the energy to do my own work. Now, I am feeling tired and my leg aches, so it is hard to walk long distances. All I can do is wait for God to do His will.

As an old woman, I try and counsel my sons now. Gatae—now that he is a man of the people [assistant chief]—I remind him that he cannot come home late at night with a family here waiting for him; he must learn to carry the country [sublocation] with *rũrigi* [strings] rather than a *mukwa* [carrying rope]. We have a saying—"*Thina ndiguaguo na mũkwa, ukuaguo na rurigi*" [Why carry it with a rope when you can use a string]. When I hear that any of my sons have quarreled with their wives, I call that son and tell him it is not good to quarrel because it will teach the children bad behavior.

Yes, I have had many roles in my lifetime. The most important roles are, first, to take care of the husband and at the same time, care for my children—cooking and washing for them. But equal with these is my role as a farmer—taking the cows to river to drink and feeding them, taking a *kibanga* to the *shamba* to cultivate and from the *shamba* carrying home firewood for the cooking fire. All these three—wife, mother, and farmer—are equally important. They are all one—they cannot be separated. Being my parents' daughter and a daughter to my husbands' parents have been less important. I could not take care of my husband's parents the way I took care of my own because now I had my own house and children to care for. When we met at the women's group, we were advised how to live peacefully in one's home without quarreling, and this helped me to keep my home happy. So that role as a member of the Mother's Union was more important than being a daughter. Being a member of the *kiama* was less important than being a member of the women's group because after the missionaries came, the *kiama* did not have as much meaning.

What has been my greatest accomplishment? All the work I have done on this earth. And I am proud of being a Christian and being saved. When I was a young girl, I used to have dreams about the young man I would marry, but now that I am old I do not have dreams anymore. My strongest character is staying at home without wandering from place to place or abusing anybody. I am also patient and follow Jesus. I used to have bad desires, like desiring somebody else besides my husband or wanting somebody else's bananas, but I called upon the Lord and was saved from those desires.

Being a woman means being one who is married and has joined her home together. It also means being able to hear things and keep them sealed inside. I think of myself as Mũgĩkũyũ before I am a Kenyan. Being Agĩkũyũ means having followed the steps of *mbuci, matũ,* and *Irua* as I told you.

It is only because you are my friend that I have given you this *kirira,* Nyina-wa-Stepheni. Now you are the one to benefit from it in your writing. I have talked all the things I have seen without refusing or hiding anything. You are learning and I am learning from you too. One can never finish learning. Learning only ends when one dies, isn't that so?

Notes

1. The goat refers to the present a father gives his daughter when she returns home after being circumcised, to celebrate her bravery.

2. Among Gikuyu, the term *mũrata* (friend) is often used to signify a love relationship between members of the opposite sex. However, in this case, Wanjiku used the term *wendo,* meaning "love."

4

Wamutira: The First Wife

Wamutira, the first of the four women in their fifties in 1983–1984, was chosen from among several women in polygynous marriages because, in addition to being a first wife, she never joined a women's group, nor had she attended adult education classes. Of those four women, she had been least affected by educational change, either formal or informal. A late convert to Christianity, Wamutira is an Anglican who attends church but is otherwise uninvolved in church activities. Her main interests are her family and farming.

When I met Wamutira, in the process of conducting the initial survey, she left me with few impressions, negative or positive. When I returned to request her participation as a life history informant and explained why she had been chosen, she listened with bowed head, thought it over for a moment, and then gave one of her indefatigable smiles and agreed to work with us. The first two sessions were somewhat hesitant—she was very shy about answering questions and kept her eyes on the ground much of the time. At the end of the second session, I asked Wamutira how she was feeling about the interviews and whether she wanted to continue. She replied, looking directly at me for the first time, "I feel good about them because they are making me think about my life." She wanted to continue.

There was a marked change in Wamutira's behavior with the third session. Her earlier shyness began to evaporate as she grasped her importance as a teacher. Further, she became more confident in volunteering information about herself. By the fourth session, a few key questions were prompting detailed retrospective responses with regard to her experience with *Irua*. Wamutira's ability to remember detail as we moved forward in her life and her candid self-perceptions enhance her autobiographical account. In fact, from her buoyant behavior I sensed she rather enjoyed the opportunity to reminisce.

Wamutira

Another positive aspect of our sessions was Wamutira's relationship with her co-wives. Both women seemed pleased that we had chosen Wamutira and welcomed any chance to cooperate. At the same time, they respected our need for privacy during the sessions and, after providing us with tea, always withdrew to work in their *mashamba.* They would reappear at the end of the hour, learn what the topic had been, and contribute their own observations and knowledge. For instance, when the topic was basket weaving, the three wives collaborated in preparing samples of basketry, using different materials, stopping at various stages of completion to illustrate the task as the women learned it as children. All three women taught me how to *gwokotha,* the process of binding together plant fibers to make a string for weaving. And all wanted an opportunity to express their views on *Irua.* In a sense, the three wives jointly accepted the responsibility of my education. They also expressed concern for my well-being, remarking that as I spent more time in the community I seemed "healthier."

Wamutira and the second wife, Karuana, are age mates and have a particularly close relationship. The third wife, Muthoni, is about ten years younger, but over the years has made a place for herself in the homestead. Unlike the older wives, she has had a few years of schooling, which seems to give her an advantage she lacks in age. Nevertheless, she always deferred to the two older women in decisions concerning the homestead. Of the three women, the second wife, Karuana, is the most self-assured, and often, when the session with Wamutira was over, she would appear and want to visit with us. It was Karuana who volunteered that none of the three wives had *cuka*—brightly colored cloth wrapped around the lower part of the body as a sarong. She asked if I could bring them each one from Nairobi the next time I visited there. Wamutira is the most reserved of the three women, often deferring to Karuana in our casual conversations. On the other hand, when we were alone in sessions, she blossomed. In short, Wamutira's story must be viewed within the context of her relationship with her co-wives; thus their perceptions of certain events, such as *Irua* and marriage, are included.

In 1989 when I returned and headed toward Wamutira's homestead, a son had run ahead to tell his mother of my arrival. I heard Wamutira from a distance running toward me through the maize fields shouting in Kikuyu, "Nyina-wa-Stepheni, Nyina-wa-Stepheni, you have come back—now I am happy." She threw her arms around me, hugging me as we swayed back

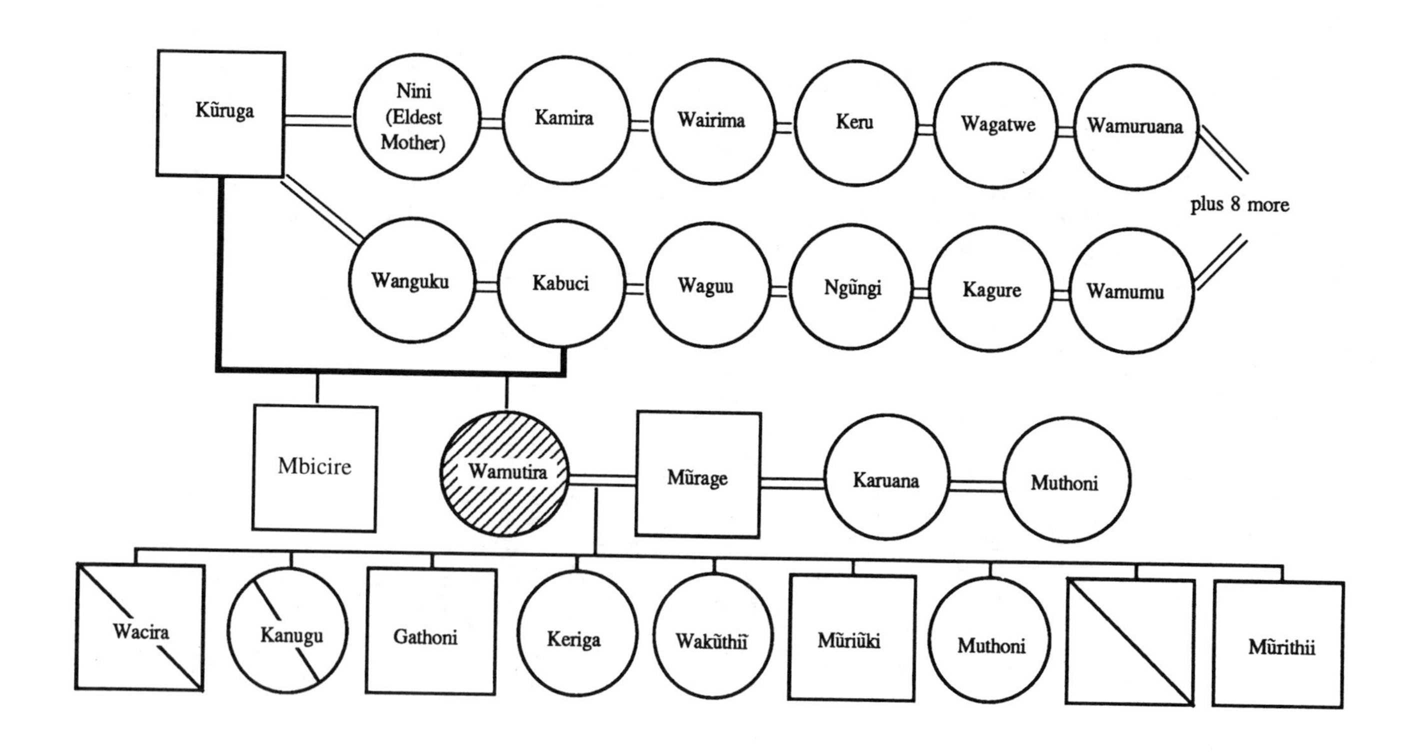

Kũruga
Nini (Eldest Mother)
Kamira
Wairima
Keru
Wagatwe
Wamuruana
plus 8 more
Wanguku
Kabuci
Waguu
Ngũngi
Kagure
Wamumu
Mbicire
Wamutira
Mũrage
Karuana
Muthoni
Wacira
Kanugu
Gathoni
Keriga
Wakũthiĩ
Mũriũki
Muthoni
Mũrithii

and forth and I tried not to cry. We ended up laughing and hugging each other again. Things were not so good at that time, economically, for Wamutira. She was not earning enough to make ends meet from either coffee or tea. She also worried about an older son who seemed to be "wasting his time and not settling down even though he has a family now."

By 1992, however, Wamutira's life had improved. One reason was that *Mzee*, as she respectfully refers to her husband, had given each of his three wives their own land and each was getting a title deed to that land. This was something little short of a miracle to Wamutira and her two co-wives, who, over tea, chattered happily about their good fortune. They also commented on the tea strike, relating that it had prevented them from harvesting. "See how bad it looks? But we cannot do otherwise or we will be in trouble [with other producers]."

By 1994 when I again returned, each wife had built a house on her own land, and so the close communal proximity of a single homestead once shared had been replaced by a new feeling of self-sufficiency on the part of each woman. Moreover, on Wamutira's parcel, her oldest son—the one who had given her earlier concern—had built a small house for his wife and two small children. Wamutira thoroughly enjoyed showing off her grandchildren.

Wamutira was busy picking tea leaves when we first reunited in 1994. I volunteered to help her but she insisted on taking a break, so we settled at the edge of her tea fields on a grassy knoll to talk. She related that she had had some medical problems but that she was better now. "Do you remember that tea strike when you were here in 1992?" she asked me. I nodded. "It finished and now people are again picking their tea. Things are better. We're earning Ksh. 3.50–4.50 per kilogram for tea now. In 1992 when you came to visit, that year there was too little rain. The harvest was poor. But 1993—that was a good year with plenty of rain—almost too much. Now we have plenty of tea as you can see." She turned her head with a small smile of pride toward the chartreuse, evenly cropped carpet of tea beside us. She still grew coffee, she confirmed, but a friend can see that her heart is in tea.

Wamutira was well aware of the escalation of food commodity prices in Mutira over the previous decade but she had little notion of why and how the change had come about. "Prices of bread, sugar, and even cooking oil keep going up and up. People are not happy with these changes," she confided. I asked her if she had heard of something called "structural adjustment." She had not. She was not alone. She attributed the worsening economy to political corruption. When I asked her about the multiparty elections of 1992, she shrugged and replied offhandedly, "Things didn't change—look, Moi is still there." She had not bothered to vote. She was much more interested in telling me about the land that she now owned, with a legal title.

The Wamutira I talked with in 1994 had grown in confidence over the decade; she was proud of what she had accomplished in building her homestead, pleased with her tea production, and satisfied with her ability to make a place for her sons on her land. Obtaining security in land and the attendant increase in her economic well-being by 1994 were the most significant changes that Wamutira had experienced over the decade since we first had come to know one another.

As a result of having their own homesteads, Wamutira and her co-wives were no longer a tightly knit band. Although Wamutira visited Karuana regularly, each was involved in developing her own property. Similarly, each had made the transition to another life stage, that of grandmother. With most of their children grown, Wamutira and Karuana were involved in maintaining heritable parcels for these children as they married. One or two sons had already married and had been given land to grow food for their families. They now had children of their own. The women who ten years earlier had been close as co-wives, sharing cooking and child care, had transferred their loyalities to grown children's families. These women had become elders, managing their own parcels. The youngest wife had joined a women's income-generating group that gave her additional income for her youngest children's school fees. The husband whom Wamutira once had described as being the "wheel and pedals of the [family] bicycle," now was a gray-haired elder living in his own *thingira* (man's house), circulating among his wives and their families.

—J.D.

I am the second child of my father, Kũruga, and my mother, Kabuci, who was my father's eighth wife. My father was a headman and very important. He had, altogether, twenty wives, but I can only remember the names of twelve of them. First, there was Nini, our oldest mother. Then came Kamira, Wairima, and Keru. Keru had two children who were my age-mates. Then there were Wagatwe, Wamuruana, Wanguku—and Kabuci, my mother. She was followed by Waguu, Ngũngi, Kagure, and Wamumu. I can't remember the names of the rest. Our compound was like a village —with so many of us growing up together. Each wife had her own house where she and her children lived. My father stayed in his own *thingira* [man's house].

My father was a good man who liked everybody and never had a bad temper. My mother was similar. I had only one older brother called Mbicire, who was jolly and would never fight. The reason I came to be called Wamutira is because I was named for my father's mother who came from a place called Mutira. It was important to name the first daughter after the father's mother, the second daughter after the mother's mother. The same was [true] for sons. This way, the grandparents would always have a place in the clan. Our clan is Waithirandu, but I married later into the Ũgaciiku Clan.

Every morning, my brother and I would wake up and go to the house where porridge was being cooked. After being given calabash of sour porridge by our mother, we went to the *shamba.* During the day, while we were working there, food was brought to us. After working some more, we would go back home and start playing in the compound. What did we work with in the *shamba?* My mother gave me a sharp, pointed stick to dig with and I never lost it.

By going with my mothers and other girls of my compound, I learned how to fetch water. I would take a small gourd and a basket, just as I used to see the women do, and follow them to the river. I would fill the gourd and put in a maize cob to stop the water from spilling out, then put the gourd in the basket and carry it back from the river. Even collecting firewood, I took some string and went to the forest with other girls and women. When I had collected enough pieces of wood, I was shown how to tie them together with the string and carry them on my back. But I lost most of the pieces on the way home.

I never started cooking until I was a big girl because my mother would not allow me to cook with her pots from fear I would break them. [Traditionally, pots were made of fired clay.] But later, when I was bigger, I watched the way she cooked—how she peeled potatoes with a knife and the amount of beans and maize she put into the cooking pot for *githeri* [a beans and maize mixture that is the staple of the Gikuyu diet in rural areas]. When I was finally allowed to cook, I copied what I had seen my mother doing.

It was my mother who taught me how to make baskets, too. I would watch her when she was making the strings for weaving. She would place a sisal thread on her lap and roll it over and then place another with it and roll them together in the same direction to make a string. This is called *gwokotha*. Here, I will show you. [She demonstrates.] You take these two threads and roll them each in the same direction with a little saliva against your leg. Now roll them together in the same direction, with a little saliva on your hands to make them stick together. I first learned to make threads using banana fibers and grass. I would make some threads and go and show them to my mother and ask her if that's the way she does it. Then she would say, "No, you have made the strings like a boy"—that's when the two rolled threads failed to join together in a tight string.

I used the tall grass to make threads at first. After picking it, I would bring it home and cut it lengthwise into long, thin strings and then I would *gwokotha* the strings and use them for weaving. After using grass and banana fibers and acquiring enough skills, then we [girls in the compound] made threads out of *migio*—a wild plant that grows around here. First, we'd strip off the leaves and then peel back the outer bark from the main stem. The inner bark was stripped back in long threads, and when it dried its fibers were good for weaving. We did the same thing with *ngutwii*—stinging nettle fibers. Later, we began to use sisal fibers when we were grown and more experienced. The baskets you see nowadays, those are made with sisal fibers and then decorated with woolen threads to form a pattern.

While the girls in our compound were learning to cultivate and weave baskets, the boys would make *mbara* [long thin branch of a tree joined at both ends with bark to form a hoop]. They would roll the *mbara* with a stick across the ground. They also made pointed sticks to throw and play with. Boys did some herding of goats and cattle, though usually this was done by old people. If a family had no sons, then a girl would herd. But me, I never herded because my father had a lot of sons. I didn't learn to herd until I got married. But nowadays, one sees more girls herding.

My brother and I were treated the same by my mother. He had his own gourd and calabash and I had my own gourd and calabash of the same size. The gourd was for porridge and the calabash for *irio* [general term used for food]. Nobody ate each other's food, but if my brother came with friends and he had drunk all his porridge and I had not taken mine, I would give it to his friends. When my brother grew big and started coming with lots of friends, then he was given more food, as I was still a child and was not able to finish as much. But when I grew up and started coming with my girlfriends, then my mother started giving me more, too. Sometimes, when I went and visited my brother in his *kithuni* I wished I could be a boy. I used to hear of a big rock whereby if you sat on it, you would change to a boy. I wondered about it, but never went to sit on it.

As small girls, we never wore very much—only a piece of blanket on the upper body and sometimes another piece for the skirt. But grown women like my mother wore a dress made out of three pieces of antelope skin, called a *njuri*. One piece was used as the front part, and the other two pieces went behind. When sitting down, my mother would wrap each of those pieces around her thighs and then tuck in the front piece.

What was I like as a child? I can't remember well, but I was told that I used to just stay at one place and mother would bring my food there. Maybe I was quiet.

We played games after we returned home from working in the *shamba*, like wrestling with each other and a game where we used to collect smooth stones from the river and gather in a group on the ground. Then one of us would throw the stones up in the air and try and catch all of them on the back of the hands. The game is called *ciũthi*.

Because there were many children in our compound, sometimes we would fight. But then any grown person nearby would come and threaten us with a beating if he or she ever saw us fighting again. That usually stopped us. It was only our mothers who were involved though, or some older son of my father. My father, being a chief, was never at home to know what happened to us children. He was always away on some business.

Mariika were important because, as one was growing up, she learned how to treat people in different age groups. People of different *mariika* would not abuse each other or even greet each other. But you, if you were of my same age group, when we met we would greet one another and laugh and tell jokes or do anything we wanted together. We would never talk with those of other age groups, especially those younger than us.

My mother used to tell me never to appear near a place where older people were gathered talking. We never stayed in the same house with my father, and when he came to visit my mother we children were told to leave so that we would not hear what their talk was about. When we got to be a little older, we went to our oldest mother, the one called Nini, and she taught us things—like not to play with boys as their games are never good and would end up in bad things, such that they would lie on top of us. Nini told us how we should behave at dances once we were circumcised. And sometimes she would tell us stories at night around the cooking fire. There is one I remember well:

Long, long ago, during the time of Ndemi and Mathathi, there was one man who used to go to the forest to make knives, spears, and shields. He was a blacksmith. When he went there one day, he left his wife pregnant at home, and as the time reached for her to deliver she was assisted by an ogre.

The ogre never used to give the woman any food. Each morning it would spread castor-oil seeds out to dry and weaver birds would come to eat the seeds. The woman tried to talk to the birds in order to send them to her husband in the forest with the news that she had delivered. But the birds did not know how to talk, and so the woman chased them away.

The following morning, there came a dove, and the woman asked it whether it would go where the woman might send it. The dove said, "Yes, I will go," so the woman told it, "Go to the forest and find my husband and tell him I have delivered and I have never eaten anything." The dove went to where the men were making things in the forest and started to sing.

Mũturi, ũgutura ĩi.	Blacksmith, you who makes things.
Cangarara ica.	Turn your head a bit.
Nduturange naĩhenyaĩi.	Make your things quickly.
Cangarara ica.	Turn your head a bit.
Mũkagwuo ara ciarire, ĩi.	Your wife gave birth.
Cangarara ica.	Turn your head a bit.
Agĩciarĩthio nĩ irimu, ĩi.	An ogre assisted her, yes.
Cangarara ica.	Turn your head a bit.
Nduke tutui ũrie, ĩi.	Get this little to eat.
Cangarara ica.	Turn your head a bit.
Warega merukie ĩi.	You refuse? I swallow it.
Cangarara ica.	Turn your head a bit.

All the men started asking themselves if there were any of them who had left a wife pregnant at home. The blacksmith said he had left his wife pregnant, and so he started sharpening his swords and spears and then went home.

On reaching home, the man found that the ogre had gone to fetch firewood to come and cook. The man's wife told him the story and how she almost died of starvation. The blacksmith cooked for his wife, and she ate until she was satisfied. Then he hid himself in the *thegi* so nobody would see him and waited for the ogre to return. When the ogre came and dropped the bundle of firewood outside the door, it started singing a song it always sang.

Wagiciiri, wagiciiri	You who have given birth
Wĩ nyumba ino?	Are you in this house?
Wogwa na mururumo wa ngu icio.	May you fall together with the sound of firewood.

And the woman replied:

Onawe wogwa nacio.	Even you may fall with the sound of them.

The ogre asked her whether the one who was in the forest making things had come back and that was why she was so brave in shouting back at him. The woman kept quiet. So the ogre entered the house, but before it could do anything it was pierced with spears and arrows until it died.

That's all I can remember of the story, but I tell you, the ogres used to scare us a lot as children. We thought they came from the forest, so we were afraid to go there alone.

While our oldest mother was telling us stories, two of my older brothers, one of whom was her son, were going to school. They were Mbicire, the one who died recently, and the other Mbicire at Kianjagi. Yes, they had the same name because they were both named after my father's father, just as my brother was. Our father did not have a good opinion of school, so he did not encourage us to go, especially the girls. But my brothers went anyway. My father did not see school as important and used to stop us from going by saying that once a girl goes there, she will become a prostitute. Yes, I had a desire to go to school, but I never got encouragement from the other girls in our compound either. None of them went to school, so I didn't want to go and be left behind [behave differently].

When Mbicire grew up and got married to his first wife, Wangeci, with a modern wedding and then built a new big house, he called all of us to come there one day. He told us that by using a *tawa* [kerosene lamp] in the house, we could start learning at night. Us, we just laughed.

* * *

What were the major events in my life? First, there was the piercing of the ears—the upper part of the ear first, called *mbuci;* then the lower part, called *matũ.* After showing signs of growing breasts, I was circumcised. I stayed for quite a long time until I got married, then had my first child. I was bigger than my daughter there [she refers to her twelve-year-old daughter] when I got my ears pierced. Piercing your ears was a sign that a girl was getting mature and soon would be ready for *Irua.* My mother told me I could not get circumcised if my ears were not pierced, and as I had seen a friend getting hers pierced, I told my mother I wanted mine done. There were two of us who went together to have them pierced, and many people watched.

A man called Kibui was the one who pierced our ears. People gathered very early in the morning to see him do it. First, the upper hole was cut. That was for putting in decorative beads called *ciuma*. Later, a hole in the lower lobe was cut for putting in shiny pieces of wood called *ndebe*. That is called *matũ*. Kibui took a sharp razor blade and went round the lobe in a circle, cutting out a piece of meat. I had seen him do this before with other girls. After the meat was removed, a round piece of wood that had been heated over the fire, then oiled, was put in the hole. In a few days, the stick was changed, and one would have to turn it around in the hole until it came out. Then another stick of a larger size was put into the hole.

After my ears were pierced and I went home, my mother spread some banana leaves on the ground for me to lie on to try and get used to the pain. Yes it was very painful. When my ear lobes got pus, I could not do anything as they were swollen and heavy on my head. I only removed the sticks, washed the holes, and put in bigger sticks. I continued this way until the lobes were healed.

After *matũ* and *mbuci*, my head was shaved with a razor blade along the front edges and then smeared with oil [rendered fat]. A sheet was bought for me to dress in. I was shown by my mother how to tie it using maize seeds to make a knot at one shoulder after folding the sheet twice to cover my body [like a toga]. Getting a sheet and our ears pierced made us feel more mature. Just recently, though, when we started wearing dresses, I paid money to have my pierced ears stitched up. Mine [holes in ears] were so big and drooping that I wanted them stitched so they wouldn't tear.

After I had my ears pierced, I didn't stay long before I went for *Irua*. I had not seen *mambura ma mũtũmia* [menstruation] yet and even stayed for a long time after *Irua* before getting it. Those times were not like today, when young girls are having their first menses at a very early age. I stayed for seven years before menstruating.

I heard about *Irua* from my mother. She told me, "You see so-and-so? She is circumcised now. You are also going to get circumcised." She told me that first we would make beer for her brothers who are my uncles and ask them for permission. The reason that it was my mother's brothers is that my father's brothers were not as important, as my mother's brothers had to be paid back the number of goats and the amount of beer that were given for my mother's circumcision. The daughter had to give exactly what her mother had given to the uncles.

I saw many people come to my father's compound, and they drank the beer we brewed and then a day was set for me to be circumcised. On the day of circumcision, I was told to go to my oldest uncle's [mother's brother] place and dance for my uncles so that they would give me money and a goat. I went and danced, holding a wooden club and showing my uncles my body. Then they gave me three shillings and a goat, and I went home with the permission to go for *Irua.*

I was never told exactly why I was going for *Irua,* but I heard from people that a certain man—who was the first to refuse having his girls circumcised—had daughters who would never marry. So we used to get circumcised so we would be able to marry, because no man wanted an uncircumcised woman.

I was circumcised at Giagato, where there is a coffee factory now. First, in the morning we went to the river where women would smear themselves with mud, and then in the river we would be washed by the newly married women with one child. The same women then carried us on their backs back to the field. We were washed to make us clean [pure] for the ceremony, and the reason they carried us was they did not want us to touch the ground—we were well taken care of.

There used to be so many people at the field, young and old, who made a circle surrounding the girls being circumcised. The women would be on the inner part of the circle singing, *"Ĩĩ, ĩĩ, ĩĩ, nĩ kiama"* [Yes, yes, yes, it is the truth]. My circumcision mother [also called "supporter"] was Nini, our oldest mother. She helped me spread the *mathangu* [leaves] on the ground where I would sit so that no blood would touch the soil. It was she who held me from behind, with her legs over mine so that my legs would stay spread while I was circumcised. Another mother held my hands away.

How were we dressed? The girls being circumcised had put on beads across the upper part of the body and a short skirt made of reeds and beads called a *thira* over our thighs. The bead necklace had gourd tops and was worn from one shoulder across the chest to the armpit of the other shoulder. Some girls were given containers called *ithitu* from the *mũndũ mugo.* These containers had *muthaiga* in them—a white powder like ground ashes or chalk. *Muthaiga* comes from herbs. It is what we call *miti dawa* [literally "tree medicine"] that has been burnt and ground to a fine powder. Having a *githitu* [singular of *ithitu*] protected one from becoming bewitched. The *muthaiga* in it was good medicine. But us, we were protected from any harm in our compound because *muthaiga* was put all around the houses—that way, there was no need of a *githitu.* So me, I did not need one around my neck when I was circumcised because I was already protected.

Kamira and another woman called Watene from Gichugu were the circumcisers. Kamira was slender and black. She did not dress in any special way. She just had a blanket wrapped around her and tied at the shoulder. Before circumcising us, she got a small gourd and emptied some *muthaiga* into her palm and touched herself with it on the face to cleanse herself for the ceremony.

The circumcisers used a *kienji,* a metal knife that was very sharp with a wide blade like an axe and a handle that was thin. But nowadays, they use razor blades because there is not so much cutting done. Each time a girl was circumcised, the *kienji* was washed in water and wiped with a *mathangu* [leaf] of the *muigoya* plant.

Our father, Kũruga, had given those of his girls being circumcised some shillings. He told us that those who never cried during *Irua* and were brave could keep theirs but those who cried would have their's taken away. Me? I lost my shilling. I was crying because I was afraid, and I knew it would hurt even before they started cutting.

During the ceremony, women of the clan sang special songs called *ndaiho,* but I can't remember how they go at the moment. Three deep cuts were made [removing the clitoris], and it was very painful. They used to cut deep until a *mathakwa* leaf fit in. But nowadays, those who want to be circumcised, only the tip of the clitoris is removed. After the cutting was done, the wounds were spread with castor oil because there was no medicine then. The oil was brought to the field by my mother in a bamboo container, and I used the oil to put on the wound until it healed. Then a *mathakwa* leaf—which is very soft—was stripped of its stem and tied over the wound, using thread, in between the legs to keep the leaf still and in place. [At this point in the interview, Wamutira stops to demonstrate how the *mathakwa* leaf is prepared for use as a bandage.]

How did I walk home with all that pain between my legs? I was being supported by those near me—by supporters who were my circumcision mothers. They were one on each side and another woman was ahead with a small gourd of water so that when I fainted she would pour water on me.

When I reached my mother's house, I went right inside. As I was not able to climb onto the bed, banana leaves were spread on the floor for me. I had to sleep on my back because if I slept in any other way, the leaf covering the wound might come off and then I would have to have another put in, which was a painful operation. So you see, it was no joke. I was told never to sleep on my sides, as the wound might close up the hole and then I would never give birth. But I only stayed that way at night. During the day, one could sit down on a banana leaf comfortably. Each evening, I would remove the leaf and smear castor oil on the wound and then put another leaf in.

All the people who had come to escort me home—who came from all places—were feasting at my home. There was so much food and beer, but it was not enough for all those people. My father had given me a goat when I went inside the house, which I never saw again.

I felt weak and light for a long time before I got back my normal health. Girls used to lose a lot of blood, especially if the uncles demanded that there were some goats that had not been paid them. The girl would bleed until the goats were given to the uncles. Then the bleeding stopped.

In those times, one never refused to get circumcised. Even those who were poor and could not afford the things asked for by the uncles, other members of the community would make sure they got them so the girl could be circumcised.

Nini told me after I was circumcised that now I would be waiting for *mambura ma mũtũmia* and I should take care and not wander about. And she told me that the calabash one eats from when circumcised—that one is never used again by another person, for it would mean contaminating the person who used it.

After I had gone through *Irua,* I felt different. I felt like I was a grown-up girl now, ready for dances. And everybody saw us as adults. People treated us differently and we were expected to act differently. Nowadays, you wouldn't know who is mature and who isn't because few girls go for circumcision, and even when a girl gets menstruation, you don't notice because girls do not have to stay in the house as we did.

Nobody ever told me about what menstruation was, and when I first saw it I got frightened because I learned that now I had to take extra care with men so as not to get a child before I was married. That was a very bad thing to happen to a girl then. I also wished that I had stayed long without it so that I would have enough time to go to more dances. [Here Wamutira contradicts an earlier statement relating that she waited a long time—7 years—before menarche. It makes for a contradictory, bumpy chronology, but older Gikuyu women did not seem to be concerned about gaps in time or the rationality of a perfect chronology.]

But now I would not want *Irua* to come back. Even the one who forbid it [Kenyan President Daniel arap Moi] did right.

* * *

[As we finished the session on *Irua,* Karuana and Muthoni, Wamutira's co-wives, learned what we'd been discussing and wanted to express their opinions. What follows is a discussion between the three wives.]

Muthoni: If it's now and I'm told to go and get circumcised, I would run away and leave all that food and beer there.

Wamutira: Yes, there is one girl who ran away and left the circumciser and beer in the gourd and even the cooked food.

Karuana: It [circumcision] was a stupidity that was liked very much by Agĩkũyũ a long time ago.

Wamutira: With Wandia, she was bleeding badly, so we took her to the hospital. When the nurse came, she wanted to beat us when she saw Wandia and told us we were very foolish to be doing that kind of thing nowadays. She told us to take the girl home and heal her. I said we were sorry and would never repeat it again. And I pleaded with her to just give Wandia an injection. But the following morning, the girl was still bleeding. What I saw that time, that was the end of it for me.

Muthoni: I feel good because the banning of circumcision means that none of mine [daughters] will be destroyed that way.

Karuana: The things nowadays are not the way they were long ago.

Muthoni: Yes, that is so. A long time ago, if a girl matured and had her menstrual period, she would never go out. She told her mother and was shown where to stay and would stay there in the house until the days given her by God were over.

Karuana: You would not go anywhere, nor cook or go to dances.

Muthoni: So your clothes would all soak with menstrual blood, one after another, until the days were over.

Wamutira: But nowadays, things are better because nobody calls another *karigũ* [silly uncircumcised girl] or *kahiĩ* [same applied to a boy], and so there are no fights between the circumcised and uncircumcised.

Muthoni: The only fights you get nowadays are between drunkards. You can't hear a girl fighting with another girl because of *Irua.*

Karuana: If you met an uncircumcised young man and a circumcised one you would not distinguish between them. It is only when he goes to school and is beaten by others [for not being circumcised] that he comes home and does it.

Muthoni: Now, you can't tell the difference between one who is circumcised and one who is not. Long ago, if you were of my age group and we met and my ears were pierced, you would never joke with me or abuse me until yours were pierced, too. There was a difference between those who had been circumcised and those who had not. Now, there is no difference. The old traditions are gone.

[Wamutira nods her head in agreement.]

* * *

[Wamutira resumes her narrative in the next session with an account of what, for most women, seems to be the happiest period of their lives—between *Irua* and *ũhiki,* or marriage.]

I stayed for quite a long time without thinking about marriage because of the happiness I got from dancing. Once we were circumcised, then we could go for dances. There was *mweretho,* where each man would dance with a girl and would throw her up in the air and the girl would shake her whole body. There was *gicukia,* which was attended by those not circumcised, and another by only those who were circumcised. We used to go to dance very far from home when there was moonlight.

I remember one dance organized by boys for their girls in the area. We would spend the whole night there dancing and then go home the following morning. Those who were a bit brave would walk home during the night. When I was a *mũirĩtu,* I used to laugh a lot and sleep out in the cold night without even a blanket after dancing. As I had nothing to think or worry about, it was the happiest time I can remember. After dancing, I would go home and meet food already cooked and would just start eating. But now the mind is occupied with where to get food, what needs to be done next—like cultivating the tea or coffee, getting food for the cows.

In those times, the man who was very attractive—who was *kiumbi*—had his own unmarried man's house, which was just one room. Girls, during dances, used to go there every night. We washed ourselves, beautified ourselves, and went to this man's house and spent the night and would not return home until morning. Our oldest mother taught us how to dress ourselves when going there to prevent anything from going wrong. This was by tying ourselves with ropes so that the skirt was tight around the body. This is how we did it—I will show you. [She demonstrates.] Take one edge of the skirt in front, gather it into a knot and tie the rope around it. Then put that knot in between the legs toward the back. Now take the end of the rope and wrap it around each thigh so that when we are fondled by the man he cannot do anything [have sexual intercourse].

A man who is *kiumbi* is the best dancer, one who is handsome and able to lead in songs. The voice, itself, was enough to make one leave a pot cooking over the fire and go and dance! We would spend the night there in his big bed being turned over and over by him all night. So in the morning we would go tell others of our agemates who had not come with us and then they would go that evening to be turned over. With agemates, you can joke about things like that—where you spent the night and who was there. But with those of other *mariika,* you had nothing to talk about.

We used to go dance just near our home, and one day afterwards Mũrage [her husband] made beer for us at his home. He never invited me but invited my friend, Kanyiba, and she took me with her. When we went there, Mũrage started talking to me on the subject of love and I told him that I was not interested in him. He realized it, too.

So, it happened that we had to pay back the beer we were given by having visitors to our place. When Mũrage came, I refused to listen to him, and he thought I was refusing him because of the beer we were taking. One night he came to the granary outside my mother's house and started blowing his nose. When I heard, I started asking, "Who is that?" I vowed not to marry him if it was the same person. I went out and told him to go home because we were going somewhere. He left, but the following night he came again. I went and told him to never come to our house again. But he started coming near the granary from day to day without stopping. He finished a month doing that.

My parents asked me who this man was who always came to the granary. I told them it was Mũrage and that I could not marry him, because I heard that at his place they beat their wives. Still he never stopped coming. So, I decided—because of his insistence—I would give him tobacco for his father. I went for tobacco from my father and gave it to Mũrage—that's the way our friendship started.

Mũrage took the tobacco to his father, and he was told to go to the sugarcane *shamba* and get some sugarcane to make beer. When it was made, it was brought to our place in large gourds by two women from Mũrage's place. Then I made sour porridge to pay back the beer, and Mũrage and his many friends came to take it. During *gũthokia* [the "gourd-having-period"], a girl would sit with a gourd of sour porridge on her lap, and an agemate, a girl who was a friend, would sit next to her passing the calabashes of porridge as she served them. So when Mũrage came with his friends, I would shake the porridge, then pour it into a calabash, and my friend would pass it to Mũrage and his friends. If a girl happened to put the gourd of porridge down on the ground, the man and his friends would not take it, because it showed that the girl was not interested in the man as she didn't respect him enough to keep the gourd off the ground.

After this period, Mũrage made more beer, and I made more porridge. When my father got enough beer, he asked for *rũracio.* It was the men of the two clans who were the ones who carried out the negotiations as to how many goats and cows would be brought to my father. The women cooked food to take to the place where negotiations were going on, and they brewed beer for the occasion. During that time, I was very far away, cultivating in the *shamba,* and was not allowed to come near. When all the goats and cows that had been agreed upon were brought by Mũrage and his helpers, a ram that was part of *rũracio* was sacrificed at our place and its blood poured into the yard. The mixing of the blood from the groom's ram with the soil of the bride's home means that peace is made between the two sets of parents and clans. *Uthoni* [in-laws] is how they refer to one another from then on. The process of mixing the blood of the ram with the soil is called *gũthinjiro.* Now I was promised to Mũrage.

I had been told by the older women in our compound that when you get married, you are carried shoulder high from your place to where you are marrying—to your husband's home. They also told me that I would go first to the man's mother's house and never come out and would always wear a veil covering the head as a bride to show respect for the mother.

So when Mũrage came to get me, I told him I wouldn't go. The following day, Mũrage and four others from his place came and insisted in knowing the reason. They threatened to carry me by force to his home. I got scared. I went into the house then and packed a few clothes, and we started walking. It was during the night, for they did not want to be seen. Sometimes, when people saw their daughters were being removed, they would refuse and would try and beat the man and his relatives because they did not want to lose the girl. I went slowly with Mũrage, sometimes sitting down because I did not want to go. Sometimes I wondered whether I could escape and go back home, but then I was threatened with a beating and I would start walking again.

When we reached the gate of Mũrage's homestead, I refused completely. I became afraid wondering what we were going to say to each other at his house—just the two of us. Then his father heard us and asked why we were refusing to go in. I had not even told my mother I was going. I knew that they would discover in the morning when they missed me. So the following day, food was brought to me from my father's place, for they knew I had been taken to Mũrage's.

I got food from my home until that time when I was welcomed to Mũrage's family by his parents with a goat. What happened is that when one married and went to her husband's home, she could not eat cooked food prepared there until she was welcomed officially. Up to that time, she was being given *kirira* [secret knowledge] by the husband's mother on what to do in that compound and how to behave. For instance, I was told by Mũrage's father's older wife not to wander about or go outside my husband [commit adultery]. She said, "You are newly married so you should not be seen outside until the time you will be allowed to." If I did go outside the house, she told me to cover my face and legs with a veil—a big sheet—so as not to be bewitched. Also, it was hard for the husband's father to see the bride that way, and [it] showed respect for his wives.

Above all, I could not eat meat during this time until a goat was slaughtered for me. I can remember it was slaughtered when I got my first child almost two years later. That was our custom. The bride would not eat any meat. Even if the husband came with meat, she would just cook it for him and not eat it.

I did not go to Mũrage's mother's house as I had been told because he had already built a house for me. After we stayed together for awhile, I learned what he wanted and how things should be done. So we stayed from that time without fighting.

I did not meet Mũrage's mother when I went to live there because she had died. Only his father's other two wives were there. Their behaviors were very bad—they refused to give me a gourd, a calabash, and a tray basket for winnowing. I had to ask for these from my father's place.

And those two did not get along with each other and used to fight sometimes, calling each other names. It made me feel sad to see them.

I stayed for one year before I got pregnant. What happened is that I was called home by my father, who was worried that I had not gotten a child yet. He called me so I would be washed in the river by the *mũndũ mugo,* just as happened to my mother when she did not get pregnant. The *mũndũ mugo* fetched some water from the river, using a calabash, and in a hidden place between some arrowroot plants, he washed me saying, "I have washed you of the bad omen that refused to let you have a child. May you have a child. I have washed you completely. I have cleansed you completely." His words worked, for I never finished that year without becoming pregnant.

Soon after the *mũndũ mugo* cleansed me I missed my monthly flow. I went to a short woman in my husband's father's compound called Waduru. She told me that I was pregnant and I would know when the baby inside was three months old. After three months, I started feeling sleepy during the day and vomiting. When I started feeling the child playing in the womb, I knew then that Waduru had told the truth.

Once I knew I was pregnant, I could not sleep with my husband anymore. He called me to come to stay with him in Nairobi, where he was working then, but when I told him I was pregnant, he said there was no need for me to come. We were told by our mothers that if a woman had sexual relations when she was pregnant, she would make the midwife vomit because the child would be very dirty.

As time neared for me to deliver, I was always feeling sleepy. When I went to the *shamba* to cultivate, I would sleep there until it was late—toward sunset—then go back home. I was not able to cultivate well. So my husband called me to come to Nairobi. His father was not happy. He told me that I should not go to Nairobi, for even here at home there was now a hospital. But I made up my mind to go because my husband wanted me to be near him so that he could take care of me as there was nobody at home to care for me—my husband's mother being dead and the other wives not friendly. When I left for Nairobi, the *Mzee* [Kiswahili word meaning "old one," a respectful term] was annoyed and started complaining and muttering.

After staying in Nairobi a short time, one day I started feeling some stomach ache and feeling like going to the latrine. A woman neighbor came, and I told her how I was feeling. She told her husband that I should be taken to the hospital because my husband was at work. It was not my wish to give birth in a hospital, but in Nairobi there was nowhere else I could have gone. People in Nairobi go to the hospital for delivery.

When I went into the hospital, there were doctors there and a woman midwife. I was put on a bed. After some more pains the baby came out, and the midwife took scissors and cut the umbilical cord and tied it using thread. Then she started pressing my sides to make the afterbirth come out. I felt pain when the afterbirth fell out. But one of the doctors gave me some medicine. A nurse attendant came and went with the child —even before I had seen him! I was taken back to my bed. I slept for a while, and then the baby was brought to me to suckle. But the child refused. I knew it was because I had made the *Mzee* angry. You know, in those days, if an old man was made angry and grumbled, the one who was the cause could be inflicted with some kind of unusual thing—like a curse. So that is why the child refused to suckle—because *Mzee* was angry that I had gone to Nairobi to deliver.

So my husband decided to go home and get *Mzee*. Let me tell you, when the old man arrived, everybody was astonished to see that the child began to suckle—suckling fast and a lot. What the *Mzee* did is he brought milk from home for the child and then he blessed the child by spitting on his own chest [a traditional Gikuyu blessing], and that ended the curse.

Because I had been stitched after I was cut to make room for the baby to come out, I stayed in the hospital about three days. We gave the baby the name Wacira, as Mũrage's father, for whom he was named, had always wanted to act as a judge and wanted people to solve their problems by consulting a judge—Wacira means "judge."

I felt nothing but happiness when I had my first child because I had always been asking myself, "When shall I have my own child?" And now, because I had a child, I felt myself a woman. My breasts dropped because now I was suckling the child. And I found that when I came home to Mũrage's place, people treated me differently. When I came here with the child, a goat was slaughtered because now I had named the child after the father's father. The women here started cooking food for me, and I could begin eating meat.

How had I been prepared to be a mother? As small girls, we were always playing at taking care of babies. We would take roasted bananas and chew them to make them soft, then feed them to toy babies. We would wash them and clothe them the way we saw our mothers do. When we got a little bigger, we chewed the bananas and fed them to the smaller children in the compound with a finger straight away without keeping the chewed bananas in a calabash the way our mothers did. We also learned how to carry babies on our backs, tying them securely with a cloth so they didn't fall.

Being a mother means having happiness and sadness too. Six of my children are alive, but many of them died before they were big—three of them. Wacira, the first born, died before he was two years old. But there was a girl called Kanugu who followed Wacira who died when she was nine years old. I say that the child who dies when he/she is very small is less heartache than the one who dies when she has fetched water and firewood for you and has cooked for you. That one is hard to forget.

What happened is that Kanugu started swelling in her stomach. We took her to Tumutumu Hospital, and she was admitted. They removed the water that made her stomach swell, and then she was discharged. We went for her and paid the hospital bill and brought her home here.

When she came home, she started telling us that she could feel her stomach swollen again, so we took her back to Tumutumu and she died there. I thought maybe she was given poisoned food, as she had come from school and got sick that afternoon. I first took her to Kerugoya, but when it turned out to be more serious I decided to take her to Tumutumu. Before we took her to the hospital, though, we had taken her to the *mũndũ mugo,* because the grandmothers were so much for him and thought he would help. We went to my father and he told us to go and buy a cow and a goat and slaughter them. He cooked beer for her to get well. But she never did.

When we went to the hospital the next morning after she was readmitted, we were told that she had died. So we went to the mortuary to see her and then started making arrangements for the burial. My husband made the arrangements for the coffin and grave, and then he came and told me she was buried.

Even after Kanugu died, I stayed for a long time thinking that it must have been somebody who gave her poisoned food so that she would have a disease that would not kill her right away but she would suffer before dying.

The one who has never lost a child has not seen any problems in her husband's house. That one might ask how one looks when one is dead because they have never seen a dead body. But me, I have been to see, so I can't go asking.

When the girl died, I went home, and my father asked me whether Kanugu felt better. I was unable to tell him because I was crying, and my heart was heavy with tears. I could not find the courage to tell him. So others told him.

I changed very much after that child's death. I started fearing that I might never be given others. The ones I had later after Kanugu's death, I took much care of so that they might not die—like making sure they were clean, had good food, and went for clinic. At times, I keep quiet and think, "I had very strong children who died compared to ones I have now"—like when the two-year-old boy died, I had just given birth to Mũrithii, my last born, and I prayed, asking, "Why has God taken the bigger one and left this tiny one?" But you see, Mũrithii is the one fetching water for me now. There are none of my children that I take for granted. Kanugu's death taught me that lesson.

* * *

After that time when I had Wacira, my first born, I returned here to Mũrage's place, but I was not happy. As I have told you, Mũrage's mother, Wagathare, who was the father's first wife, had died, leaving the other two wives here. I found these two women would not give each other food, nor did they share food with me. They never wanted to talk to me, and they hated each other. But it was their husband, Mũrage's father, who was at fault. He liked one more than the other and bought her better things, like clothes. The other one stayed feeling bad. Another thing, if the two wives made beer, *Mzee* would not give the second wife the beer but would share some with the younger wife. Those two women were very uncooperative, and I began wishing I had somebody I could talk with. I remembered how I'd seen my father's wives having good talks when sitting eating their evening meal together after the day's work. Then one day Mũrage came home from Nairobi to visit. He had been working for some Europeans as a houseboy. He told me that he could see the child and I were not very happy, so he was going to marry another wife so we could be working together. I agreed with him. "Yes" I told him, "that is a good idea, because now I will have somebody to talk to and work with." So we started looking for a bride.

Mũrage heard about Karuana from another woman who was her neighbor. We were told that she was a very good girl—hard working and not naughty. She knew how to control her mouth. So I told my husband to marry Karuana, because if he married a woman who was *ng'aa*—a woman who didn't care and wouldn't listen to me—then the home would collapse.

When I saw Karuana, I liked her and wanted to have her as my co-wife. I knew she would help with the work and was one I could communicate with. From then on, I felt a lot of happiness. Like today, when I'm visiting you, she is the one home cooking for the children, and when I return home I will meet things well taken care of. That's why I like Karuana so much.

I am able to remember well the day I went for Karuana, even though it was a long time ago. It is only that I don't remember the year, but I know it was during the start of Mau Mau [1952]. I can remember Mũrage and me taking beer to her father's home near the Kariko Coffee Factory, where there was a homestead of some Britons. And it was me who went for her on the day that was arranged for her to marry, because the husband was in Nairobi.

The first night after I brought Karuana home she spent the night here with me in my bed. Then, the next morning, I escorted her to the bus stop to go to Nairobi. It is me who married her. After becoming pregnant,

Karuana came back here. When she came, my son got sick, so she told me to go to Nairobi so the child could be taken to the hospital. I went and left Karuana here. But I was only in Nairobi for a short time. Then I came back here and stayed with Karuana until the husband wrote a letter telling me to go back to Nairobi. Karuana and I, we each had our houses here, but she would always cook with me—even now.

At the time that Karuana came to live here, there was no coffee planted, only cultivating of food crops like maize and beans. We had our own *shamba* in different places, but we cultivated together. I never felt any jealousy toward Karuana. I was happy because the husband was finding children with her, which I also wanted. And he would also come and give me mine. And after one of us got pregnant and was unable to work, it was the duty of the other to cook for her, cultivate her *shamba,* and feed and wash that one's children. Jealousy? That would be a waste of time. Mũrage would spend the night with Karuana and then come in the morning and ask me to warm his bathwater, and I would gladly do it. And the same with Karuana if he spent the night with me. The thought of where he slept and what he did was never in us. When two or three wives are good friends, that home is always warm and lively. But if they hate one another, there is no home.

* * *

[In order to find out Karuana's perceptions of her marriage to Mũrage and her relationship with Wamutira, I interviewed her on a day when Wamutira had gone to the clinic in Kerugoya. This is Karuana's account.]

First Mũrage came to our home, and we talked with him about the marriage. So when he came for tobacco, I gave it to him and he went and took it to his father. Then he brought beer, after which came *gũthokia.* Finally, the negotiations for *rũracio* were completed. My people had talked with Wamutira and she told them she had asked Mũrage to marry a girl who would keep her company. So he had that pressure from Wamutira because she wanted a co-wife.

After *rũracio* had been brought, I stayed at home until the day Mũrage said he would come for me. As I was told when the day was, I washed all my clothes and got ready. It was Wamutira who came, about three in the afternoon, carrying the child who was her first born on her back. We stayed at my home until dark because I would not agree to go in daylight. We met Mũrage at Karia coming to get us, as it was dark. The following morning, Wamutira escorted Mũrage and me to the bus stop in Kerugoya.

When Wamutira escorted us to the bus stop she was pregnant with that girl, Kanugu, who later died. When I went to Nairobi, I never changed in my feelings about Wamutira—I liked her. While we stayed there, a letter came telling us that she had given birth. At this time, there were difficulties in traveling because of the state of emergency during the Mau Mau times—the British put up roadblocks. Mũrage feared to go home, as he was a Mau Mau supporter. I felt very badly that he was not sending anybody to take money or soup to Wamutira. I reached a point of quarreling with Mũrage until he sent somebody home.

I had gone to Nairobi in May, and the following May I returned home to Mũrage's place and was three months pregnant. When I came here, I met Wamutira and we stayed together in the same house. You could even see me carrying her child when I needed to go somewhere. And if I went for a visit to my parents' home and was given something to eat, I would not eat it but instead carry it back here to share with Wamutira. We stayed together until we were taken to the villages run by the British during Mau Mau.

During that time, Wamutira was called to Nairobi with the *komerera* [type of bus that secretly transported Africans], and she left me here. When we were forced into the villages, it was me who carried all our things. Then I went back to my parents' home and there gave birth to my firstborn girl. When Wamutira returned home, we lived in a house with two rooms, but the doors were very close together. We are still good friends. Even if the husband would not wish it, we would still be close, and he would not be able to separate us, for Wamutira and I are of the same clan. But Muthoni is from another clan.

* * *

[Probably the other major change in Wamutira's adult life in addition to the births and deaths of her children was her relocation to Nairobi during the Emergency. She describes her trip.]

It was the beginning of Mau Mau when I went with other women to Nairobi. We were taken by a bus called a *komerera*. It was a vehicle that had canvas covers for hiding people underneath. I walked with other women wanting to see their husbands up to Baricho and got into the *komerera* to Nairobi. I had left Karuana here that time. When we reached outside Nairobi, those who went further into town were taken prisoners by the British and taken to Lang'ata Police Station. But us, we got off very far from town at a place that was all forest. We walked awhile and then were met by an old *mzee* who told us there was no roadblock near the railway station. So we passed through there. At the station, we met a man who was Mũgĩkũyũ, who took us to his house. The man cooked for us, and we washed and slept there overnight. We were very tired. In the morning, the man sent messages to each woman's husband, telling him where his wife was waiting. So each husband came to that house without being noticed by the police.

While in Nairobi, Mũrage and I stayed in two rooms of the "railway houses," which were many rooms in a row built for Africans by the British. The rooms had concrete floors and were built of stone. Mũrage was a supporter of the Mau Mau freedom fighters, even though he was working for a *muzungu* [European] at the time. The supporters of Mau Mau had made groups, one at Karatina, another at Sargana, another just before reaching here. The last one was at Nairobi. These groups would communicate with one another and tell each other when the roads were clear of roadblocks. That way, Mau Mau people would move from Nairobi to here and back without meeting government soldiers. Mũrage was part of the Nairobi group.

Before I went to Nairobi to join Mũrage, I had already taken the Mau Mau Oath, but Mũrage took it while in Nairobi. The Oath was being given by force to everybody here. Even when going to take it, one did not know that was what one was going to do. Somebody would come and tell you to accompany him to go and eat rice and broken maize. When you got to the place, it was a bitter experience. If one had plaited her hair, it was cut off using a blunt *panga.* If one made an attempt to refuse, one would be slapped hard. Also, we were made to take off all our clothes, and if one tried to cover her private parts with her hands she was beaten. The meat eaten in the ceremony was rotten, and one had to swallow it and could not spit it out. One would not even utter a word in that hut. It was bad. You only hear about the Oath. You do not know how it really was. Me, I know.

I went to Nairobi when the trench was being dug, so I never had to dig it. But I was involved because my husband was. The Mau Mau supporters brought money to me, and I would go and buy soup to give to the freedom fighters.

We returned home from Nairobi while the fighting was still going on but was not as great as it was at the beginning. Mũrage lost a lot of money when he left Nairobi and his job there. When we got here, we discovered that the goats and cows that he had left here were *gũtaho* [commandeered]. They had been taken by British government soldiers to Mwea and Ndomba to feed government soldiers. It was that time when people were just being released from the villages [1958–1959]. We began to build the houses here and they were not yet completed by the time *Uhuru* came.

I was feeling very happy the day of *Uhuru* because now we would not be beaten again. I could not eat anything, because I was excited that we were no longer slaves. There was a lot of dancing and singing that night and all the next day. People were ululating and telling Munyao to raise the flag on Mt. Kenya. We were not sad to see the British leave.

* * *

After Mũrage came to settle here, he became a tailor. He worked at a tailor shop on the other side of the market. Muthoni was sewing there, too. So it happened that every night he would visit her in her room next to the tailor's shop on the pretext that he was staying there to keep watch over the machines—that's what he told us. We did not know about it until Muthoni, who was only a girl, got pregnant, and then Mũrage came to tell us that he was going to marry another wife. Karuana and I, we told him that he couldn't marry again because we wanted to stay just the two of us. He told us he could not leave Muthoni, because she was already pregnant and she was a good girl—even had been to school.

We told Mũrage to go and hear what his father had to say. When he went, the father told him that he would not allow him to marry another wife. But Mũrage went and made beer and bribed his father with four gourds of it. And so the father gave his consent to go ahead and marry Muthoni.

Before, when Mũrage came home from Nairobi, he often wanted to beat Karuana and me because of our friendship. He would ask me, "Is it me who married Karuana or you?" This was when he found Karuana always staying at my house. Karuana told him it was me who married her because I went for her at her father's homestead. The husband would try and separate us, but he was unable to. It is our hearts that like each other—Karuana and me.

When Muthoni came we just kept quiet. But later, we reasoned that even if we three lived together feeling bad because of one another, there were none of us who had the power to take another back to her father's home. Karuana and I stayed for almost one year feeling bad about Muthoni, but we found that even if we fought with her or tried to abuse her, we were doing nothing because she was there to stay. Karuana knew Muthoni because she comes from the same place, but I did not know her. Finally, we agreed between ourselves to get united together as wives, the three of us. Like now, if a visitor comes and I'm not around, the others will welcome her and entertain her for me. The husband has never told us to be friendly, but it is our wish and what our hearts want—to like one another and be friends.

* * *

[Karuana, when interviewed, had a different perspective on Muthoni's arrival as a wife, as she relates here.]

When Muthoni came she found me with only one child. When the husband told me that he was going to marry Muthoni, I never felt bad.

During that time, Wamutira and I never used two pots to cook—we always cooked together. The houses were two, but if you were told that one had an owner you would not agree. I only went to my house to sleep. Sometimes Mũrage would come and ask me, "Karuana, are you unable to get firewood for making your own fire?" Then I told him, "Wamutira is my mother, and she is the one who came for me from my mother's house. If you want me never to go to Wamutira's house, then take me back to my mother's. You knew very well we would stay together when you came for me. Leave us alone to do our work."

When Muthoni came, we welcomed her. At times, you cannot differentiate which children belong to whom here. Those children who are away, when they come home they always go to Wamutira's house. So sometimes you might say, "Wamutira has a lot of children." In my house, there is never a child. If there is food to eat from my house, the children will carry it to Wamutira's and eat it there. There is no difference between the way we treat the children—they are all the same.

* * *

[Having heard Karuana and Wamutira's perceptions of Mũrage's marriage to Muthoni, I approached Muthoni to hear her version.]

When I first came to live here at Mũrage's, I met Wamutira and Karuana. I was eating and drinking without seeing anything bad about the home, and I decided to stay. When I first met Mũrage, he was a tailor. I stayed with him next to the tailor's shop, and then I got pregnant. After seeing me, he would go to his other wives at home. They would cook food and send it to me at the shop. When time reached for me to have my baby, I came here and gave birth as I never went to the hospital. My co-wives were the ones who caught the baby—my first baby girl. They cooked for me for a long time and treated me well until my body got back its strength. So I started helping them in their work, and we stayed together, eating together and laughing a lot.

When I first knew Mũrage, he did not tell me he was married, because he wanted us to be friends [lovers]. But when I stayed with him and got pregnant, I pressed him for more news of his home, for I knew my fate was to marry him. He told me that he had two wives and I was going to be the third. I felt very bad inside and even wanted to leave him then. I went to my parents' home and stayed for two months. But Mũrage came and told my parents that I was free to go and marry elsewhere but I should not take his child along. When I thought about it, I decided to marry him. And when I came here, I never found him changed. If he brought anything home, he would give to each of us the same.

When I came here in 1962, I was a young *mũirĩtu* [newly circumcised] and a child to the other two wives. I was not even cooking. I started cooking when I had my second child. There have never been three houses for cooking. In this house, each wife has her own sleeping room and one for the children, and the other separate room—that one with a lock—that is the husband's. So there is no discrimination.

We help each other with the work here, but each wife has her own *shamba* and knows its extent. But when it is plowed, we plant together, and during weeding, when the plants are young, we do it together with the children. But when it comes to harvesting, one knows where her *shamba* reaches and harvests that one only.

Before we had the cart with the bullocks, we used to carry the coffee harvested in sacks on our backs to the coffee factory—all three of us. Now that Mũrage has the cart, our work is easier. When there is pay from the coffee harvest, if Mũrage gives one wife 100 shillings, he will give the other two the same. If he thinks of buying meat, he buys it and divides it equally, giving each her share.

* * *

[Karuana, in a separate interview, agrees that Mũrage treats all wives equally.]

When Muthoni came here nothing changed, because the husband never started to differentiate. If he had something to give, he gave it to all of us. The same with the children. If one of the girls' dresses gets torn, he will buy a new one for that child. But if he is buying new clothes, he buys for all of them when he has the money. If the children are sent home from school for lack of school fees or uniforms, he will not differentiate amongst them but will help them as they need it. He treats us all the same. You are not the only one who is surprised, Nyina-wa-Stepheni. Many people ask what makes us stay such good friends—all three of us.

* * *

[Wamutira, in a separate interview a week later, agrees.]

Each of us wives has her own portion of land to cultivate, but Karuana and I work our lands communally with the children. We start with one of our portions then go to the other one. The food that we cook, all three of us, the food cooked first is given to the children and husband. Then the food that is cooked later will be saved for cooking again the next day.

If disagreements occur, the husband calls me and shows me the mistake. But if we three wives have quarreled amongst ourselves, Mũrage calls us all, starting with me, and hears each one's account. Then, later, we talk and solve the problem with him. He never likes seeing us quarrel. He asks what we are missing here that makes us quarrel.

Mũrage treats us all the same. If it is school fees, he pays for all the children. He takes all the children to get new school uniforms, and also he loves all the children more than he loves us three. No, it would not have been so peaceful at home if he had favored any one of us over another, but he is equal in the way he treats us.

* * *

[One day when I was visiting the homestead, Karuana made the following analogy of our occupations.]

Nyina-wa-Stepheni, you see how you use a pen and paper and that machine [she referred to the tape recorder] as your tools for work? Well, Agĩkũyũ women use the *mũkwa, kibanga,* and *ũma* as their pens and pencils in the *shamba,* and they use the *nyungũ* [pottery cooking pot] and *muiko* [long stick that is rounded and flattened at one end—used for mashing food] in the house.

[The *mũkwa* is the woven rope carried by all women to haul containers of water, bunches of bananas, sacks of potatoes, and firewood home on their backs. The *kibanga* is the machete used for weeding, planting, cultivating, and digging out tubers. It also serves as a cutting tool around the homestead. The *ũma* is a short-handled pitchfork, with the fork set at a right angle to the handle, used in cultivation. Finally, the *kiondo* is the term used for any woven basket used to carry produce home from the *shamba* or market. Karuana's analogy is perceptive, because the tools she refers to provide a rural Kenyan woman with the ability to support herself economically, just as my pens, pencil, and tape recorder provide me a means of support. Mutira women are full-time farmers who cultivate not only subsistence crops but have major responsibility for the two cash crops grown in the area—coffee and tea. Wamutira describes how she learned to grow them.]

We first began planting coffee after Mau Mau. We were shown by government agricultural officers how to plant the coffee, take care of the bushes—pruning them when needed—and how to pick the ripe seeds [coffee berries]. They showed us that we should pick the seeds when they are red. Before, we were fearing to pick coffee because we were afraid that it might not sell. But now, we do not fear it, and through practice we have learned to pick better and faster. Coffee is picked twice a year, in late May and again in November. Everybody helps then. We put the seeds in large sacks and carry them to the coffee factory for processing. The coffee factory is a cooperative. When the skins have been removed, we collect them and use them as fertilizer around the bushes.

With tea, it has to be picked year-round. The government took us to a training course at Kagosi to learn how to cultivate and pick it. We learned from extension workers that we should pick two leaves and a bud. At first we used to pick using one hand, as though picking vegetables, but now we are able to pick using both hands at the same time, putting the tea leaves into *gikabu* [large baskets] on our backs. Because we have learned how to pick better through practice, now we get a bigger yield. So, more kilograms of tea and coffee are sold now than when we first started. We take tea to the weighing stations and are paid at the end of the month according to the number of kilos picked. One of the things I am proudest of is that it was me who planted all these coffee bushes you see here. From what we earn, we can pay for the children's school fees.

Yes, it is true that school has taken our children from the *shamba*. When I was a child, we were expected to help our mothers once we learned how to handle a digging stick and a hoe. Nowadays, children have to go to school, so they can help us only on Saturdays and holidays. But I think it's important for children to go to school so that they can get educated and get the good things I see—like more knowledge and the ability to read road signs so one doesn't get lost. Those who go to school are able to get employed and support themselves, unlike us who were foolish enough not to go to school. School might have helped me, because I would know some things I do not know now—like how to write letters to people whom I want to write. Like now, if I had gone to school, I would be writing to you, Nyina-wa-Stepheni, and even talking to you in English.

Nowadays it is just as important for girls to go to school as for boys. Even a girl can do a lot of good things to develop her home. It is not like the old days, when people used to say that they would not take their daughters to school because they thought they would become prostitutes. Our fathers were foolish then.

My daughters did not get enough schooling. When we tried to force them to go like other people, they preferred to get married. But they do not have the best marriages. I know they regret, now, that they never finished school. Even my sons did not get much schooling.

What do I think is important to teach my children at home? To teach a child obedience—that is important. That means waking your girl very early in the morning so she can wash herself and go to school. It means when I send her for something, she should obey me. If it is after school, I tell her to go and fetch water for me and cook. I tell the younger ones to respect the older ones because they are just like their mothers. I would also like my daughter to be hard working and somebody who is able to rely on herself later on. After educating herself, she should be respectful to me and her father, knowing that she was able to go to school because of our hard work. It is the same with a boy, but, above all, a boy should be clever and study hard to be a teacher or an officer in a big company somewhere.

I taught the girls how to cultivate with a *kibanga,* how to pick coffee, cook, and wash their clothes. But I remember I never showed them how to dig with a hoe. They used to follow me in the *shamba* with a hoe and do as they saw me doing. That way they learned how to use a hoe. But for picking coffee, I had to show them how to do it. They learned how to pick just the red berries, putting them into their baskets without spilling them on the ground. Sometimes one of the children would find a chameleon on one of the branches and become frightened. Then I would take that child away—for a chameleon is a bad omen.

The main difference between being a grandmother and a mother is that my sons' children are told to go to *Cũcũ's* [Grandmother's], but the children of my co-wives are told to go to their eldest mother's house. But there is no difference when I'm taking care of all of them. If it is giving food, I share it equally amongst them—they are all my children. The most important thing is to take care of *all* children, regardless of whether they are yours or not. When giving tea or food, one should not discriminate—that way the home will stay in good harmony. To be a good mother is more important than being a good wife.

Which do I think is my most important role? The one of cultivating, picking coffee, fetching firewood and water, and cooking. Also that includes feeding the cattle. It is a difficult thing to think about the rest, but I told you being a mother is more important than being a wife because my children depend upon me very much. I only need to obey my husband as a wife. But now I am not very interested in him sexually. The next most important role is being a co-wife, which is more important than being a daughter, as that was long ago.

When did I become a Christian? It was after Mau Mau. Everybody had joined, and I was left behind like a fool. I found that so because when somebody died, she was buried by the church she belonged to. And me, I did not have any church, and so I would not be buried properly. So I joined the Anglican Church at Mutira.

Before I started going to church, when somebody began quarreling with me I would fight back. But now I don't do such things, even if somebody abuses me. The things I used to do—like nagging or feeling bad when my husband came asking me whether the cow had been given food and water, and I'd tell him to go and take the cow to the river himself—I don't do anymore. Now, I never talk back rudely to him, because I know he is the wheel and pedals of the bicycle and if he can't take the wheel and push the pedals, then we wives can't move.

* * *

[I asked Wamutira if when her first child was circumcised she had gone through *nyumithio* in order to achieve elder status.]

My oldest son went through *Irua* not so long ago, but there was no ceremony for me like in the old days when a woman's head was shaved and she got new ear plugs. And the tradition of the *kiama* for elders I never met—it had passed, too. Not long ago, I went through menopause, but I never got any headaches. I got some hot feelings and chills and sometimes I felt low. But I never felt sad when menstruation ended. I felt only happiness because I had layed down a burden that I did not want anymore.

What am I proudest of having achieved? I'm proud because I planted all the coffee trees you see here. I do not have any future dreams because I am satisfied with my life the way it is. My strongest character is being hardworking. I work in the *shamba* all day and feed the cows. I generally like working. My weakest is that I have a very bad temper when somebody does me wrong—but everybody loses her temper at times. The thing in my life that changed me the most was when my children died. I started worrying and wondering whether I would ever get others to keep. I was not able to eat or drink anything, and even working was a problem. I started taking extra care to see that my children were well fed, clean, and when they got sick, I took them to the clinic.

What does being a woman mean to me? A woman is one who plants herself firmly at her own homestead without wandering. Being Agĩkũyũ means that I took the Mau Mau Oath—for if you did not take it, one was not considered a true Mũgĩkũyũ.

I liked the way we talked, Nyina-wa-Stepheni. The things you have asked me about my life make me think. I will keep them in my heart and never forget.

Watoro

5

Watoro's Story: Poverty Is Like Dust

Watoro, the second woman in her fifties, represents another aspect of polygynous marriage, one in which the relationships are not copacetic. Watoro's case is atypical because she decided to leave marriage in the early 1960s, a drastic step in a society that does not look kindly on marital separations. I hypothesized that such a change might prompt unique experiences in Watoro's life, a hypothesis that turned out to be wrong. In addition to separating from her husband, Watoro had had minimal experience with an adult education class and belongs to no women's groups. She was the poorest of the women in their fifties in 1983–1984, although by 1994 her situation had improved somewhat.

My relationship with Watoro proved to be difficult in two ways. First, as we began to know one another, Watoro's extreme poverty caused her to make material demands of me that I found difficult to meet over time given my own limited resources; her demands left me with a certain sense of guilt and resentment. Second, her acute bitterness toward her estranged husband prevented her from discussing her marriage or him in any detail. The bitterness is woven into the fabric of her narrative, and she refused to tell me the man's name, referring to him only as "the husband."

By 1994, Watoro's bitterness was less apparent, her economic condition had improved, and she was more relaxed with me. She actually welcomed me in her coffee fields with some enthusiasm, asking why I had not come to see her in 1992, as she had heard I was back then, too. I had tried to locate her but she was not in her home or fields on that visit.

In 1984 Watoro was the only woman in her age group who had no land of her own to till, and to be without land, say the Gikuyu, is to be nothing. A woman's access to land once she marries is through her husband. Watoro lost that access when she left her husband. Instead, she cultivated her absentee brother's land. In 1984 she earned enough from the harvest of coffee to buy books and uniforms so her two youngest sons could go to school. Watoro was the major economic provider for her four sons, then aged ten to twenty-four. Beyond what she earned from coffee, there was little financial security. As a result, Watoro was constantly under stress. Her two oldest sons were married and living with her in the overcrowded compound, rather than with their father as is customary. Both had young children, adding new mouths to feed.

Because the survival of Watoro's family depended upon her labor in 1983–1984, we usually met during her midday rest hour in the middle of the coffee fields under a shade tree. After the session I would spend an hour or so working with her in the *shamba*. The two times I met her at home, she willingly shared what little was available with her visitor. Such a gesture is characteristic of the hospitality one finds among rural Kenyan women.

One day, as we were sitting in the coffee field talking about what led to Watoro's drastic decision to leave her husband, I remarked that often a crisis can turn into a learning experience. She gazed off tiredly, fatigue and disconsolation showing in her dusty face, and then retorted, "If you are cultivating here in this field and a big wind blows over you covering you with dust, would you say that is a learning experience?"

In 1994 when I returned to Mutira for the fourth time, I found Watoro again in her coffee fields. Having missed her the previous visit, I sent a message that I wanted to see her. I found her with a daughter-in-law and niece who were helping her pick coffee berries. In contrast, in 1984 she had often worked alone.

By 1994 Watoro had come to view her brother's land as a source of security. She said, "The sisters received letters that my brother is not coming back. This means that I can continue to cultivate it but because it belongs to my brother it cannot be divided. That means my sons cannot inherit this land." When I asked her about her father's land she replied, "My father sold the land that was not given to my brother before he died so there is nothing to inherit."

She related that the increase in coffee prices in the mid-1980s had helped her to send her children to school. "But now," she says in an aside, "primary school fees are Ksh. 600 [US $17 at 1994 exchange rate] and school uniforms are required, which is an additional expense. It is cheaper to take the boys to school

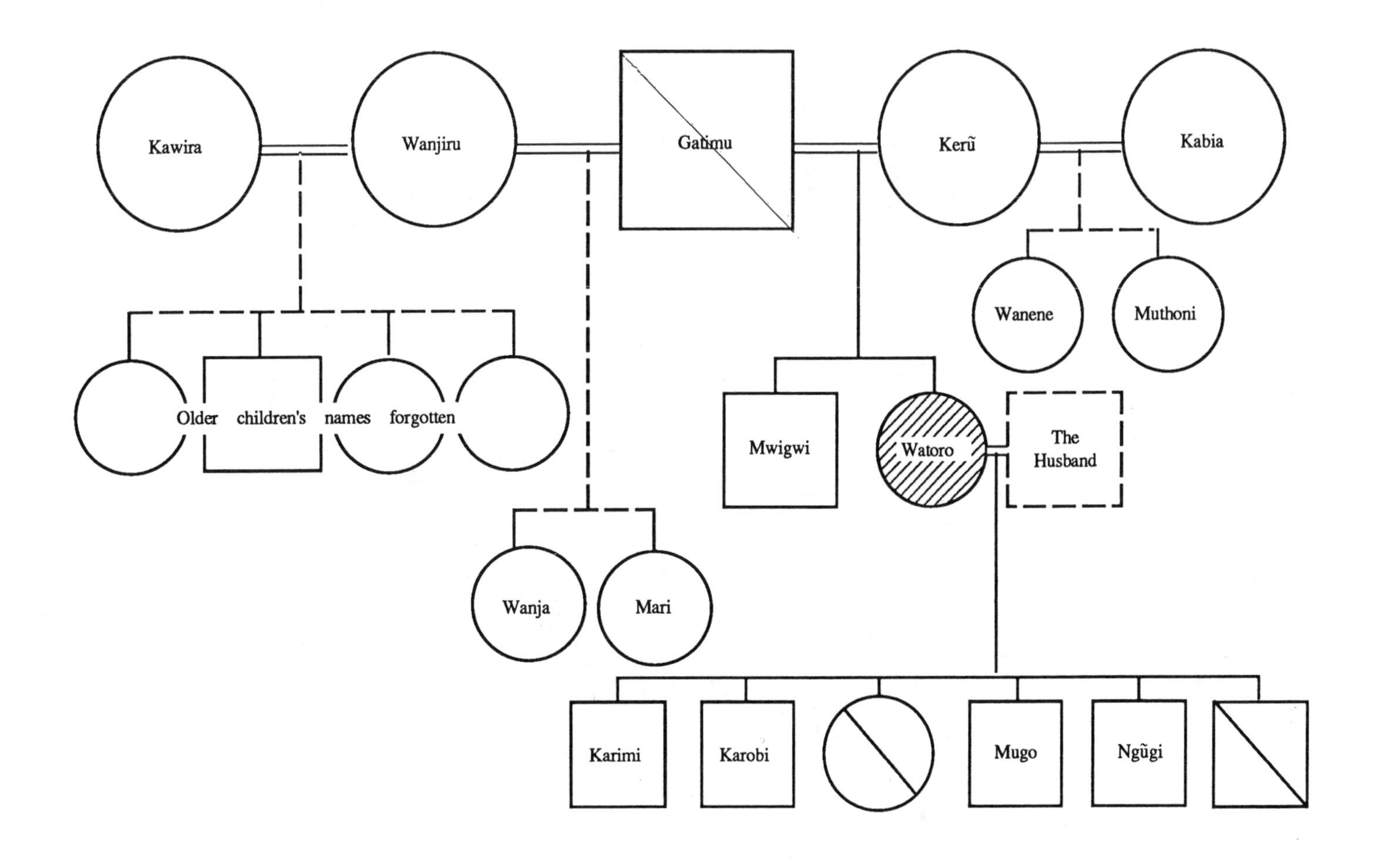
Kawira
Wanjiru
Gatimu
Kerũ
Kabia
Wanene
Muthoni
Older children's names forgotten
Mwigwi
Watoro
The Husband
Wanja
Mari
Karimi
Karobi
Mugo
Ngũgi

because the uniforms cost less but if someone has a girl, they will be taken too. Secondary school is very costly so if one has more children some will have to go for vocational training, depending on their marks."

Watoro related that since 1988 the price that small growers were getting for coffee berries had not been good. In 1992 there had been a drought and it had adversely affected the coffee harvest that year. "Because of the poor price," she observed, "people [in the late 1980s] were not taking care of their coffee trees so they did not yield a lot of berries." In order to make ends meet and pay for her children's schooling, Watoro told me, she went out and worked for other people in their *mashamba* to earn money. In the early 1990s the price had gone up a little, and also growers were being paid four times a year instead of twice a year, which helped marginal growers such as Watoro.

Illness had also been plaguing Watoro. She had been having a bad cough, she said, that came in combination with pneumonia. Despite her illness, however, Watoro's earlier depression born of constant stress seemed to have dissipated, replaced by a much more positive attitude about her life.

Since 1985, all of her sons had been living at home, with four building houses for their wives and children. Only one son still was unmarried. Her grandchildren are now of school-going age. Speaking of her situation, Watoro was proudest of the fact that she had managed to send all of her sons through school, testifying that it had been worth the earlier sacrifice. Education, she now believes, is the key to economic security. When asked about the elections of 1992, Watoro, like Wamutira, showed little interest, maintaining that all politicians are alike—only interested in lining their own pockets.

Of the major changes in Mutira over the last decade, Watoro observed, "Long ago it was good because people had many things to give to others. But these days they don't. There are a lot of problems because people don't share—there is more competition with people doing for themselves." When I asked if she meant to include 1984 as "long ago" she said yes, but that she was referring to time even further back. She clarified her point by explaining that the tendency toward individual competition had increased in the last decade.

—*J.D.*

I was named Watoro for the mother to my father. My clan is Ũnjiru. My father, Gatimu, was a black man who was not very tall and not fat either. He was of medium size and jolly. He had married two wives before my mother came to live with him. They were Kawira and Wanjiru. The first wife, Kawira, had three girls and a boy, but I don't remember their names because they were big by the time I was born and had already moved away. The second wife had two girls. My mother, called Keru, was the third wife. She was a good woman—hardworking, always cooking, and she did not talk badly to people. After some time, my father married his fourth wife, Kabia, who had two daughters who were my agemates—Wanene and Muthoni. I have only one elder brother called Mwigwi. These are the children I grew up with in the compound. I can remember that all my father's wives were similar in character, because when you went into any of their houses you were given food to eat—they never bothered to ask if you were hungry.

Our homestead was at Gatitu. Also living there was my father's mother whom we called Cũcũ. She was a short woman, neither so black, nor so brown. She was a patient woman who did not show a bad temper. She would never scold us if we bothered her with questions like "Where does the mongoose hide his house?" I can remember she would cook millet porridge and drink it while she was singing.

We children would ask Cũcũ lots of questions like "What is the best food to cook?" She would answer, "Porridge and *irio.*" Cũcũ's food was always good and sweet, so we used to go to her house and eat when we were small. We also used to ask her how one looks for firewood and ties it together with a *mũkwa* [tumpline], and she would show us how to wrap the rope around each end of the firewood, leaving a long loose piece in the middle to put at the forehead. She was the one who showed us what kind of work a girl does and which is for boys.

Long ago, when boys got to be about eight years old, they would only go herding and after that they would come and sit near the fireplace outside—the one set for old men—warming themselves and waiting for food to be brought to them. But us girls, we used to go to the river to fetch water, go with our mother to cultivate, and when we were older, help with the cooking.

I was shown how to fetch water using a very small gourd. When we went to the river, the mothers would fill the gourds for us to carry home. Later on, we learned how to tie a larger gourd on our back with a *mũkwa* until now we carry big barrels of water. After we were through our work, the girls would go inside and sit near their mothers and the grandmother at the cooking fire when the sun disappeared and it began to feel cold. This is how we learned to prepare food—by watching how the mothers chopped the greens and added them to the big pot of *githeri* [maize and bean mixture] cooking on the fire. Sometimes they would add some chopped onions or carrots to make it taste good. We still do that now and some people even add tomatoes.

It was my grandmother who taught me good character from bad—like when I go along the road, I should not abuse anybody. We learned through songs and stories and sometimes through wise saying. I remember she told us, "*Utemuhe nĩ mũigĩre*" ["The one who has not been given already, hers is stored"]. It means that if you have not been given something, do not dispair, you will be given a chance of getting it.

I can remember a story my grandmother told us about being a good mother:

Long ago, there was a man who was a *mũturi* [carpenter]—a man who makes and molds things. He had two wives and each wife had a son. The two boys loved each other very much and they were both called Mwĩra after their father's father.

One day, the first wife died, leaving her son behind. After a short time, the husband went back to his place of work leaving the two boys with the second wife. It happened that the second wife did not like the other boy and so she planned a way to eliminate him. She dug a hole in the *thegi*. Then she sent her own son to his grandmother's place and put the other boy in the hole and kept quiet. When her son returned, he asked where his brother was and his mother told him that she had sent him also to the grandmother's but he had not returned.

The boy took the goats and cows to graze. When evening fell he asked his mother again, "Where is my brother?" But his mother scolded him and told him to go and sleep.

The following morning, when his mother had gone to the fields to cultivate, the boy began singing:

Mwĩra ũĩ Mwĩra,	Mwĩra, oh Mwĩra,
Kaninindume na nja	Small one come out.
Ũĩ, Mwĩra	Oh, Mwĩra
Baba mara guka	Our father has come
Ũĩ, Mwĩra	Oh, Mwĩra,
Na tuthanju twĩrĩ	With out herding sticks
Ũĩ, Mwĩra	Oh, Mwĩra
Gakwa na ka Mwĩra	Mine and that of Mwĩra
Ũĩ, Mwĩra.	Oh, Mwĩra.

His brother, in the hole, heard him and sang in reply:

Mwĩra, uĩ Mwĩra	Mwĩra, oh Mwĩra
Kanini ndurarĩmuuru,	Small one you are not bad,
Ũĩ, Mwĩra	Oh, Mwĩra
Nĩ nyukwe urarimuuru,	It is your mother who is bad,
Ũĩ, Mwĩra	Oh, Mwĩra
Kwenja irima thegi	Digging a hole in the *thegi*
Ũĩ, Mwĩra	Oh, Mwĩra
Ria guguĩkia Mwĩra	For throwing Mwĩra in
Na tunyungu twao	With all the pots
Ũĩ, Mwĩra	Oh, Mwĩra
Na tuuga twa nyina	And mother's calabashes
Ũĩ, Mwĩra.	Oh, Mwĩra.

So the boy came to know where his brother was and he stayed near the hole singing that song and not eating anything. So he lost weight and grew sick.

At his place of work, the father of the boys started getting feelings that something was terribly wrong at home. He decided to go home for a visit. He reached there in the morning before the boy had taken the goats outside but found that his wife had already left. When the father did not see his other son, he asked Mwĩra where the other Mwĩra had gone. The boy told his father to follow him into the *thegi,* and he would show him. Mwĩra sang the song again, and the other son answered from the hole. The father removed the soil from the hole until he found his son. He pulled him out and went and slaughtered a goat and gave the boy *tatha* [contents of intestines], and the boy vomited all the soil and dirt he had eaten in the hole. Then the father roasted some of the meat for his two sons and hid the boy who had been in the hole in his own house and waited for his wife to return.

When the wife returned, she welcomed her husband and he gave her some meat to cook and went to his house. The wife told him that the other Mwĩra had gone for a visit to the grandmother. The wife's own son refused to stay at his mother's house and followed his father to his *thingira.* When the meat had cooked, the wife brought it to them. The man ate with his two sons and then smeared both with animal fat.

The next morning, the father told the wife to go and get his other son from the grandmother's. If she should not find the boy there, then she should come back with all the family members of both their clans.

So the two clans met and the elders told the wife to give them the child because they knew he had not gone to the grandmother's as the wife had told everybody. The boy who had been hidden was brought into the presence of the clan members, and the story of how he had been put into the hole was told. The family members told the wife that because of what she had done she could not stay there anymore, and she was to go back to her own people. But her own people refused her when they heard the story and killed her. The father went to his place of work, taking his two sons with him.

That is the end of the story. You see, a hospitable woman is the one who, when she marries away and meets young children, she takes care of them as her own. Our grandmother told us that if one marries she should not go abusing the children she meets, and when she cooks, she should give food to all children she meets. We were told, "*Gũtanaha na kũigwanira tha mũndũ ndagaga mwoi*" ["To be hospitable and merciful to others, one will not miss somebody to collect her"—help her in times of need].

As a child I was very playful, but I wouldn't provoke other children as some do. I remember we sang and danced a lot. We had one type of play where we would pass a ball around a circle of us, singing, "*Marombo na Mwarau*" three times, then "*Mwendi gũceca nĩa cece rĩngĩ*" [The one who wants to play can play again], then "*Marombo na Mwarau*" again as we passed the ball around.

When I grew up to be about four or five—still a child—a *mũndũ mugo* slaughtered a goat, and the skin was spread out for a bed for me, and *rũkoro* [a strip of goat's skin] was put around me. It was taken off the next day, after it had hardened. The elders gathered for the ceremony, then ate the goat's meat to celebrate. We called this *mambura ma twana* [ceremony of the children]. It usually occurred when the mother wanted to remove the youngest child from her bed so she could have sexual relations with her husband again and get another child. Up to that time, a child would sleep with the mother until it was weaned—no matter how big. All this time, the father was staying in his *thingira.* I don't remember too much about *mambura ma twana* because I was still small, but I was told about it.

The first major changes that I remember were *mbuci* and *matũ;* then, after these healed and I grew up some more and showed signs of growing breasts, I was circumcised. Then I was a grown person and could go to dances during the night. After many dances, when I was more mature and had begun to menstruate, I got married. Later, I separated from my husband and went back to my father's home—these were the big changes in my life that I remember clearly.

When I was about fifteen, that is when I went to my mother and told her I wanted *mbuci.* The reason I wanted my ears pierced was for beauty and putting on beads and decorative metals. Also, one would not be very happy to see her agemates with decorations in her ears while she had none. The ones who did not have their ears pierced were like fools, because they were trying to cut themselves off from the community. We would not joke with them, nor could they joke about with us.

As soon as I told my mother I wanted *mbuci* she went to my uncle to get permission. He was the brother to my mother who was born together with her [her twin]. It was the tradition that every girl had to get permission from her mother's oldest brother. My upper lobes were pierced with small holes, using thorns of a tree called *mũthũthi* [a type of acacia]. Then sticks were put in. When mine were pierced they began to swell, and so the sticks were removed and the holes joined together and disappeared as you can see. Like me, you would not say that I had *mbuci,* because the flesh grew back.

When we were to have our ears pierced, it was an old woman with experience who did it. She did not have any fear. But I felt pain when she poked the holes in my ears. After my upper lobes had healed, my mother again went to the same uncle and told him that I was ready for *matũ*—that is the large hole made in the bottom lobe. A goat was slaughtered, called *ndonya matũ,* and was eaten by my uncles. When I got the bottom ones pierced, hot pieces of wood were put into them to make them bigger—like these holes you see now. It was painful, but we wanted to have it done. Later, after a woman's first son got circumcised, she used to put beads in the upper holes, called *ngoni,* and *mwikwo*—large plugs—in the lower lobes. After I got *matũ* I felt more mature, for I had already started getting breasts. It meant that now I could go for *Irua,* so I was excited.

I went for *Irua* before I had gotten my first menstruation. We were told by our mothers and grandmother that *Irua* was a way of buying maturity. It was me, together with my agemates, who decided when we were ready. When a girl feels ready she tells her parents to go and tell her uncles and ask for their permission. In return for the favor, the uncles are given a goat or beer. That was the custom. Then preparations would begin—one month before the actual ceremony. Dances were conducted at the homestead of the girl being circumcised and people would hear the sounds of the drum, rattles, and singing from far away and come to join the dancing. It was a festive time. Beer and porridge were prepared by women and taken freely until the day reached for the ceremony.

From the time of *mbuci,* our eldest mother had been counseling me that I should take care of myself and not be a wanderer. She told me that now that I was to become a grown girl I should be careful when moving about with boys and not do anything else apart from dancing when I attended the dances. She told me, "Soon you will go for *Irua* and will be discovered that day." By this she meant that people at the ceremony would discover whether or not the root I came from was good by the way I behaved that day—"A good club grows from a good root" is our saying.

Irua occurred after the harvest, when the main work was done and there was plenty of millet and sorghum to make sour porridge for the celebration. The first day of *Irua* was the "Day-of-*Mugumo.*" Boys and girls were circumcised on the same day—boys in the morning and girls when the sun had begun to go down. On that morning, we went to the *mugumo* tree [sacred fig tree—enormous in size—that was similar to a shrine where prayers on behalf of the community were made by the elders], which had been singled out for that occasion. The candidates for *Irua* would go there and throw pointed sticks with dyed cloth tied to one end through the branches of the tree. Then branches were cut by newly married women for the candidates to take home. If the candidate was a boy, five or nine branches were cut, and if a girl, four or eight. [The number five of something is associated with the male sex, whereas four is associated with females.] The branches were carried to my home as good medicine and to sooth me after I had been circumcised.

It was on this day that one put on *mathangu* [leaves] tied around the waist so they rustled when dancing. We also had a skirt made of beads, called a *thira.* The one whose circumcision was well prepared had people to borrow beads and other decorations from to make her appearance beautiful. Then the dancing would begin.

During the circumcision dances anybody was free to do anything—abuse another person, chase a woman, or any other social evil until the next morning of *Irua.* If a man had a desire for a certain woman, he could try and take her by force, so women would prepare themselves and come armed with sticks and clubs and move only in groups. We used to hide a club behind our sheets [tunics], putting them down the back so when somebody tried to attack us he would be beaten. [The behavior Watoro describes refers to young, circumcised women, not the initiates.]

On the morning of *Irua,* we who were candidates were taken to the river by women of our clan to wash. The reason we were washed was to wash away *mũgiro*—the dirt the girl was coming to *Irua* with. That state of being uncircumcised was termed "dirty" and had to be washed away. Newly married women were singing songs as they washed me and then escorted me back home, where I stayed until it was about three in the afternoon and you could see the sun starting to go down. While at home, we were given small gourds of porridge and *ngima ya mũhĩa* [made from sorghum flour]. These were fed to us with a spoon by our circumcision mothers. It was as if we had become children again.

We were eight girls who got circumcised together that time. The field where we were taken was cleared of brush and was made of grass. It was the same place where other dances took place. There were so many people who came to the field to watch us. They were all ages.

The one who was my supporter was the one who told me how to sit on the *mathangu* [leaves] and what to do during circumcision. My mother brought castor oil to put on the wound after we had been cut. The circumciser was an old woman who was fat and very black. I felt a bit scared when I saw her. She had been paid money for the task—my parents gave her 3 shillings. To do the cutting, she used a *kienji.* My supporter, who was our oldest mother, held me from behind so I would not move about. The circumciser cleansed the knife with water and then smeared it with castor oil each time she circumcised a girl. Those who were brave did not feel anything—they just looked away. That is what I did—I just looked away when I was being cut. But those who were cowards started crying, even before being circumcised!

After it was over, castor oil was put on a soft leaf, and it was put over the wound to cover it until it was healed. If a girl bled a lot the parents would decide what to do, because it meant there was a dispute between her parents and her uncles, and before it was solved—by slaughtering a goat—the girl would bleed. So uncles were given in advance the number of goats given for the mother of the initiate when she was married—that way there were no problems.

On the way home, I walked slowly with no one to support me. There were so many people going with me, cheering and singing songs for me on the way to my mother's house, where sour porridge had already been prepared. But me, I was so weak and tired, I went straight to bed and slept.

After three days, a small girl came and shaved my head, and from then we called each other "*Wamathaga,*" which means that as you have shaved my head, you are my mother, and so I can't call you by your name—only *Wamathaga.* It took me a month and then another to heal completely.

After it was over, I felt grown up and walked around proudly. When a girl got her ears pierced, then was circumcised, she was looked upon as a grown-up and was treated like one. No young boys would dare joke about with her or abuse her, for the boy's father would beat him. Circumcised girls were very respected, and those who went for *Irua* earlier than us, they were considered our mothers, and we would not disobey them or we would be beaten.

The girls who are circumcised together, of the same age, are *riika* [agemates] and are friends always. We used to go to sleep at our house and other times at theirs, working in the *shamba* together and cooking soup for each other. After going through *Irua,* we made beauty marks on our faces by rubbing ashes into cuts we made. We also made some on the breasts so that when dancing naked, the marks made our bodies more beautiful. That was our tradition. Later, some missionaries tried to stop traditions like this, but we said, "The one who puts on a dress and goes to school is a prostitute." My father refused to let me go to school, because he said I would become a prostitute. I never felt sad about not going to school. I was happy going to dances, because I was not alone.

When I got my first menstruation after *Irua,* nobody had told me about it. I was scared when I first saw the blood, because I had never seen it there before. I went to my mother, and she told me that it was normal and it was a sign that I'm a woman so I should start taking care of myself with men.

Nowadays, girls are getting pregnant when they are still at their parents' home. This is because they have no way of knowing when they are grown-up. Girls continue to joke around with younger boys even when they are grown. Now, a boy of my son's age [twelve years old] can abuse me and give no respect. It is not like long ago, when we refused to have any dealings with anybody who was not an agemate. And now, young uncircumcised boys are being called "men" by girls, so they feel grown-up and can joke about with the girls. All this was brought about by school and when we threw away the traditional way of becoming adults through *Irua.*

* * *

I stayed for ten years before I met my husband. During that time I was going to dances and learning how to do things around the homestead and be responsible for the house. During the night, when we were sitting around the fireplace, my grandmother would teach me things I needed to know before marrying. Above all, she said, one should be obedient to one's husband without being stubborn. Also, one must cook good food, and she taught me how to do it. During the day, I was fetching firewood, washing the children in the compound, and helping in the *shamba.*

I would think about the kind of man I wanted to marry in those days. I wanted a good man who would not wander about, a person who was able to take care of things like the goats and cows at home so that eventually we would be rich and have many things.

I first met my husband when dancing—that is where people used to meet each other. The men would later escort the girls back to their homesteads—that way, a man came to know where a girl's home was, and if he wanted a certain girl he knew where to find her. That is how my husband came to know my place, because he lived far away from where we were.

My grandmother had told me that if a man was interested in you, he would come near the granary and start blowing his nose—that is just the way it happened. One day, the husband came near our granary and blew his nose, and I went out to greet him. After talking for some time, we agreed to meet again. We met at my home many times during the next few months, then I decided to have him so I went to my father for tobacco. Later on, the proceedings started for *rũracio* between our two fathers. I never knew what they agreed that my husband should give, but when we separated he still had not paid anything to my father.

On the day he came to get me, he came alone because I had agreed to marry him. When we got to his homestead, I found nobody there because it was at night. But in the morning everybody in the compound came to see my husband's new wife. You see, I was his second wife, so they wanted to see how I looked. Wangũi, the first wife, was there, and I could tell she was not happy to see me. That scared me. Right away she started screaming and abusing me. She had known me before, but now she had different feelings because she didn't want the husband to marry another wife. He insisted. I knew that I would be the second wife, but I didn't know Wangũi would be so bothered. But I learned she had had no say in the marriage when I went there to live. So she and I were not on good terms, and we just stayed that way, abusing one another.

One day, the husband's mother gave me a new *sufuria* [Kiswahili word meaning pot] to use, but Wangũi took it from me. I was angry, but I did not show it. I never allowed our quarrels to reach the point of physically abusing each other, but we did tarnish each other's names in public. Like she might abuse me by saying that I had poisoned her children—that's a very bad insult, because it's like bringing a false witness against another. In fact, that is the worst insult one woman can give another! But the older women in the compound would intervene when we were fighting, and so we learned to just keep quiet.

When I looked at Wangũi, I saw she was not happy, and after staying there awhile, I found I was not happy either and I began to hate the husband. Neither of us wives were happy. It wasn't just that he beat us, he was irresponsible. If you have a husband who is not caring about you—so that when the children are hungry or sick he's not bothered—then you feel angry. Even when we wives began to fight, we'd ask for his help, but we didn't get it. I began blaming him for bringing me to his place.

When I first went to his place, I was staying at his mother's house, but later he built a house for me. When I moved there, I found a big change because now I was required to fetch my own firewood. Before marrying, I used to cook, but younger ones would have already fetched the firewood. [One of the duties that Watoro mentions in an earlier interview that she had to do after *Irua* and prior to marriage was gathering firewood, which contradicts what she now states.] Now I was fetching my own water and washing my own utensils and keeping the house clean all by myself. I did not like being alone to do all that.

When disagreements came up between the husband and me, people in the homestead, especially his mother and father, would bring us together to talk. Sometimes I used to be beaten, and if it was me in the wrong I would try to change and never repeat that thing again. When a wife is beaten, it is because she has not made her husband happy, so she tries to change her ways. Do they beat wives in America? No? How do you know when you are doing something wrong?

So now I stayed about one year before I had my first child. I found I was pregnant when I stayed for two months without menstruating. I was feeling very sick, and my husband called his mother when the child was ready to be born. She came and assisted me and tied the umbilical cord and washed the child in a piece of broken pot because there was no basin then. She also called "*ariririti*" five times to let people know that it was a boy-child. Later, I washed and rested.

Now that I had a chid, I felt a little bit light—and older, because I realized I had become a woman. It took me about three weeks before I came out of the house, and during that time women were bringing firewood, bananas, porridge, and other food. Those at home would cook for me and came to work in my *shamba.*

Who prepared me for motherhood? It was my grandmother who told us that we should feed a child bananas, arrowroot, sweet potatoes, and porridge. All these were roasted, then chewed and fed to the child. We would see Cũcũ feed the babies, and the children grew up very big and fat, so I knew that was the right way to feed a child. She also told me that if I got children I should never mistreat them and should shape their characters by watching the types of children they moved with, and if those children were not well behaved, I should prevent mine from moving with them.

After staying in my husband's compound for awhile, a third wife came and met me there. But this one finished only one year and then went away and left us. She left because of the same kind of mistreatment and lack of care and cooperation from the husband. I never felt badly that the husband was taking another wife. I had my own *shamba* at his place and my work to do. I didn't feel jealousy—I was not interested in who he was marrying next.

By now I had two sons to care for, and then a daughter came. After the daughter, I had two more sons. But when I think of my daughter, I feel pain in my heart. There was a time when she got very sick, and there was no help that the husband would give. After some time, she died. She was five years old then. When my daughter died—that was the time I made up my mind that I would leave that place. The problem of my husband not helping me, even when the child was sick, and other things made me realize I could not stay there any longer. He wouldn't even help me take her to the hospital.

That child—the daughter—disturbed me for three months. I was always taking her to the hospital, and she was getting three injections every time I took her. Then she was admitted and only spent one week in the hospital before she died. The doctors would never tell me what disease she had, so I never learned what was the cause of her death. When the child died, I felt as if I had lost direction, and I started feeling that now I could distinguish between bad and good. You hear, when I talked to my husband, he seemed not to care and started being uncooperative. He did not like to hear me speak of the child's death or sickness. I began to see him as bad. Now I had no daughter—her death left me very weak, with no energy. Then I knew I could never stay there. I did not tell anybody, but kept quiet to wait for a time when God would help me to leave.

Then one day my father came to visit us and he saw me unhappy, so he insisted on me going back with him to our home—that was when we were just released from the villages at the end of Mau Mau. Because I had been waiting for such an opportunity, I went with him back to my home, and my problems with the husband were solved. The husband could not insist that I stay with him, because when my father asked him for the part of the *rũracio* that he had promised, the husband refused. So I returned home and now I only get the ordinary problems here.

I left the husband when my oldest child was about eight years and the youngest was newly born. When I reached home, I felt my heart grow better because the problems I had known were gone. My father gave me my brother's *shamba* to cultivate, and after awhile I began to get food for me and my children. Then after the harvesting of the coffee, which we had just started cultivating then, my father would give me a share of what we earned and I could help my children by taking them to school.

One does not always know when changes are occurring, but realizes later on that the things she is seeing are different from what they were before. You see, after I came home and these children of mine started asking me for their life necessities, I noticed there was a big change. There was nobody else they could go to for their needs except me. If they had their own father, they would have somebody else to go to. But now it is just me. At times I feel sad, but I remove the sadness by knowing in myself that I'm not waiting to marry again. When I left the husband, I decided never to marry again or even to be good friends with a man.

* * *

When my daughter died, we were living in the village—it was during the Emergency. When Mau Mau started [1952], I had just married. During that time, things were hard. We were put into villages, and all around us a trench was dug and spikes were put into it, so that if one tried to jump or if one fell in the trench, that person would die. The British were trying to prevent the freedom fighters from being fed by the people in the villages—that's why the trench was dug.

We were put into a village at Kibingo. After two years we came to another one here at Karaini. Our days were hard—I would wake up at four in the morning and walk up to where the trench was being dug and get there when the sun was just coming up. We would be given the number of feet to dig, and we'd work all day and come back sometime in the afternoon. While working on the trench, the soldiers would line up, and they beat those who became lazy and were not working as fast as they wanted us to.[1]

During that time, my husband was a government soldier—he was a Home Guard. He was one of those supervising the work on the trench. He was given his portion to supervise, and sometimes I could hear him using hard words to make people work. By that time, we were not friendly, and he would not treat me as a wife but just like any other woman. When we were released from the work of the trench, or other communal work in the afternoon, then women would go running to their *mashamba* to work. First, one cut maize for cooking that evening, then cultivated in a small area, then came running back to meet the deadline [curfew]. When we reached the village, there were guards already there to prevent anybody from going out at night. Because the houses were built in lines, the Home Guards would start from the first house in one line and go from house to house looking for freedom fighters—Mau Mau—and they beat the residents of the house sometimes, trying to force out any hidden fighters they might be hiding. During that time, we were being beaten and told to show where the Mau Mau were. But at the same time, supporters of Mau Mau were coming and forcing us to take the Oath, and the one who refused could be killed. If a Mau Mau came and found me cooking, I would gladly give him food, but if one refused, one could be beaten and, we heard, cut up into pieces and locked inside the house. We were in great trouble then.

Finally, when freedom came, we rejoiced because we knew that would be the end of the beatings and mistreatment. When we heard about the fighting at Nairobi, we were happy because we knew the fighting would soon be over.

Uhuru changed things, because I started seeing new things coming that were different from the old. *Maendeleo* [progress] was beginning and soon we began to forget the old days, when things were so bad. As that was the time I left my husband, I found that now I could rely upon myself to buy certain things that were becoming available—such as corrugated iron sheets—that I needed in life.

* * *

After Mau Mau, I was raising my children on my own. Caring for your children isn't easy. When you see your children trying to take others' things, you tell him not to steal because it is bad. If the child brings something strange into the house that you haven't bought yourself and you tell him he's stealing, he might say that he's doing it for you and that makes you feel badly. Then you take him to school and pay the school fees without delay. Going to school keeps my sons out of trouble. If I see one of them moving with bad characters who are influencing them to do bad things, then I talk to that one and tell him to stop moving with such people.

Boys should be taught to be obedient and hardworking. If they are working hard at either grazing the cows or working on things around the homestead, it stops them from going and spending their days and weeks at another boy's place—it keeps them from roaming. A girl should be obedient, too—doing what she is expected to do. And she should respect others, especially the elders, and be hospitable to everybody she sees.

All of my four sons have been to school. If one is schooled, it is a good thing because he can read signposts and know where he is. And after school, with the help of God, one can be employed and have a good job. My firstborn reached Standard Seven [seventh grade] and the next born reached Form Two [second year of high school]. But the younger ones you see here working with me in the *shamba,* one is in Standard Four and the other is in Standard Five. The reason the firstborn dropped out after Standard Seven is because we had less money for school fees. Before there was school, we used to exercise our brains by playing games and singing songs and trying to learn from our parents the things they were doing. But now, children need school to better their lives. This is because a schooled person can read, so he knows where there are jobs by finding them in the newspaper.

Yes, I have observed that those who have been to school know how to get a job. Like now, if you and I walked together into an office seeking a certain job and you are schooled and I am not, you will be taken and, me, I will be left behind. Those who live in a place like Kagumo should finish up to Form Two, because that is the level of education needed to bring progress here. If people want more money they can still go on to Form Four, but I think Form Two is enough. And today, it's just as important for a girl to go to school as a boy.

When we were children, all of the girls knew they would marry, and so we did not need school. But today a girl may get pregnant before she marries and have to get a job to feed her children. If she happens to get pregnant and there is no husband, she will have to depend upon her parents to feed and take care of her children, or she will find a job.

When I married, a woman got a *shamba* from the husband—not just one piece but several pieces in different places. One plot would be for maize and beans, another for sweet potatoes. Each kind of food needed a different soil and amount of water. But now women have only two or three plots, and women without husbands must depend on their parents to give them land to cultivate for their children. I grow maize and beans in two different places, but it is barely enough to feed my sons and their wives and children. No, the older sons do not cultivate at their father's *shamba.* They stay here with me. If my daughter had lived and she had no husband she would be living here, too. Sometimes I worry about how all these children will be fed.

* * *

During our time there was a big change when a woman's firstborn got circumcised and there was a lot of feasting. The woman had her head shaved completely and became an elder. But today, there is nothing like that being done. No woman's head is shaved nor does she get *ngoni* in her ears. That ceremony for elders is gone. Awhile back, I finished with menstruation. I had a lot of headaches and chills for a time, but I felt happy because God brought menstruation to an end. I was not in need of it anymore.

Now that I am a grandmother, I find there is a difference between being a mother and a grandmother. Take this child here [grandson in her lap], I never chew roasted bananas for him and I can only give him the food left by his mother. If it is porridge, I feed it to him using a cup. If my grandchildren fall asleep, I take them to bed. A long time ago, you know, one used to carry a baby everywhere one went. I try and teach my grandchildren some things—like this girl here, she is learning how to peel potatoes by watching me. And if I happen to see any of these children doing something bad, I will stop them. They have to obey what I say. Their mothers are too busy working in the *shamba* to watch them all the time. When my sons—the ones in primary school—are home, they take care of the older children, but these two small ones need their mothers or me. And now one of my sons' wives is pregnant.

It is good to have many children, but we do not have as much land as we used to and this means problems. When there is a good harvest we have plenty of maize, but when the rains do not come we have to go and buy maize from the market, and then there is less money for school fees. Do I think my daughters-in-law should use family planning? No! I have heard a woman can bleed to death from taking those pills. It is God's will to have as many children as one is given.

* * *

When did I become a Catholic? When I was a mother with grown children. It was just recently when the old church was being reopened. The reason I joined is that my mother had joined, and she found her life better. As you know, "Where the goat goes, the kid also follows." Another reason is that my conscience convinced me to leave worldly things alone and join the church. I guess you could say that it is the Spirit that called and directed me there.

Before I started going to church, if I went along the road and somebody abused me, I would abuse that person back. If one started talking to me in dirty language, I would reply and not be ashamed. But now, if somebody comes and starts abusing me, I just let her continue until she gets tired without abusing her back. The church teaches good things—like we mothers are told to respect our children, and in turn they will respect us. When you do it, you see it's true. I never joined the Catholic Women's Group or any other women's group, but I did join the adult education class for a short time. Then I had to stop because the work at home got to be too much. That's the same reason why I can't join a women's group—I have too much work.

I first heard about the adult education class about eight years ago when it was announced by the government. When the teachers for the class came to Karaini, we learned through rumors that we were required to go. I finally joined last year so I could learn how to read and write my name. I went for one month only. If I had continued I would have learned how to write my name. But one is really helped only after completing something to the end. If one leaves it halfway, she does not get as much help from it—isn't that so?

The adult education class was just here in Karaini. If I had been coming from here at my home, it would have been a short distance. But I was coming from way down at the *shamba,* and it is quite a distance to walk. If I started class at four o'clock, then I reached home late.

When I get home, I go running to the river for water, then cook, and by the time I'm through, there's no time left for me to attend class. I can see that it has helped others because they are able to read books and write their names, but I didn't have time with all the work.

If I had to choose between joining a women's self-help group and the adult education class, I would choose the women's group because there one learns good things from one another and the money given each woman enables her to help herself by buying things she needs. If I had enough money, I would not always be worrying about school fees. I would also buy a cow so we would have milk for the children.

* * *

Six years ago, my father died—that was a big change for me. When I separated from the husband and when my father died—those were when I changed the most. My father never got sick. We had spent the day together here on the *shamba,* and then he went to take beer in Kagumo. When he came home, he started vomiting, and when he was taken to hospital he never recovered. He died the following morning. It was hard to believe that he died, because it had been my father who had helped me and it meant that now I would have to start helping myself alone. When he died, I started having many thoughts, especially when my children started growing older and needed clothes, food, and above all, schooling. Now there is nobody to help except me. I have been thinking a lot about these things lately.

Of all the roles I've had, the most important are cultivating, fetching water and firewood, and being a good mother. Next is being a good wife. After that comes being a daughter, then a student—that is least important, but it never ends.

My greatest accomplishment is that I have built an iron sheet roof for my house and have moved out of my grass-thatched house. This kind of roof is better because the gutters catch the rainwater and it runs into the petrol drum, so we don't have to make so many trips to the river. Also, a thatched house has to be repaired every year but *mabati* lasts longer.

At times I dream of coming to cultivate here and producing a lot of food crops. Other times I dream I'm holding bundles of money notes and I'm laughing. I normally feel sad when I wake from this dream and discover that I don't have anything. I like it that I am self-sufficient with the use of my *kibanga,* my *kiondo,* and my *mũkwa.* They help me to keep myself and the children fed. The only thing I don't like about myself is that if I abuse anybody and they abuse me, I find it difficult to ever talk to that person again. I see this as bad, but there is no way I can change it.

Womanhood means to me taking care of one's things at home and caring for the children. It means supporting the children and home together. Being Agĩkũyũ means knowing that I generated from Gikuyu and Mumbi, the first man and first woman of the Agĩkũyũ.

Now it is starting to rain, and we better run from here [*shamba*] to Wambura's before that machine of yours gets wet. It's always good when it rains after cultivating—like a blessing.

Note

1. Kenyan writer Ngũgĩ wa Thiong'o has described a similar scene in his novel *A Grain of Wheat* (1967).

6

Wangeci's Story: A Widow Among Women

In 1992 when I visited Mutira, I learned that Wangeci had died two years earlier of an illness. I had not seen her in 1989 and was deeply saddened to learn of her death. Most of all, I remember her playfulness and sense of humor. At the same time there was continuity in Wangeci's homestead: her oldest son's wife and daughters now drew water from the well that Wangeci had built in 1984.

Unlike Watoro, Wangeci maintained control over land that her husband had given her even though her social status changed after his death. Not all widows have been so lucky; some find themselves at the losing end of a battle with their deceased husband's brothers over rights to land. It was only in the last decade that a law was passed in Kenya to ensure that a widow's rights to inherit a portion of her husband's land are legally protected. However, in Mutira, Wangeci's right to manage her husband's land was not contested. She remained on her husband's land, increasing its value over the years through tea cultivation. In doing so, she knew that she was protecting her children's future.

Wangeci's monogamous marriage to a man who encouraged her to be self-sufficient helped prepare her for widowhood. In addition, Wangeci in 1984 was actively involved in two women's groups that provided her with some mutual aid.

My choice of a widow was based upon prior counseling experience in the United States, which led me to postulate that the death of a spouse among Gikuyu might be a transformative experience—one leading to new self-perceptions, knowledge, and skills. Wangeci's case is illustrative.

Of the four women then in their fifties, Wangeci achieved the most in developing her homestead. She began by building a timber house with cement floors and a corrugated iron

Wangeci

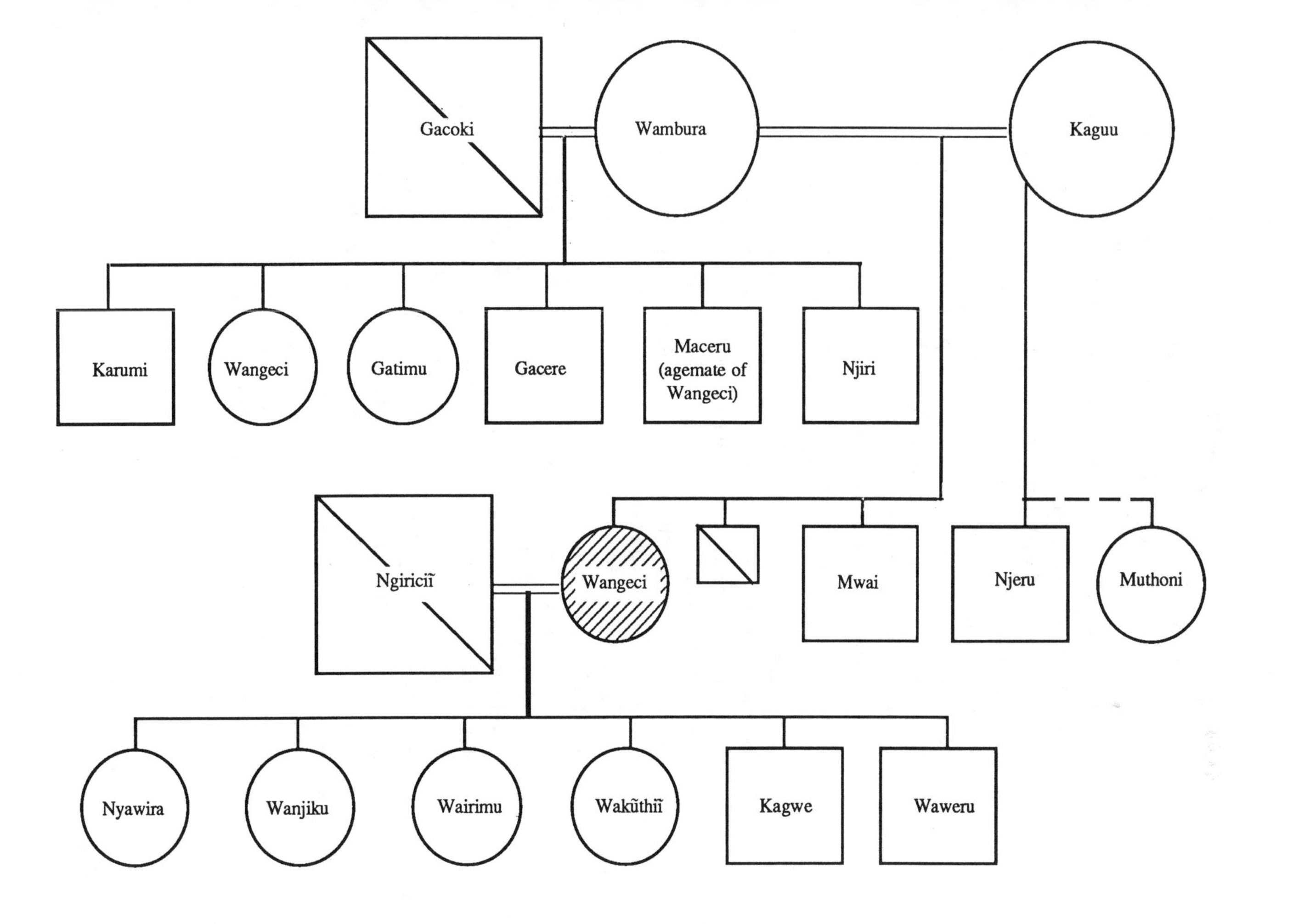
Gacoki
Wambura
Kaguu
Karumi
Wangeci
Gatimu
Gacere
Maceru
(agemate of
Wangeci)
Njiri
Ngiricĩĩ
Wangeci
Mwai
Njeru
Muthoni
Nyawira
Wanjiku
Wairimu
Wakũthĩĩ
Kagwe
Waweru

roof, using money saved from tea harvests. In late 1984 she was having a well dug so that she and her daughters-in-law would no longer have to fetch water from a stream. By 1985 when I first returned, the well was completed and she was enjoying the benefits. Wangeci was proud of the accomplishments acquired through her own hard work.

The word that comes to mind in describing Wangeci is *industrious.* She was a small woman with the boundless energy of a hummingbird. During our sessions her hands were never still—she was weaving a basket, peeling potatoes for the family's lunch, or pulling up buckets of mud from the borehole that would soon become the well.

Wangeci agreed to become one of my "teachers" because she felt that God had chosen her for such a role. Her narrative accounts were well organized and full of detailed description, often told with a sense of humor. She illustrated particular events in her life by donning attire appropriate to the occasion and acting out the scene with whatever props she could find. To simulate the circumcision scene, she donned an approximation of the circumciser's costume and then staged my research assistant and me as initiates and demonstrated how the circumciser had leaped toward each girl with her knife three times. The effect was highly convincing!

Wangeci demonstrated a keen sense of self-awareness that enabled her during our sessions to view her own life span development in relation to that of her cultural group. She perceived herself as unusual rather than typical of Gikuyu women, partly because of her status as a widow and partly as a result of her own personality. Of all the women, Wangeci was the most goal-oriented. She liked setting specific economic-related goals, and then worked hard to meet them. Halfway through the sessions she let me know that her next objective was to buy a sewing machine for a son trained as a tailor. She wanted my help in selecting one. I gathered the information and at the end of our sessions took her to Nairobi for the final purchase. This, then, is "the widow's tale."

—*J.D.*

I was named Wangeci for my father's mother because it was me who gave birth to my father. I was the firstborn and our clan is Ũnjiru. My father, Gacoki, was a brown man who was very hard working in the *shamba.* I can remember him bringing food to us children when we were herding the goats and cows. My father died when I was about ten.

My mother, Kaguu, who was the second wife of my father, is a jolly woman. Even now if you were to meet her, you would not think she is my mother—you would think we are of the same age. Besides my mother, there was my father's first wife, called Wambura. We shared everything with her children—it was as if we were all children of the same mother. And our mothers liked each other's children as their own.

Another woman who lived in our compound and was important to us as children was our grandmother—the co-wife of my father's mother—because I never met my real grandmother. We always called this woman *Cũcũ,* but her name was Wakarira. She was most responsible for me. You know, at that time, all children were left with the grandmother and older children during the day when the mothers went to the *shamba. Cũcũ* was a hardworking brown woman who was jolly with children.

I was the oldest child in my family. There was a boy who followed me, but he died when he was about four. Then Mwai, my brother, was born. My mother was pregnant with Mwai when my father died. Njeru, the next born, and my sister Muthoni are from relationships my mother had with other men after my father died. Mwai was about six years [old] when Njeru was born. I was responsible for looking after the younger ones. But Maceru, who was my agemate and the son of my older mother called Wambura, would help because he had to look after his brother, Njiri. The older children of Wambura were all big by the time I can remember them. Karumi, the firstborn, was in the Italian war [World War II]; Gacere, the next, was working; and Wangeci was married.

My grandmother taught me many things growing up—like how to fetch water in a gourd and how to fetch wood. But it was my mother who taught me who I was related to. She would wake me up one morning and tell me, "Today, I'm going to take you to your Uncle So-and-so's." Then she would put things into a basket for me to carry, and we'd go to my uncle's place. When we reached there she would tell me how I was related to each person there.

Was I raised differently from my brothers? Yes. When you are small, everyone sleeps together in the mother's house. But as you reach a certain age, around five or six, your brother cannot sleep in your mother's bed anymore. Then boys go to their father's *thingira.* You, being a girl, stay at your mother's, learning what women do. When eating, the boy's food is carried to the father's house, but you stay with your mother.

When we were young, sometimes the girls used to wish we could be boys. We would pretend that we were *anake* [young men] and make beer from maize-stalk juices and then divide ourselves up—some being "men" and others "women," as the older married people did, and then we'd drink "beer" and laugh a lot. We would make small houses to play in, but we never did sexual imitations. Even if a boy came and tried to raise one's dress to see the thighs, one would run and tell her father and that boy would be beaten.

After my father died, I started staying alone quietly under the granary. Sometimes I would cry, thinking of all the things my father used to do for us. I thought that he would come to life again, but then I realized he never would. Now my mother and I were alone.

My father's death changed my way of looking at things because now I came to learn that people die and it's not that they are just asleep. Also, his death brought a lot of changes in my life because the good things he used to do for us children came to an end. He used to roast bananas and yams for us and chew them so we could eat them when we were small—that was good. He would bring clotted blood and cook it for us when the men had taken blood from the cows. When we went to herd goats and cows when we were bigger, he brought food to us to eat where we were herding. So after he died, we never went far to graze, for we did not have anybody to bring us food. Sometimes, the cows and goats would go and feed in other people's *mashamba* because we'd leave them alone when we got hungry and went to find something to eat. Then those people would become angry.

After my father died, I could see my mother with nobody to help her now. She would take a hoe and go and dig in her *shamba* by herself, take the cows to the river and feed them and other things. I remembered this later, and when I became a widow I knew that I, too, would have to do things for myself.

* * *

As children, we had many games we used to play when we were not helping our mothers. There was one where we used a broken piece of pot and drew lines in a rectangle on the ground. We'd divide the rectangle into two smaller rectangles at each end, then draw two crossed lines [creating four diagonals] in the center part. [At this point in the interview, Wangeci got up from the stool she was sitting on and drew lines on the ground with a stick to show what the game pattern looked like.] Now, you take a stone or broken piece of pot and throw it into the first square and then hop over it with one leg. On the way back, while still hopping, you have a kick the stone out. [The game is similar to hopscotch.] Another game we played is *ciũthi*. We used to collect stones, then throw one up in the air, catching it with the same hand before it touches the ground. We'd start with one, then two, three, four, up to five. Then we'd try and throw them all up in the air and catch them on the backs of our hands without spilling any.

We learned riddles from our grandmother. "Catch a riddle," she'd say. And we'd tell her we were ready—here's one for you.

Mwarĩ mũtune rware.	A red daughter in the field.

You don't know? It is easy. If you don't know, you say, "Take all my cows," as a way of paying for not knowing the answer. Here's the answer:

Kirayo kia njahi.	Blossoms of peas.

[At this point, I had the uncomfortable feeling of a student in a classroom who has missed the answer to an obvious question. However, when given the answer, it was easy to see how beautifully the problem cast as a metaphor fit the context of peas in bloom.]

* * *

Usually when a child was about five or six, a ceremony to remove the child from her/his mother's bed took place. But for me, it didn't happen until I was about eleven, because my father had died so it was not necessary for me to have a *rũkoro.* A goat was slaughtered and its skin was dried in the sun to spread out for my bed. But I don't remember *mambura ma twana* as being a big occasion like *mbuci.* It usually happened when the mother wanted to get another child. It meant she could resume sexual relations with her husband. During those times, a woman would not have sexual relations while she was suckling a child, and we used to suckle our children for three to four years. It's not like now when women are having babies almost every year. We had our own kind of family planning then.

My mother and grandmother were the ones who taught me good behaviors as I was growing up. *Cũcũ* told me, "Bad things have no product in a good life"—that is one of the wise sayings the elders gave us. Bad things are like standing on the road and abusing people or getting into somebody's house when they are not around and removing something from there. Good people are those who are obedient to their parents and grow up listening to them and the advice they give.

I remember one time, I removed a gourd from the granary and went to the river with it. I fetched water and on the way back I broke it, but I did not say anything when I reached home. So when my mother discovered the broken gourd she beat me because I had hidden it and not told the truth. That time I learned that hiding the truth can be bad. Among

Agĩkũyũ we say that cheating somebody is like killing them, because if they found you had cheated them they could very easily stab you with a knife.

Cũcũ used to say, "An obedient child eats his/her mother and father." By this she meant that when you obey your parents and respect them, all they have saved for you in the future will be yours. She used to send us to get something from a neighbor's house, and she would put saliva on her hand and warn us, "If the saliva dries up before you have returned, you will surely die." So we'd run fast. We learned to obey.

Sometimes *Cũcũ* would tell us stories at night in her house around the cooking fire. We were never told stories during the day because hyenas would come and eat us—that is what we were told. If we happened to mention stories during the day, *Cũcũ* would tell us to touch the three firestones that make the fireplace to prevent the hyenas from coming.

Though my grandmother taught us many things, I learned how to weave baskets from my mother. She used *migio* [type of bush] when I was very young, and then later she began using sisal. *Cũcũ* made baskets out of *ngutwii* [stinging nettle fibers]. I would sit on the ground and watch my mother and grandmother carefully to see all that they did, including *gwokotha* [process of rolling plant fibers together to make strings]. But me, I started making baskets using banana fibers because they were easier to use. I collected those that were left after feeding the cows and tried making a basket. Then my mother would help me. She started the basket and I watched how she did it, then I did it just the same way. Sometimes, when the *migio* trees were pruned, we would peel off the red bark and make strings from it. The red strings were used as decoration. Sometimes strings were dyed with soot to make a black design. My mother showed me how to collect soot from a blackened cooking pot to decorate a basket.

We started to make baskets from *migio* strings just before we were circumcised. We used to spend a lot of time with a migio plant trying to get string from it, then drying the string for *gwokotha.* We learned how to *gwokotha* well and made small baskets that looked like a bird's nest. But in those times, women did not make sisal ropes for carrying things [tumplines], because our ropes then were cow's hide cut into thin strips and then joined to make a *mũkwa.* It was as we were growing up, learning how to weave, that we began to think about going for *mbuci* and *matũ.*

* * *

When my agemates began to have their ears pierced *mbuci* and then *matũ,* they told me not to follow them around. I went to *Cũcũ* and told her what they had said. She said it was because I did not have my ears pierced, and she went and told my father to brew beer so I could take it to my uncle to get permission for *mbuci.* [When Wangeci refers to "father," she means her father's younger brother. Brothers to one's father are called "*Baba*"—father. "Uncle," in this case, refers to her mother's brother.] It was not the Agĩkũyũ tradition to ask permission for *mbuci* from where the child was born, but from the oldest uncle's home where the mother came from.

When my oldest uncle agreed and gave permission, I went to have my ears pierced *mbuci.* Before we had our ears pierced our heads were shaved with a knife—*kienji*—all around the edges, with hair left in the center. It was *Cũcu* who shaved me. At that time, too, our mothers' heads were shaven, but not completely because none of them had a child who was circumcised yet. It was another grandmother, called Waturi, who did the piercing at the top of the ear using a sharpened stick of an acacia tree. After the piercing, castor oil was smeared in the holes and sticks were put in. *Cũcũ* would change the sticks about every four days for me until the holes were healed. I don't remember that the piercing hurt—it was just something one did to show she had reached another stage of life.

When *mbuci* healed, *matũ* were cut in the lower lobes. There were many children there watching us have our ears cut, but no grown people. By watching us, the younger girls would know what to expect when they reached our age. I didn't cry, but I squeezed my eyes shut. It hurt, but the pain has faded in my mind.

After *matũ* healed, big sticks were put in the holes. They were wider than your earring [over an inch in diameter] and made of wood or curved stone. Sometimes a cassava—when it was still fresh—was cut and kept and dried in the sun and put in. Once put in, the earplugs would shine from far away and one looked very beautiful and people would talk about how beautiful so-and-so's daughter looked. Another kind of earplug was black. These were called *ndebe.* They had holes in the center and were wide at both ends like a spool of thread. They were put in by rolling them over the drooping lobe of the ear so that when a girl danced, the *ndebe* jingled.

After piercing the ears, one knows that she has left the childish things behind. I began removing myself from the childish games and began acting more grown-up, because now the days were being counted for me to go for *Irua. Irua* was the most important ceremony among our people. Between *matũ* and *Irua,* I was not allowed to go to the forest to dance but could only dance outside the houses and was careful not to be involved in any sexual relations. You see, I was being prepared for the time when I would become an adult. There were so many of our agemates from the whole village who moved together, abusing [in this case Wangeci means "teasing"] one another and sharing our secrets. We were very playful. But then an elderly lady came and if she suspected we were becoming loose in our ways, she took us in a mother's house and made us sit down with our legs apart so she could look at us. I can remember her doing it once. She was investigating our private parts to see which ones were becoming sexually involved. Knowing that she would investigate us kept us from becoming active sexually. Even up to the time of marriage, after *Irua,* the older women would keep an eye on us like that.

After staying for some time, *Cũcũ* went to my father [father's younger brother, who was the head of the family] and told him that I looked suitable for *Irua* and asked if he could make the necessary arrangements. This was before I had begun menstruating. If your first period came before going for *Irua,* it was a bad omen, and your father would not be given the first goat during the *rũracio* negotiations when you married.

After eight gourds of beer were taken to my uncle, I went to his place and was given a goat and a cow. These were taken home by the women from my clan.[1]

I learned about *Irua* from my two grandmothers—the mothers to my father and mother. They sat down with me and told me that it was time I got circumcised before I got any bigger. They told me it was the Agĩkũyũ tradition—to mark the end of childhood and the beginning of adulthood. One had to undergo *Irua* to be separated from the other children. To Agĩkũyũ, nobody could carry out a sacrifice unless that person was circumcised. We say, "A goat which has not shed blood cannot offer a sacrifice." It means that, like the goat, the person has not yet shed blood.

After taking beer to my uncle's place to get permission, he told my mother and father [father's younger brother] to make some more beer so he could go to their home to drink it there. Then my father took over the preparations. He told the women in our homestead to go for sugarcane, and the following day the juice was removed from the sugarcane and it was used to make beer.

The way women prepared sugarcane for beer is that once the stalks were cut, they would be *gũkiro* [passed over a piece of hard metal that had percolations all over it], so that thin thread-like pieces of sugarcane were left. Then the thin threads were put in a skin bag filled with water and put in a hole in the earth. Young men would remove the threads and press them into a ball. They tied the ball with strings and started draining the juices from the sugarcane threads into the skin by tying the strings tighter and tighter until the threads became dry, hard, and white. The juice left in the skin bag was now ready to be put into *itumbi* [huge egg-shaped gourds]. The women strained the juice, using leaves from an acacia, as it was poured into the *itumbi.* I can remember women doing this. The *muratina* [a special bean pod that was a fermenting agent] from a tree was added to the sugarcane juice, and the huge gourds were put near a cooking fire—all around it—to cook. The heat of the fire helped *muratina* to release its juices, which mixed with the sugarcane juice. The women had to keep the cooking fire going all day so the juices would boil. It took one whole day, sometimes two, and by the next day the beer was ready.[2]

When the beer was ready, a boy was sent to tell my uncle. He called his clanmates, and they came to drink the beer. When they got drunk, they would start singing *Irua* songs as a way of showing that they were giving permission. Just before going home, the uncle set the date for *Irua* eighteen days from that time.

During the next eighteen days, you could hear women singing the *Irua* songs. These songs could only be sung at this time, and they were naughty. [At this point Wangeci burst into laughter, and when I pressed her for details, she described them in only general terms.] They were songs about intercourse and things like that, which you didn't hear talked about ordinarily.

When the day came for circumcision, I was told to go to my uncle's place for the blessings called *karathiro.* We went singing slowly to his homestead, and on reaching the gate, I was hidden in between the women of my clan so nobody would see me. So we entered the homestead that way and were singing.

When we reached the place in front of my uncle's house, I started singing:

Nĩndutangĩrũo	Bring out for me quickly
Ndĩwamathiĩ.	I am in a hurry.
Ndĩwamagendera.	I am on a journey
Na ngũndio iria	And give me some milk
Gũtihindi ciomire maitũ	For my mother could not have come from a place
Ita ciaraga.	Where cows never calf.

When my uncle heard me singing this song, he came out of his *thingira* holding a goat, and he gave it to me to take back home. He also gave me four shillings and his wife gave me two shillings. Afterwards, they brought sour porridge that they had made for the women of my clan who escorted me there, and, I can tell you, those women enjoyed it. After they had taken the porridge, we started the journey back to my home with all those who were at my uncle's homestead accompanying us. At home, the dancing continued all day up until the time we should go to the field.

Slightly before three in the afternoon, all the girls going for *Irua* were taken to the river to wash. We washed together with the women from our clan. Then one woman, who was a young bride with only one child who came from my father's family, carried me on her back so that I would not touch the ground back up to my home to dress for the ceremony. The reason a young bride carried me is that they had been carried by young brides of the mother's family to the homestead when they were married. So, during *Irua*, it was time for them to do it for somebody else.

Why wasn't I allowed to touch the ground after being washed? To keep me clean and pure—it was the clan's way of showing appreciation for one of their girls who is maturing. When I reached home, a *mũndũ mugo* was there, and he put a mark on my face from the forehead around to the chin and back up on the other side with *iria*—a white, chalklike substance that signified mother's milk, because it was as if we were being reborn—this time as adults. Then I was dressed with beads on top and a *thira* and two pieces of cloth called *retho* tied around the shoulders, so that when I was swinging the beads against my breasts on the way to the field where we were to be circumcised, the clan would be happy because I wasn't shaming them. During the operation, the *thira* and *retho* were removed, except where a girl had big breasts—then her circumcision mother would leave the *retho* covering her.

When we got to the field, it was crowded with people who had come to see the girls get circumcised. The men from the clan were chasing away those near the girls until a distance was made between the girls and the crowd. So the people were surrounding the girls with old women on the inside, then the rest behind them. Of course, children were there, but if any misbehaved they were carried away. At the center of the circle were the candidates for *Irua*, who made a line like we plant maize nowadays. Men, women, boys, and girls were all singing as the girls took their places in the center. They were songs like:

Aya yoi ĩĩ ndirĩ ndũgũ	I have no relations
no mũthuri ũnyitĩrĩire mwana.	only the old man who is holding my child.

I had been eager to go for *Irua* so I could become a mature girl like the ones at home and be loved like them. I also wanted to be able to wear beads and have my sheet smeared with oil and acquire a *mũthuru* [a skirt with slits] and finally be able to go to dances. So I was not afraid of the pains I had heard people say were experienced during *Irua*—I was excited and eager.

When the circumciser came into the circle, she was dressed in two sheets, one tied on one shoulder and the other tied with a knot in front. She came hopping and jumping toward us, holding her *kienji.* She would make the first cut, then go back again and come jumping forward again to make another cut. Each of us were cut three times—first one side of the clitoris, then the other side and in the middle so that a V-shaped [triangular] wound was left where the clitoris had been. By the third time, the circumciser would get set in her work, and those girls who were cowards were screaming and crying. Usually, a circumciser was given three shillings for doing her work, but the parents of a girl who screamed and shitted in the field had to give the circumciser a goat, too.

If a girl cried or screamed, the others in the line could beat her after the operation. And later, when we went home and were healed and started visiting each other, she was given the leftovers to eat. Each girl in our *riika* would leave some little food for her and after all of us had eaten we would put the leftovers together in a calabash and give them to her. She would never eat from a full calabash when visiting us.

Where I got circumcised at Karaini, there were only two of us—Wambaca and me. We were the first in our age group to go through *Irua*. When I sat down, after spreading my *mathangu* [leaves], I was held by my two supporters. One was my older grandmother, called Ngunju, and the other was my "sister." I call her sister because she was a grandmother where I was born [one of Wangeci's grandfather's co-wives]. Among Agĩkũyũ, a grandmother can be your sister because your mother can have a daughter who is your sister and was named for the grandmother. So your sister and she have the same name. The one I call sister was like a mother to me—that's why I chose her to be one of my supporters. Both of those women held me while I was being circumcised—one from behind, sitting down with her legs over mine, and the other holding my hands. But when the circumciser came jumping toward me, I was not watching.

I had been told by my supporter to look away so I wouldn't see the circumciser and become frightened. So I was looking up at the sky. The first thing I felt was a sharp pain like fire—just like you feel when you cut yourself badly with a *kibanga*. Then I felt my body numb and did not feel pain again until three days after the operation, when the wound got pus. But when the circumciser was doing her cutting, I was brave and did not cry. I was the one circumcised first, and as I had been brave, the other girl braved herself and also didn't cry. She knew I would beat her if she did.

Though there were only two of us that time, sometimes there are many. Another day, at Kariko, there were eighteen girls who got circumcised and six others who were circumcised near where the primary school is now. At that one, two girls cried. So those who got circumcised earlier went out and started beating the two who had cried until we were bribed by the girls' supporters not to beat them again. They gave us a bamboo container containing castor oil, which was used for medicine in those days.

The two of us who were circumcised together, we never showed our pain—even if you met us you would never know. When you realize that men, boys, girls, and women are watching you, you make yourself brave and afterwards get up and walk home even though you are feeling weak. I would not want the people to see me as a coward. Not even my supporters were helping me walk home. I wanted to show people that now I was mature and could endure pain.

When I reached home, before going into the house, I was told to hold a goat by my mother, and she gave me six shillings. Usually it is the father who gives the girl a goat, but because my father was not alive then, my mother gave it to me. After entering the house, I slept first. Then I was given sour porridge to drink and ate potatoes and bananas mashed together. Later, I was taken behind the house by my mother, and a leaf that the circumciser had put on the wound was removed and I was washed with warm water. A piece of old soft blanket was smeared with castor oil and put on the wound. It took only one month for me to heal.

After it was over, I felt that now I was a mature girl. Then I started waiting for my first menstruation. Others treated me differently. Because I was growing big breasts and was circumcised, they started to respect me and treat me like a grown person.

Irua taught me how to move from childhood to womanhood. It helped me to leave my childish ways and start acting like a grownup. There was nothing that was as important as *Irua* during our time, because after *Irua* one learned how to act and behave like a mature person. Today, one is born, but she does not pierce her ears like we did and she does not go for *Irua*. Where does she shed her childhood acts and behaviors? She grows with them, matures with them, and even marries with them. Her acts are childish. She is not clever, nor is she mature in her mind.

Irua was our tradition. There was the time for women to go for *Irua* and so we did. It had much meaning, as it was a way of doing what the ancestors had done. It was a way of staying part of them. *Irua* was a tradition and something one just did—just as we eat every day and never stop to think about it.

Irua has no meaning to Agĩkũyũ girls today because now they have become people of a different culture. The only important thing to them is schooling—to pass or fail. After marrying, they carry the childhood behavior to their new homes. Take this girl I have here [granddaughter, aged 14], she is now mature enough to go for *Irua,* but I can't bother to take her because her mother would not like any mention of it. I wouldn't want her to go either because it has no meaning nowadays—it is useless.

There is nothing that can take the place of *Irua* to help a girl make the transition from girlhood to womanhood today. Big girls who are grown and mature are playing with girls of their daughters' age. There is no separation of age groups. You can see a girl swinging her hips in front of her father and mother nowadays. During our time, when my father was alive, I could never bend to pick up anything or do work when he was around because I would not like him to see my thighs. Even when sitting in the kitchen, I would never sit in a way to show my thighs. I would pull down my skirt to cover my knees. Today [Wangeci goes into an adjacent room and comes out dressed in a short, tight-fitting dress], a girl is washing clothes or dishes in a basin, and she bends with her back to her father and does not feel ashamed to continue washing, showing her father her naked thighs!

At times, young girls come here and ask me questions that we would have never asked an older woman—like how one becomes pregnant. I tell them one has to wait and see for herself. And if a girl gets pregnant, the only thing I can advise her is never to take abortion tablets, for if you take them you will surely die. Now younger women are getting two or three children, but they come close together. Us, we would get the number one was able to get, but we never got another until the smallest one was three or four years and able to be a little independent—until it was weaned. We would space them out that way.

Even if we tried to change back to the old ways, everything would go up in the air—it would have no meaning. In my time, one's *riika*mates were important, but today *mariika* have no importance to younger women. For us, they still have meaning. Like the woman called Wambaca in Karaini that went for *Irua* with me, we still help each other. If I'm in any need I call her, and she gathers people and comes to help me in the *shamba.* When my daughter got married she paid for most of the photos taken, and when her sons get married I will help her with the same. She also came and helped me with preparations for my daughter's wedding—like what to cook and buying the gifts. Sometimes, we give advice to each other when one knows more than the other. Like after my husband died, Wambaca came and said, "Now that your husband is dead, if I were you, I would not have another child by any other man and would only look after the ones your husband left." So I felt advised. But now, a younger woman will talk and joke with a man—even a younger one. In our case, those who were younger than us, if we met with them, we had our own way of greeting them that showed the separation between our ages. Now, it is different.

* * *

After *Irua,* I stayed for only one year before I got my first menstrual period. Because I was not at my father's home, I got a handful of soil and went and threw it under my bed at home. *Cũcũ* had told me that when one was expecting menstruation, her body would start feeling tired and lazy, and after a day or two one would see a flow of blood. If that happened at another girl's homestead and not ours, I should take a handful of soil from that girl's homestead and go throw it under her bed at her home to make it appear that I had started menstruating at home and not at another's.

Cũcũ also told me to stay in the house while I was having *mambura* [menstruation]. So I stayed there, and when *Cũcũ* noticed that I was not moving out she came and asked me why and I told her. She told me not to go anywhere until the bleeding had stopped. There was nothing we used to cover ourselves with—no cloth—so we just sat on a stool, bleeding. The stool on which one sat while menstruating was not kept in the open where anybody could sit on it because it was considered unclean [contaminated]. Because I did not have my father, there was a hole dug for me to sit over as with other girls. I was with my mother only, so the other children did not know what was happening. When it was finished, *Cũcũ* fetched some water for me from the river and after washing myself and my clothes, I washed the stool and then threw it under the bed where it was kept. Afterwards, I was given oil to apply to my body, and that day I spent at home. The following day, I could go out and visit my friends.

I started to take care of myself where men were concerned. *Cũcũ* and my mother had told me not to move with men, because now a man might spoil me for nothing and then I might end up being a *mũkoma ndi* [unmarried pregnant woman] if I got pregnant while at my father's place. Then I would never have the chance of being someone's first wife.

It was during this time of being young circumcised women that we began to make ourselves more beautiful. When we were younger, we had had our two bottom teeth cut out with a knife and stick once the new ones grew in. Now we would file the upper ones, curving them to make them look better. We would also make these marks you see here [short, dark vertical lines on the cheekbones—cicatures] with a razor and then put in soot from a cooking pot. Also we put marks on the breasts because we used to dance half-naked, and our breasts were very straight and so they were beautiful when we danced. We never thought of ourselves as "naked." Even now, women go about naked because of the dresses they wear that show their legs.

The marks on our breasts were made using the inside of the maize stalk that covers the kernels. A small piece was cut and one side was covered with saliva to make it stick to the upper part of the breast here. Then the other side was lit with fire and when it healed it left a raised place. Yes, it was painful, but you did not feel it so much because you wanted it done to look beautiful.

During this time we were going to dances. We would spend the day dancing and even we could decide to spend the night at a *thingira* and nothing would happen. We would go to the *thingira* of a *mwanake kiumbi* [a handsome, well-liked young man]. Before we went there we would tie our clothes with a rope. We would get one edge of the skirt at the front and tie it between the legs and round each thigh with the rope—that way you were protecting yourself. We would spend the whole night at this young man's house being turned over by him on the bed. He would only touch our breasts and nowhere else. At times, we would be so many on the bed that the man would ask his friend to come and help. But if we disliked the friend, we would not let him touch us. The *mwanake kiumbi* was the one who was a good leader in songs, who was the best dancer, had a nice voice, and cracked a lot of jokes, and was handsome. When we went to that man's house, we would never go back home until very early in the morning. The mothers would not see us at all—that was our way of giving them respect.

I kept going to dances for a long time before I got married. It is not like now when a man comes to a girl's place one day and the next day they get married—no, it took years. Many used to come and visit, and I would go meet others at dances. That is the way I saw my husband—there in the dances.

He did not know our home, so he asked his friends. Then he came near the granary in our homestead and stood there. Us, we were in the kitchen giving stories and cracking jokes—making a lot of noise. Then he started blowing his nose for the first time. My mother heard it and told us to keep quiet. When we did, we heard him blow his nose again. We kept quiet and he blew it a third time—like this [she covers one nostril with her thumb and blows loud]. Our mother told me to go and see who was there, because I was the only girl in the kitchen with the women.

I went, and after seeing who it was I asked him why he had come. He told me, "To visit." I asked, "To visit whom?" Then he told me, "To visit you." He thought I would not mind. Because it was the first day he visited, I did not ask him a lot of questions. I told him to go in peace and that he should not be abused—meaning that he was welcome to come again.

He stayed for three days without coming back and on the fourth day he came again. He did the same thing, blowing his nose. Because I knew who it was, I went out to see him. We talked awhile, and then he left. After the fourth time of visiting me this way, my mother asked, "This man who is always coming here, who is he and what does he want?" I told her about him.

The next time he came, I asked him who he was—his mother, his father, and his clan, all the particulars, even if I knew them already. I knew that if he was really interested he would come another day and tell me what he had been told by his parents, and I would tell him what I was told by mine. Then the friendship [relationship] would be established. When we had done that and he had gone and told his parents about my parents and clan, he came back and said that our clans intermarry.

From then on, he began watching my steps—when I was cultivating, he would send a group to come and see how much I could work to know if I was hardworking or lazy. He even watched to see if I stayed at home and did not wander. He did this until he learned about me fully. Finally, he came one day and asked for tobacco. I went for it from my father [father's younger brother] and gave it to him. If I had not liked him, I would have told him to go away. He took the tobacco to his father, and his father told him to make some beer to take to my father to pay him back for the tobacco. That is how we used to get married—not like today when a boy loves a girl, they go to his home and she starts cooking for him right away.

Before I met my husband, I had an idea that I wanted a man who took good care of his father's things. He had to be productive in the *shamba* and know how to take good care of a person. Knowing a man sexually was not in our thinking until the time when one was officially married. But if he turned out to be sexually inactive at that time, we would not hide our displeasure—we would leave the man in broad daylight and return home. The reason is that as you are a woman, you would not want to stay married to one who is a woman like you. Sometimes, a woman would stay for the first year after marrying and then tell her mother if her husband was sexually inactive. The mother would tell her daughter to wait, and the second year, if there was still the trouble, the mother would advise the girl to come back to her own homestead. So she would go to her father's compound and take back all the goats and cows given for *rũracio,* returning them to the husband's father. The husband would be left holding his head in his hands, because he knew he could never marry again now that everyone knew his state.

The purpose of having sexual relations is to have a child. If the husband was inactive, it meant that you would not get a child. Any other time, sex was just like eating dirt. After you got a child, your husband would not have any sexual relations with you until after you had stayed for four years—he would not even sleep in your house during that time. Until the child was big and old enough to have a *rũkoro* put on him/her and was officially removed from the mother's bed, the man could not have sexual relations with his wife. If you look at a man of my age now, he is still strong because he did not use up all his sexual energy. Look at young men nowadays—they are tiring easily and growing old fast because they think all the time they are enjoying sex, but they are not. The girls, too, are growing old very fast using up a lot of sexual energy for nothing.

Now people are doing what they feel they have the right to do about sex, and they do it in their own way. A young girl marries today and gets a child year after year, and after five or six years she looks older than her mother and dies early because she is wearing out. In our time, one waited for four years before getting another child, giving time for the body to build up strength, all the time eating good food like green vegetables.

One can go to the river and fetch water, but can you fetch blood and energy from a river? We knew these things, and we had our own kind of family planning. People had only the children they needed, and there was plenty of time for the body to heal between children. Nowadays, people talk about family planning with pills and medicine, but we didn't think about such things. I would not like my daughters to take the pills or other things because we hear stories about them. But I hear that some women who have had all the children they need go to Tumu Tumu to the clinic to get fixed so they don't have any more children.[3]

Some of our men take other wives—it is true. Then they have more children. But some, like my husband, only had one. A man would wait until those four years while his wife suckled the children were over and be patient, because if he went and had sexual relations with any other woman he would be called *githaria* [adulterer], and a song would be composed about him and it would be sung openly by his *riika*mates and those of his wife. They would shame him.

During the time my husband and I were coming to know each other—when he came to visit—we had to be careful. When I escorted him from the compound, I would throw his walking stick to him at the gate and come back running. When walking to some place, I could not go alone but would always be with my mother or *Cũcũ* or a small child. Even if Ngiriciĩ saw me and accompanied us partway, he would not talk to me.

It was three years after Ngiriciĩ first came to visit that the negotiations for *rũracio* started. Finally, the men from both our clans met and settled the number of goats that Ngiriciĩ would give to my father. In the morning, twelve goats were brought to our compound, and right behind them were the women of Ngiriciĩ's compound carrying six large gourds of beer.

On the day Ngiriciĩ came for me, he was accompanied by somebody named Kabuu. Ngiriciĩ came saying that he was coming for a visit. I welcomed him and gave him food. After that he told me to escort him to the gate. When we reached our gate, the other man held my hand and told me that I would have to go with them now that all the *rũracio* had been given. I did not scream. I just went with them to Ngiriciĩ's father's place without trouble. When we reached the gate, though, I refused to go in. A woman from the compound came and escorted me in.

During the old days, we were married when our parents still wanted us, so the man would have to find a way to take the girl without her parents realizing it. My mother was not left happy. But the following day, when she guessed that I had gone to Ngiriciĩ's homestead, she cooked food and sent somebody with it to my husband's place. At that time, I could not eat anything cooked in his homestead, because I would be considered greedy if I did. I had to wait until a goat was slaughtered and I was officially welcomed into a new house built by my husband later.

It was a women called Wanjira who welcomed me that first night. She was my in-law now, because her husband's father and Ngiricii's father were brothers. After Wanjira welcomed me, she took me to Ngiricii's mother's house. Ngiricii's mother lit a fire, but I went into the room where the bed was and never came out to warm myself at the fireplace. The reason I went to the bed was to show that now I had become her child.

The following morning, Ngiricii's mother asked me to come out to the fireplace. She went and brought sisal threads for me to make into strings for a basket. She gave me threads, because if I didn't start making my baskets then, when I went to my own house later and needed to get food from the *shamba,* I would have nothing to carry the food home in. It was not until three years later that I moved into my own house. The mother loved me because she didn't have a daughter and I was a companion to her. You see, Ngiricii went to Nairobi shortly after I went there to work as a sweeper in a European's store. During the three years I stayed with Ngiricii's mother, she treated me well and taught me many things—like when a married woman starts menstruating, she should not sleep in the same bed with her husband.

Before Ngiricii and I moved into the house he built for me, his father—who was a *mũndũ mugo*—blessed the house by sipping some beer, then spraying it from between his teeth into the house. Then he poured some of the liquid near the fireplace in the center of the house. But during this time, I was told to go the *shamba* so as not to interfere—I was told about it later. After that, Ngiricii's father could never enter the house again, because now I was one of his children and a father does not enter his grown child's house.

Ngiricii's mother went to the river and collected three good stones to make the fireplace in the new house. Then she went and got some *ndũma* [arrowroots] and bananas. She lit a fire in the fireplace and placed a pot of water on the fire over the three stones she'd brought. Then she put the *ndũma* in the pot to cook. She peeled the bananas and started to roast them. So now I was put in my own house, and I stayed in that house for three days without moving anywhere. It was like getting married again, so I had to hide my face from people. But now I could have sexual relations with my husband.

Another thing, during those three days, *ndũma* was not given to any outsider, because we believed that if it was given to somebody outside the compound, the new house would be contaminated. After Ngiricii had stayed with me for a few days in the new house, he went back to Nairobi. I was given a *shamba* to cultivate. At that time, a woman's *shamba* was not all in one place. I had two pieces of good land down by the river and four up here, where I planted maize and beans, sweet potatoes, and millet. I would get up very early while the ground was still wet and cook some gruel for Ngiricii's mother and me, then sweep the house out and hurry to the *shamba*, where I worked until the sun was going down. I liked working hard—even then. Sometimes a letter from Ngiricii would come, and his brother would read it to us. Then I missed seeing him. But usually I did not think about him with all the work to be done. A few months after Ngiricii left, I found I was pregnant.

* * *

I first learned I was pregnant after staying for three months without menstruating. When I noticed I had missed three times, I went to my home and asked *Cũcũ* what could be happening. She asked me whether I had had any sexual relations with my husband before he went back to Nairobi, and I told her yes. Then she told me I was pregnant and now I should stop greeting the *anake* [circumcised young men] I had danced with before I was married, for they were known to cause one's pregnancy to abort due to jealousy. You see, if you had refused one of the young men who had tried to woo you, he might take some herbs called *ngunga*. He would drink some of them in a tea and hold others in his hands so that when he came to greet you, the *ngunga* would cause an abortion. So I had to avoid those *anake*.

During that time of being pregnant, I could only eat certain foods like green vegetables, and, at times, I cooked bananas. When it came time for the birth of my first child, I had spent the day comfortably, cultivating in the *shamba*, and I had carried one and a half *ndebe* [large containers] of potatoes home with my mother. When we got home, my mother told me to go and light the fire—by that time I had gone to stay with my real mother because my husband was in Nairobi, and when I felt my time was near, I moved in with my mother because I could not figure out how I would tell my husband's mother when the time was reached. As my mother was cooking for others at her fireplace, she asked me to go and make a fire for my cooking in a house where she used to store things. After cooking my greens and eating them, my mother came and we stayed together. She fixed porridge, and instead of carrying it to her house, we just took it there. Then we went to sleep, each in her own house.

At around midnight, I called my mother and told her that I was having a stomachache. She told me to go and take some water. At that time, I didn't know what labor pains were. I told her the ache was severe and it couldn't be stopped by just taking water—it felt as if it was way inside near the backbone. She told me to sleep on my back and not to lock the door. So I did what she told me—she knew what was happening.

When I tried to sleep again, I couldn't, so I called again and told my mother I was going to sit up and warm myself by the fireplace. She woke and came and lit a very big fire and told me to get a mat from my bed. When I tried to get one, I couldn't. I was in too much pain. My mother went into the bedroom and came out with a mat and placed it on the floor and told me to lie down on it and sleep on my back. I told her I couldn't sleep. Then she decided to send for my husband's mother. I told my mother I felt like my abdomen was swollen, and I had to push hard. My mother began pushing on my stomach and the baby just came out. My husband's mother arrived just in time to cut the umbilical cord with a razor. Then my mother washed the child. It was a girl, so the two women called "*aririririti*" four times.

When it was daylight, my mother sent my brother to go and call other people from my husband's homestead. They came with bananas, potatoes, porridge, and firewood. The women from my husband's homestead didn't take me back to my husband's house immediately but told me to stay and get a little strong and then we would go back there. I stayed for some time and then left to join my husband in Nairobi because that's when Mau Mau first began [1952].

* * *

I was still a *mũhiki* [bride] with only one child when I heard a rumor that there were Mau Mau people giving the Oath, which consisted of eating the meat of a dog. At that time the baby was sick, and my husband heard and told me to bring her to the hospital in Nairobi. So I decided to get away from the oathtaking and go to Nairobi. After taking the child to the hospital, I stayed on in Nairobi during most of the fighting. What happened is that we received a letter from here telling us not to come home, for people were being killed and it was not safe.

During the time we were in Nairobi, my husband was working as a cook for one of the many Europeans that lived there. I used to stay at home in the place where Africans stayed, locked in the house the whole day while my husband worked. I did not like it. If it was cooking I needed to do, I cooked with a *jiko* [charcoal cooker] instead of using a fireplace as at home. It was hard to get things like food. Ngiriciĩ had to have a passbook, which was like an identity card but was carried in the pocket. He had to carry it always wherever he went.

Ngiriciĩ never told me whether he supported Mau Mau or not. He never wanted to tell me his secret thinking—he kept that to himself. So we stayed in Nairobi without problems for some time. I do not remember our stay there as being a big change, but a temporary one, because I knew when the fighting stopped we could go home. When we heard that things were better here, we decided to come back—that was a year before *Uhuru*. Then, soon after, we heard that Kenyatta was released from Maralal, where he had been held in detention, and we were being granted our freedom—*Uhuru.*

On the day of Jamhuri [Independence Day], we watched for Munyao to climb Mount Kenya and raise the flag. During the night before, we watched the fireworks being shown at Kamuruana Hill and guns were fired. In the morning we started singing, cooking a lot of food, and slaughtering chickens to celebrate, because it was a holiday. I felt so happy that day because now we were free. Some tried to tell us that *Uhuru* was just for the rich Africans, but I realized that it was given to everybody who had any brains and was hardworking. We had just planted tea here, and I knew we would not be cultivating tea—as much as we wanted—if *Uhuru* was only for the rich. The government would have told us that if you picked tea you could only pick one kilo like the British used to tell us before we got our freedom. So it was the lazy ones who said that *Uhuru* was only given to the rich.

* * *

I first learned to pick tea before *Uhuru* when Brook Bond Tea planted it at Kianjagi. That was just before the Mau Mau trouble started. We had not planted any tea here yet, so we used to go there and were taught how to plant and cultivate tea by a *muzungu* [white, European] and his workers, who had come from Britain. We also learned how to pick—two leaves and a bud—and how to use the old leaves to make new plants [cuttings] for more tea.

Then, when we returned here from Nairobi, we decided to plant our own tea just before *Uhuru.* Everyone was beginning to plant it, and we thought we would try it. We learned that people could earn a good profit with tea to buy some of the new things that were becoming available in the shops—like iron beds, wooden tables, and clothing. Government extension workers came to our *shamba* to see our tea and show us how to make it better by pruning and picking it using a long stick to make the tea bushes level with each other on top. Where did we grow it? Up here. Before Mau Mau, part of the *shamba* was planted in maize and another part in yams. But it was not well kept during Mau Mau, so we cleared part of it for tea and kept other parts for maize and beans. And we cleared some new land.

At first I picked only 3 kilos [6.6 lbs.] of tea a day, then increased to 4 [8.8 lbs.] or 5 [11 lbs.] and finally got so I picked 10 kilos [22 lbs.]. When we pick maximum is when we have picked 11 [24.2 lbs.] or 12 kilos [26.4 lbs.]. But young people can pick up to 40 [88 lbs.] or 50 [110 lbs.] kilos a day. Us, who are old and our bones are getting stiff, we cannot afford to pick faster than 12 kilos [26.4 lbs.] or so.

I'm always learning new things about cultivating tea and developing my land. I've learned to put manure around the tea bushes and how to trim the edges. I use manure either from the goats, cows, or chickens and mix it with rubbish from my house to increase growth of the bushes. Fertilizer is necessary to yield better production of the tea. I have learned all this from the *baraza* [outdoor meetings] held by the KTDA—Kenya Tea Development Authority. I also use manure on the gardens where I have maize and potatoes growing. And now I am planting cabbage and *skuma-wiki* [kale], too. Before, we just used to collect wild spinach.

When did I become a Christian? I started going to church before Mau Mau. Neither of my parents were Christian, but when some of my agemates and I saw others going to Sunday Service at the church in Karaini, we decided to go, too. We were already mature girls by then who had gone for *Irua.*

Then I saw that the sister to my mother had become a Christian, and I could see her staying peaceful and having good things that I longed for, like cleanliness and being able to take care of one's home and a good relationship with the husband. I began thinking that I should join the church, too.

Becoming a Christian changed my life—even my soul—because in the days before I became a Christian I used to cook and drink liquor. I would cook *njohi* and sell it to people. But after becoming a Christian, I stopped cooking *njohi* or drinking it. Before, I would abuse anyone who tried to abuse me—like if they came demanding something that was mine and I refused to give it to them, they would abuse me. But now, even if somebody comes and abuses me or tries to fight with me, I will not fight back. I believe there is only one who fights for me—that is God. That is why I say that Christianity is good.

I did not get baptized until I was a married woman. I had been going for catechism at the Anglican Church, and after mastering those lessons of the Bible, we had been told to learn the Apostle's Creed and know a prayer before being baptized. So I learned those things, and a day was set for our baptism. I can remember that day. We went to church very early in the morning and sat in the front seats with our baptism "mothers." We got up then and made a line around the basin of water and each baptism mother would give the Christian name of the woman who was her "daughter" to the vicar, and he would baptize each of us, saying our new name and putting drops of water on us. I was the one who chose my name, "Peris," and told it to my baptism mother.

After staying for twenty years married the Agĩkũyũ way, my husband and I renewed our vows in the church. Then I became a member of the Mother's Union. I find that going to church now feeds my soul with words and prayers that help me forget about doing something wrong and console my soul when I am feeling badly.

Shortly after the renewal of our vows, I went with other women from the church to Mutira, and we were initiated into the Mother's Union group and were given certificates to show our membership. The Mother's Union helps in teaching about good home care and how to bring up one's children by giving the women advice. The teachings of the group show us how to advise our children and to correct their mistakes in a good way. We are also taught how to stay in harmony with our daughters-in-law by not interfering with their affairs and not desiring the things our sons have bought for them. We are reminded not to abuse one another and to be obedient and keep our Christian beliefs.

Sometimes the teachers in the Mother's Union are the wives of Bishops. These women are trained to deal with family problems. I can remember one called Gathoni who came from Nairobi and taught us to refrain from desiring other people's things. She said the minute you ask to borrow something and you are given it, if the owner comes for it and you refuse to give it back, it will cause a fight.

Every year the Mother's Union has a rally at Embu where members from all the churches in the area go, and we are given teachings by trained people from Nairobi and other places. The lessons are on how to keep harmony in the home and how to use Christian teachings to solve our problems. Through the Mother's Union I learned how to be self-sufficient without desiring other people's things.

I joined the Mother's Union first, then later I became a member of the *Uritu wa Gatwe* Group when it started about three years ago. The Mother's Union and *Uritu wa Gatwe* are sort of connected, because it was members of the Mother's Union that started the women's self-help group. "*Uritu wa Gatwe*" means "Power of Gatwe." Both the self-help group and the Mother's Union have helped me save money for my needs. Since I joined the Mother's Union, I no longer waste money on going to buy beer for myself and my friends. In the self-help group, we all contribute so much each month and at the end of the month that contribution is given to one woman—a different woman each month. If your child is sent away from school because he lacks school fees, then you can use the contribution money to pay that child's fees. With money given to me by the group, I have built this house you see, fenced with barbed wire, and am now digging this well for water.

Sometimes, the government sends extension workers to teach us new things in the self-help group—like how to raise pigs to make money. We are also part of the *Maendeleo ya Wanawake* [Development of Women] Organization. Maendeleo sent an extension worker to show us how to raise pigs. We have a male and a female and after the male mates with the female, we will slaughter the male and sell the meat. In the future I would like to see us build better sheds for the pigs and a trough for food and water. Pig raising is our main project.

Today, the sub-chief is coming to talk with our group about a plot of land that we would like to purchase. You can see that our group is doing a lot to help us improve our lives by making us more self-reliant. The group has been important to me, because now that I am a widow I can only depend upon myself, and the group helps me get what I need.

* * *

I became a widow when Waweru, the last-born, was twelve years of age. [Wangeci has four older daughters, who are married and living away. The two youngest children are sons in their early twenties, both married and living with her at the homestead. She lost one child before it was a year old but does not consider its death significant to her life history.]

I think I was about thirty-seven when my husband died. He had been sick and stayed in the hospital at Kerugoya for a long time. But the doctors never told me what disease he had—they never said. I can still remember well the day he died. It was the third of March.

I was at the hospital, visiting him, and he was saying, "Wangeci, the only thing I can tell you is to take care of yourself, the children, and the things you have that are enough to help you. I feel now that my time has come." He said this softly.

I asked him, "How should I take care of myself?"

He told me, "A widow has a lot of advisers. Take care not to be deceived out of what you have—the cows, the tea, the *shamba,* and the children. If you are not watchful, somebody may try and take them from you by force."

"Who is the one who will dare to take them from me?" I asked.

He said, "Wait, and I will think." He said this slowly and then he was quiet. So I kept quiet and waited for him to think. But when I looked at him, I saw that there was nothing—he had died. I was shocked because I had been waiting for his answer. That was the last time we talked.

Now I felt cold at heart and my body shook. I lost appetite and felt very thirsty in my throat, like sand. For the next few days, anytime I took water or tea, the thirst was never quenched. I was shivering even though it was hot outside. I was scared, so I prayed. There and then I just decided to stand on my own with Jesus without thinking of anybody else to help me. Yes, my faith helped me to see that.

When I came to tell my children that their father had died, I did not know what to say, because they had loved him very much. I told them that I had left him in the hospital. They asked whether he was feeling better, and I told them that he was not feeling well and was not getting better—I told them this the morning after he died. When I went back to the hospital that morning, I found they had kept him in refrigeration. I never told the children what was happening, because one was only in Standard

Seven and the other in Standard Five—the two boys. I felt that the news of their father's death would affect their learning at school. After three days—that's when I finally told them. The children cried and cried, and they looked changed, too. They felt very sad and found the hole in their lives deep to try and cover.

The hardest change for me was to refrain from moving with women who had their husbands, and learning to stay alone with my work. When I made friends with a woman who had her husband, and the wife would tell her husband that I was getting a good house and he should build a better house for her, he would tell her that it was me, Wangeci, who told her to say this—putting the idea in her head. He'd tell her, "I can see you want me dead so that you can own a cow" or "You want me dead so you can be talking with your children like Wangeci." The husbands thought that I showed their wives that I was having better things now as a widow, so I had to take care there. I also refused to move with married women because I realized that I might be beaten by women who had their husbands, because they might think that I was moving about with their husbands. So I decided to keep to myself and be self-reliant.

I stayed for about four years, still thinking about my husband before I began to get used to his absence. I changed then and stopped thinking about how he had helped and began to forget about his good work. It took me those four years to learn to do all the work myself.

It is different being a widow, because there are some things you cannot do when your husband is around, but then when you are widowed, you are forced to do them and you discover for yourself you can do these things. For instance, trapping moles—women leave that to their husbands. But a widow has to do it to stop moles from eating up the tea plants. So she learns how. If a married woman finds a banana tree falling down, instead of finding a post and putting it in the ground to hold it up, she calls her husband to do it. A widow has to do it by herself. Feeding the cows is usually the husband's job, but I have to do it myself. And I milk them as well. Yes, the learning is different for a widow.

When I was married, if a child was sent home from school for some reason, I could tell the child to go and tell his/her father why she/he was sent from school. This is normal. But now, being a widow, I have had to take care of my children and their school fees so they wouldn't be sent home. A widow, therefore, has a lot of work and a lot to think about.

What advice would I give to a woman recently widowed? I'd tell her to stay self-sufficient, taking care of her children and the things at home. I'd say, "Don't wait for outsiders to come and advise you on how to run your affairs. Do not follow what others are doing blindly. Make yourself a *mũtũmia ngatha*" [a self-sufficient woman]. Another thing I would tell her is, "Do not join forces with any woman who has her husband, for you might lose a lot. If you go to help her with her work, your work is still there waiting for you when you get home, and nobody is there to help you." Like now, since I started digging this field, if my husband were alive he would have dug up the rest. But now the field has to stay the way it is until I get time to finish it. "One cannot defend and at the same time fight." So being a widow, one needs to do her work first, single-handed, slowly by slowly, before she can help others. That way, one will win the respect of the people in her area. This is the advice I would give.

Nowadays, in our society, widows do not get help. They say each has his mother. It means that even the father's [deceased man's] brothers can't help, as they are interested only in their children. It is the mother of the child who takes care of the child, and a man helps only his own children today. But long ago in Agĩkũyũ society, if there was a feast somewhere, a share of meat would be brought to the widow, and the father's brother took over the dead father's role—like my father's younger brother became my father after my real father died. But nowadays, the brothers to my husband have never even thought of buying a kilo of meat to bring to my children. They say they have their mother to care for. Even in the community, people say that you, a widow, are rich with all the things left to you by your husband. So they never think to help someone like me.

What do I remember best about Ngiricĩĩ? I am happy when I remember how he brought me here to his place and told me that if I worked hard I would be able to support myself. I also remember that he was very hardworking in the *shamba.* He liked, and took good care of, the children. At times, when I had a new baby to care for, I would not cook. He would be the one to cook or, at times, hold the child while I was cooking. He showed me that women can also plant bananas. So whenever we went to the *shamba,* he would plant one and then force me to plant the next. He taught me that I could also do things that men normally do, and I am grateful because that way he helped me to be self-supportive and stand on my own after he died. He was a good person, and that's why I'm always proud to say that I was his wife—*mũtũmia wa Ngiricĩĩ.*

* * *

When my children were growing up, I taught them to respect their elders. I told them, "Any woman married to somebody of your father's *riika,* respect her and call her 'mother.'" Respect should also go to the father's brothers and the uncles.

A child that does not do what he/she is told to do is wrong. A child should be taught that his/her parents are there to be obeyed and respected, for they are the people who have given birth to the child. I tell my grandchildren this now. I say, "Obey your parents, for they are the ones who have given birth to you and are caring for you while you are growing up. They are wiser than you who are small. You are their child, and you will always be so until they die. Obey your parents so that days may be added to those which you are going to live on this earth."

Now, I raised four girls and all are married. The important things to teach a girl are how to cultivate, to clean the homestead, sweeping the house, and not throwing the rubbish under the bed. Rubbish can be saved and mixed with manure and put around the tea bushes for fertilizer. I showed my daughters how to cultivate, digging the soil with a *kibanga*, how to plant, and when the plants grew to take care of them, weeding and turning the soil. That way I was taking them to high school.[4]

It is important to show a girl how to respect people anywhere she goes, to teach her that when she goes and marries in another place, she should show those parents she meets at her husband's home that they are just like her mother and father and so need respect and obedience. It is also not good to laugh while other people are talking, because they will think she is laughing at them and become angry. Finally, she should not forget God—always pray for the good food given before eating.

A boy needs to learn that he is the cornerstone on which to build a homestead. He should be taught to cultivate cabbages, carrots, and potatoes, as well as maize and beans. He should go to school, and as he gets more knowledge, he should bring that knowledge back home. For instance, he can get himself trained as a mason or carpenter, and those skills will help him develop his home and will provide money to bring up his children well. He can also help his parents when they are old that way.

Now, when I was growing up, our mothers and our grandmothers in the kitchens and *mashamba* were our teachers, showing us what to do just as we show our sons and daughters. The *shamba* and homestead were the school. A woman would wake up early, cook whatever she had to cook, then sweep the outside around the house and inside, collecting the rubbish and throwing it in a certain place to be used as fertilizer later on. The young girls near her would learn that it is good to keep the compound clean and the rubbish swept and saved for fertilizer. If the mother was cooking, the girl would learn how to make *irio* and the right mixture of maize and beans for *githeri*.

The bigger and older girls were our advisers, telling us how to behave with people younger than us, how to take care of ourselves in front of men, and to respect the elders. We'd learn certain ways of behaving, just as young girls learn these things in school. Even nowadays, girls are still learning from their mothers and grandmothers at home.

Even though school was not important when I was growing up and our parents thought that if a girl went to school she would become loose and a prostitute, today it's important for girls to go to school, so they will learn how to become self-sufficient and not depend, when they are grown, upon their parents or others. The highest grade any of my daughters achieved was Standard Seven, but the son who was supposed to go to Standard Seven refused—he got malaria, and so he said he could not go to school again.

I thought I would try to learn how to read and write so I could become more self-sufficient. I decided to join the adult education class at Gatwe—I was looking for more knowledge and how I could develop my land better. If I could learn how to read and write, then when going to withdraw money from the bank, I would no longer have to put my fingerprint on the bank slip in the place for a signature.

The class was held at the school—it was not so far away from here. The first day, I did not know what time the class met, so I went very early, before four P.M., and stayed there waiting for people to come. Then I only saw letters written on a blackboard, and looking at them made my eyes water. The following day, as I had been too early, I decided to stay home and work a bit longer. When I went at five o'clock, I met the class ending. I was told that the class meets everyday, Monday through Friday, at four P.M. But by that time, I decided it was better to stay home and cultivate and forget the adult education class. The reason is that I could go and cultivate a piece of land or even cook during the time of the class —to go and waste time at the class and not understand anything seemed useless. Well, I decided just to continue putting my fingerprint on the bank slip.

If I had a choice of going to either adult education class or the women's group, which would I choose? The women's group! In that one, we do work that helps us—like building the pig's pen or buying their food or even contributing money to each other. That's not like being told to learn letters that are hard for me to see. I dropped that class because I did not understand what was being taught, and not understanding, I decided it was better to stay home doing something else to help myself. But there are some women who have gone, and they say they can read letters and are never cheated at the shops because they know how to do maths. But me, I do not care.[5]

The way I learn best is seeing how other people do things. I will attend *baraza* like the one for tea growers held at the biggest factory at Kagozi. By going to the *baraza,* I learn better ways of increasing my tea yield. By being taught new ways of doing things and using my own head, I try to do things that will improve my work and my way of living.

* * *

Which of my roles in life is most important to me? Now, the most important is cultivating my farm and doing the work of the homestead, because those are needed before all else. Then I would say being a member of the Mother's Union and *Uritu wa Gatwe,* because the women's groups help me a lot, as I've said. Being a mother or grandmother is next most important. Then the one of being a wife to my husband, because the role of being a daughter was a long time ago.

Long ago, before the missionaries came and started changing things, the role of an elder was important, too. During my mother's time, when a woman's firstborn went for *Irua,* her head was shaved and a *mũkwa* was put on at night, and she got *kirira* from the other women. But when Nyawira, my firstborn, went for *Irua,* it was after the missionaries had come, so the ceremony for elders was not observed.

I have not gone through menopause yet, but at times I stay for three months before I menstruate. Sometimes I get headaches and hot spells, but I never experience chills. I think menstruation will end soon.

Of all the transitions in my life, I think the death of my husband changed me the most. I started keeping to myself, as now most of the work in the homestead was all mine. I could not move with other women for marketing or other things, because by the time I came home, I'd find the cows not fed, there was no water, and I had to cook. Also, I was having to learn how to do new things I never had to do before when my husband was alive. So I changed the most when he died.

My greatest achievement has been to build this house of timbers with a cement floor. I don't really dream of the future. I know that someday, some hour, I will die. But I don't think about that. For now, I am satisfied with my life the way it is, except for getting the sewing machine I want to purchase for my son who is the tailor. At times, I feel that the headaches I get are due to thinking so much about how to buy this son a *kibanga* or a *jembe* [hoe] and that one a sewing machine.

My strongest character is that I like people and I'm hospitable to all—even when calling you to come and eat my food, it is with a clean and happy heart that I do it. I can't think of anything I'd like to change—I feel satisfied with myself. Being a woman means being able to keep things to myself, to go ahead and do them but not talk about them.

I think of myself first as Mũgĩkũyũ, because I was born in the Agĩkũyũ tradition and brought up in it. I had *mbuci* and *matũ,* then went for *Irua*—those were part of the tradition. After that I think of myself as Kenyan.

I have given you this knowledge freely—and given a lot of it. Now I hope you will help me go to Nairobi and buy that sewing machine for my son. [We went the following week.]

Notes

1. Wangeci is the only informant in her age cohort who relates being given a cow in addition to a goat. According to culturally recognized "experts," a goat is the norm. When I asked about this later, Wangeci insisted that she had been given a cow. My suspicion is that she was exaggerating a bit.

2. As taking beer is an important aspect of any ceremonial occasion and because women are largely responsible for beer-brewing, they perform an important function related to Gikuyu ceremonial events, and their skill as beer-brewers is recognized and appreciated by their male counterparts who depend upon them for the supply.

3. Wangeci refers to tubal ligation, which was, in 1984, fast becoming an accepted form of family planning among older women of childbearing age who had the number of children they desired—usually six to seven—and wanted to prevent additional births.

4. Another woman I interviewed referred to this as the "shamba school."

5. Five months after the interviews were completed, I made a follow-up visit to the adult education class that Wangeci referred to and found her in class, squinting at the letters on the blackboard as she tried to sound the words—she had decided to give the class a second try.

7

Wanoi: The Many Facets of a Midwife

Wanoi is a creative woman. Whether using her skills as a midwife, weaving a basket, or composing political lyrics to be sung to a traditional Gikuyu song for a campaign rally, Wanoi demonstrates an exceptional ability to innovate. Her peers refer to her admiringly as "clever." Said the leader of a self-help group to which Wanoi belongs, "If Wanoi was of the age when she could have gone to school, she would have learned very fast. She is somebody who is teachable, and even now with the adult education class she has been able to learn a lot quickly. She is the leader in our singing. She is one who is clever and creative." Not afraid of change, Wanoi is willing to take risks to try innovative ways of doing things. As openness to change and willingness to risk are both dimensions of creativity, Wanoi's life is, indeed, creative.

In 1983–1984 Wanoi typified Mutira women in their early fifties who had converted to Catholicism shortly after Kenya's independence. Similar to other Catholic women, she persuaded her husband to remain monogamous. She participates in both a Catholic women's group and a self-help group. In addition, she was attending adult education classes in 1983–1984. Her uniqueness stems from her role as a midwife. The only woman I met in her early fifties practicing midwifery in 1984, Wanoi had fewer opportunities to apply her skills because more women were beginning to seek hospital births. By 1994, she had given up the practice. Mainly she cultivates coffee and some tea along with maize and other staple crops.

Wanoi is an excellent basket weaver. Her ingenuity is expressed in the elaborate patterns she weaves and in color combinations that remind me of a Guatemalan cloth appliqué. In 1984 she was experimenting with new basket shapes using banana fibers, and gave me one to take home in 1985. It acts as

Wanoi

a visible link with a woman whose life became interwoven with mine in the 1980s and who continues to share my interests into the 1990s.

Physically, Wanoi is a beautiful woman with sharp, chiseled features and high cheekbones accentuated by piercing, intelligent eyes. She has three short, dark slashes (cicatures) on either side of her long, straight nose that enhance her beauty. It was Wanoi's beauty and self-assurance that first attracted my attention in an adult education class. She appeared an experienced student who was willing to help other women with the skills of writing and mathematics. I approached her at the end of class one day to schedule an interview, and she invited me to her homestead.

It turned out that Wanoi was as intrigued by me as I was by her. Not only was I of a different color and culture, but she saw in me a means of learning about a world that lay beyond Mutira Location and Kenya. We discovered similarities: our oldest children were born in the same year, and we had both been teachers—I of high school and university students, she as an expert in traditional Gikuyu culture for University of Nairobi students who visited her once a year.

Wanoi is a self-assertive extrovert, eager to teach anyone willing to learn. At the same time, her role as a teacher complicated our work at first because she thought I was interested in a generic picture of Gikuyu women rather than her personal narrative. It was not until the third interview in 1984, when we began to talk about circumcision, that I was able to communicate successfully that I wanted to know about her life as an individual. Even then, there were times when I felt that Wanoi was idealizing her roles—presenting an ideal of the person she felt she ought to be.

During our initial interviews, Wanoi was direct and clear in her explanations, but as I delved more deeply into her life, contradictions arose that, at first, confused and frustrated me. For example, in the initial survey interview, Wanoi stated that all her children were living: thus, she was counted with the women who had lost no children. During the later interviews, I discovered that she had lost her first three children—two as infants and one as a boy of seven who died of a disease. Such a revelation amplified for me the hazards of quantitative research. To a stranger, especially from another culture, an individual may protect herself by revealing only what she wants the social

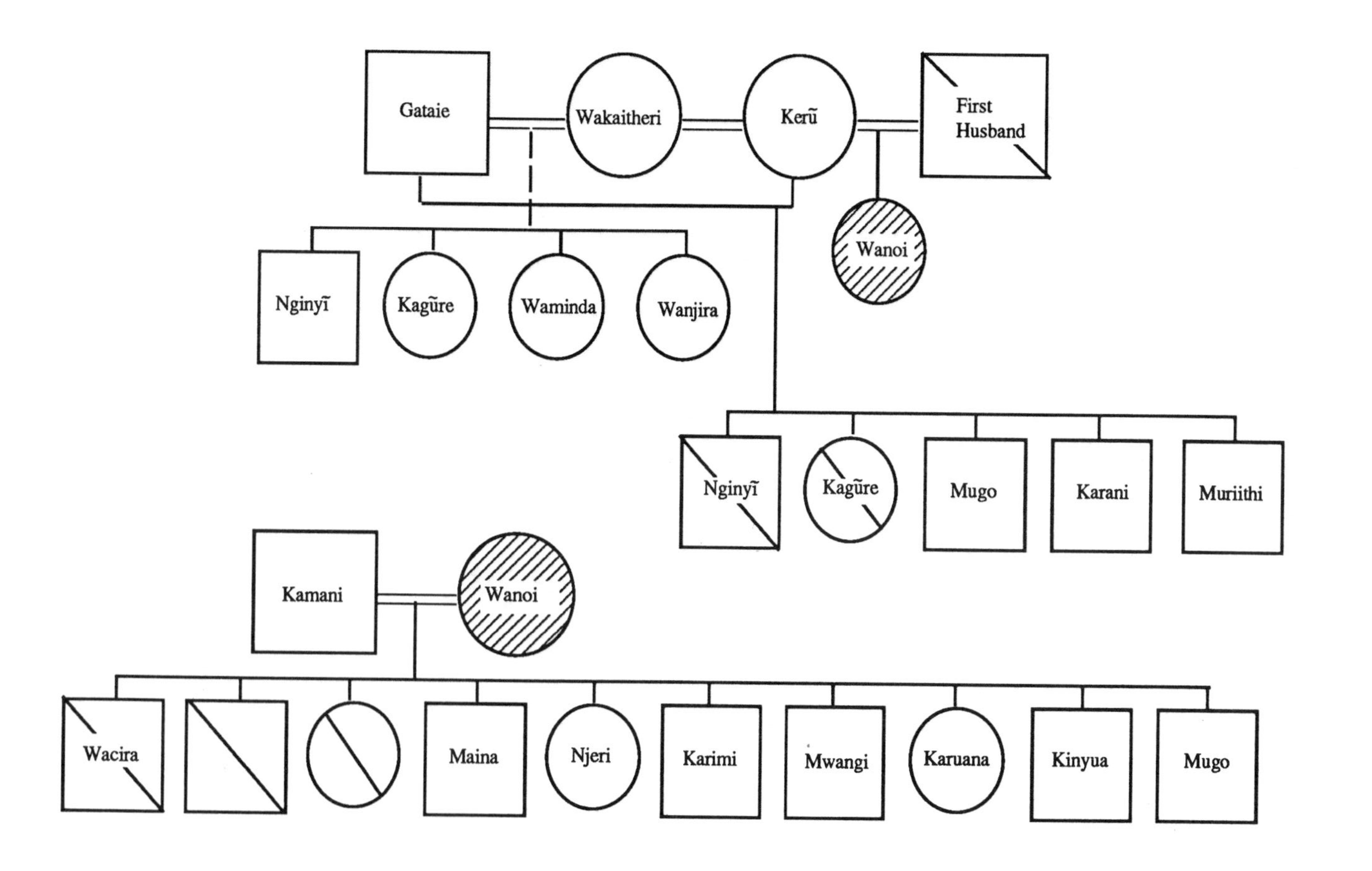
Gataie
Wakaitheri
Kerũ
First
Husband
Wanoi
Nginyĩ
Kagũre
Waminda
Wanjira
Nginyĩ
Kagũre
Mugo
Karani
Muriithi
Kamani
Wanoi
Wacira
Maina
Njeri
Karimi
Mwangi
Karuana
Kinyua
Mugo

scientist to hear. Only through long-term interviews and observation is one able to scratch beneath the surface and learn about other dimensions of an individual's personality.

Another complication in working with Wanoi arose from my inability to fit events together as a chronological sequence rather than as conflicting stories—this was *my* problem, not hers. Undeserved expectations creep up and surprise us when we least anticipate it. When I asked Wanoi how she had learned her skills as a midwife, she told two different stories over a three-week period. It was not until several weeks later, through probing, that I discovered both stories were true but for different periods in her childhood.

Wanoi's apprenticeship as a midwife did not occur in isolation. Rather, her exposure to her mother's profession as a midwife was an integral part of the rest of her indigenous education, just as her continuing education as a midwife was only one aspect of her many-faceted adult life. Nevertheless, for purposes of clarity, I have chosen to present Wanoi's experiences as a midwife in a sequence of events beginning at one point in her life.

Of all the women whose life histories I collected, it was the most difficult to end the sessions with Wanoi. In the process of collecting a life history, a transpersonal relationship may develop that resembles both a counseling relationship and a friendship. In some cases, the narrator may feel a sense of loss when the sessions terminate. It was critical in Wanoi's case that I prepare her for the end of our formal weekly sessions. When I introduced the subject prior to the last session, she became agitated and wanted to know if termination meant the end of our friendship. I assured her that it did not. In succeeding months, after the research had ended, I made sure that I visited her whenever I went to the research site, up until the time I left Kenya in 1985.

Each time I returned to Mutira thereafter, we would inevitably run into each other, in front of a shop, at the market, on the way to Gatwe. She was overjoyed the first few times, insisting that I come to her homestead—which I did. I was a real visitor. By 1992, however, her economic and health circumstances had changed. A drought had affected food as well as cash crops and she complained of stomach pains. When I returned for follow-on interviews in 1994, she was forthcoming with information, but obviously was not well. She said the greatest change in her personal life in the last decade had been "growing old" and poor health. She expressed frustration over not being able to do most of the things she once did, attributing it to illness; she had been diagnosed as having a stomach ulcer.

By 1994, most of Wanoi's children had grown and moved away. Only the three youngest children remained, and the youngest now reached my shoulder. Wanoi related that her husband had become much more helpful with harvesting tea and coffee than he once was. He also was more often at home. However, in 1995 she wrote through friends that he had fallen out of a tree trimming branches and had broken a leg so that he was unable to be of much help.

As Wanoi is more interested in politics than the other life narrators, on my visits in 1992 and 1994 I sought her opinions of the changing political scene in Kenya. In 1992 we talked about the upcoming multiparty elections in December, and Wanoi related that she was voting for the Democratic Party (DP) candidates. At the same time she knew that the Gikuyu in Central Province were split politically and that this would hurt their chances of defeating Moi. She was right.

Whereas in the 1983 elections, Wanoi had taken an active role as women's song leader for a particular candidate, by 1994 she was more indifferent to becoming actively involved. She had voted for DP's Mwai Kibaki for president and Kinyua Mbui for Parliament in the 1992 elections. Neither had won. At the same time she observed that in contrast to previous elections there were "no incidents" (harassment or intimidation of voters by competing candidates' supporters) at the polls in the 1992 elections. The voting process, at least, had run smoothly. She believed, however, that Moi won because he "rigged the votes." She claimed that many people she knew did not vote because they had already sold their votes to the Kenya African National Union (KANU) in exchange for food or money. When asked if she thought the DP had a future in Kenya, she said, "If the opposition united and if there was no rigging in the next election, the DP might have a chance of winning."

Wanoi also observed that Central Province's support for the opposition parties in 1992 had caused it to be neglected politically after the elections. "Nothing has been done for us; no new hospitals built, no roads constructed, and no new schools." Development has, indeed, lagged in Kirinyaga.

Wanoi related in 1992 and again in 1994 that things had gotten economically worse for her—low prices for tea and coffee through 1992, and higher prices for necessary household commodities. Whereas in 1983, a producer got 80 cents per kilo for tea leaves, by 1992 the price for production had increased only to Ksh. 1.50–2.50, she related. After the three-month tea strike in 1992, the price increased to Ksh. 4.00, and by late 1994 producers in Mutira were earning Ksh. 4.50 per kilo. She believes that the tea strike had a positive effect. "One day," she states, "we staged a peaceful demonstration at the DC's [district commissioner] office in Kerugoya to air our grievances. We also forced shopkeepers to sell foodstuffs at the correct price and not an inflated price. Our demonstrations helped a lot since the KTDA [Kenya Tea Development Authority] began paying Ksh. 4.00 per kilo for tea." The producer price for coffee berries also had improved after 1990. By 1995, according to Wanoi, producers were earning Ksh. 60.00 per kilo of picked berries.

In the decade between 1984 and 1994 the prices of food commodities in Mutira skyrocketed. Wanoi explained that in 1984 a kilo of sugar could be purchased for Ksh. 16.00, but by 1993 the same amount of sugar cost Ksh. 50–60, although the price dropped in 1994 to Ksh. 40.00.

Citing further fluctuations in food prices, Wanoi used *nga'no* (wheat flour) as an example. *Nga'no* cost Ksh. 27.00 at the beginning of 1993, went up to Ksh. 60.00 in 1994, then dropped down to Ksh. 50.00 in early 1995—a sign that overall inflation was finally slowing. However, Wanoi does not attribute the drop in prices to macrolevel economic adjustments. Rather, she attributes the lower food prices to the existence of a political opposition that has forced KANU to make changes to stem the downward slide of the economy. "Now with the help of the opposition, prices are going down and we can afford to buy some things again," she explained.

Another economic constraint is lack of money for schooling, so that more parents are unable to send their children to school, Wanoi continued. "These days if one does not have more than Ksh. 20,000, one cannot send a child to secondary school. And in Standard 8, the books alone are very expensive—even up to Ksh. 2,000 for a child. I am lucky to have only one child in Standard 8—the last-born." Of the others, five completed primary school, two have completed secondary school, and two have gone for technical training. Wanoi then filled me in on the oldest children. "David Maina is married now and has a family of three girls. Njeri, whom you remember, completed Form 4 and trained as a secretary. She works in Embu and is married with two boys."

All of Wanoi's sons have settled at home, building houses for themselves. Yet Wanoi worries about having enough land to share among her children. "Take me now, I have only five acres and five sons. The one who is married has been given a piece of land where he can grow his own food for his family. But that means I'm left with a smaller piece to grow my own food. The time will come when I have to divide this piece between the other four sons and may be left without any myself. But for now we are using the land communally."

We turned to a discussion of AIDS. She noted that people in Kirinyaga were beginning to talk about it. She was aware that it was a socially transmitted disease (STD) and that people could die from it. She talked about how people used to treat STDs before Western medical treatment—a woman tied a special kind of string around her belly to ward off such diseases. She also volunteered that razor blades and intravenous needles could be sources—the latter made some people afraid to go to the hospital.

Wanoi's observations of changes in her own life and changes in Mutira were helpful because she was willing and able to give more details than the other two remaining women in her cohort. Wamutira gave some details about changes in the prices of tea and coffee, but Wanoi's was the most complete account. Watoro noted that food prices had escalated but she was more interested in talking about her own improved life circumstances. Wanoi's observations, then, were critical in reconstructing the impact of external forces on the lives of the narrators now in their early sixties.

—J.D.

My name is Wanoi. When I was born my mother named me after my mother's mother who came from a place called Inoi. Mary is the name I was later baptized in the Catholic Church. I am of the Ũnjiru Clan.

My father, Gataie, had two wives. The first was my older mother called Wakaitheri, who was co-wife to my mother. She had four children. The first was a boy called Nginyĩ or Maina, and the other three were girls. The older two, Kagũre and Muthoni, used to smear us with oil and plait our hair. Kagũre was beautiful, and men used to like her, but she had loose morals. Muthoni was a good girl. The last born of my older mother was

Wanjira, who was my agemate. My mother, Keru, which means "brown," used to take care of Wanjira after her mother died, so we were raised together.

My mother was a widow when she married the man I called *"Baba"* [Father]. I never knew my real father, because he was killed for stealing someone's millet shortly after my mother married him. My mother was pregnant with me when she went to live at Gataie's—the man I knew as my father. Gataie and my mother had five children together, but the first two—Nginyĩ and the girl Kagũre—died when they were very small. The others are Mugo, Karani, and Muriithi, who are my three younger brothers. My mother did not have another girl apart from me.

My father was first a big man in the village, then he became an elder, then a chief and retired only recently before he died at the age of a hundred and twenty. I never knew him much because he was always away on government business.[1] My older mother died before I was a mature girl—I can still remember when she died. We were getting arrowroots at the river with her, and a big bird came and sat on her head. She was so scared that she never survived that day. But my mother is still alive. You will meet her. She is a small, jolly woman who likes people.

My mother was a circumciser and midwife. She was very good at her job. She was a woman who worked fast, without delay. But nowadays, she no longer is a midwife. When I was growing up, she never used to nag, though she was talkative. My mothers and my grandmother—the one who was my mother's mother—were my teachers. My grandmother did not live with us in the same compound, but I would visit her. She did not live far away.

My mother would often take us to stay with our grandmother while she did her work. During these times, our grandmother would show us how to make porridge, cook *irio,* peel beans, and fetch firewood for the cooking fire. She did not say much, but we could see how she was doing these things. She would also advise Wanjira and me. Once I remember her telling us how one sits when she goes to get circumcised, and how one takes care of herself after circumcision.

Those *wazee* [Kiswahili term for "old people"] like my grandmother, sitting around the fireplace at night, would teach us a lot of things. They told us stories about ogres, but I can't remember those well. There was one story, though, that I remember about a greedy wife. Let me think.

Once there was a girl who when she got married and went to live in her husband's compound, a goat was slaughtered and the meat was hung inside the house where she was staying with her husband's mother before being officially welcomed into her own house. She got hungry and went and cut a piece of the meat and started eating it in bed where she had to stay. This was before she was allowed to eat meat, and while she was still eating the piece, somebody came into the room where she was in bed and saw her. She dropped the piece of meat right in the bed. People were angry when they heard about her greediness, and so they took her back to her parents, because nobody wants to marry a greedy wife.

There is a song that is sung with that story that I will sing for you. It is called "The Greedy Wife Who Showed You the Meat in the *Itara* [rafters of the house where firewood is kept to dry]."

Mũhiki mubio,	Greedy bride,
Mũhiki mubio,	Greedy bride,
Nyama iriitara wonirio nu?	Who showed you the meat in the *itara?*
Ĩi, wainaga.	Yes, we sing.

That story was important because it taught us that we should be patient when we went to live at our husband's home, until his parents were ready to welcome us officially with a goat. The song was sung if any bride showed she was greedy. I would have sung this song to my brother's wife, because when she was newly married, I met her stealing chicken meat from our house and also ripe bananas. If it was long ago, she would not have remained married. She would have been sent back home for being so greedy. It is only recently that this tradition is not followed, or I would have sung the song.

What was I like as a child? I was one who never used to stay at one place but moved around from place to place. As children we were not naughty and we liked each other, but we used to fight sometimes. We would fight with a blunt *kibanga* and if somebody provoked me I would fight that one with my teeth and scratch him/her with my nails. I had so many friends I wouldn't be able to count them. I was always looking for those who were like me—those who were talkative and daring and did the things I wanted to do. I remember once when we were jumping with tall poles over a huge fire outside. Then one of us fell and got her legs badly burned. From that we learned that fire can be dangerous. Also, when you are smashing food in a cooking pot, if you bend down to look inside you can be burned. Another time, when we were roasting maize, the seeds [kernels] started popping off and burned me on the chest. So I learned that being so near roasting maize is dangerous.

I used to want to make porridge as a small girl, but when I cooked nobody ate it because it was always undercooked. I was teaching myself how to cook by watching my mother. I used to cook over the fire with small pots bought for me in the market, and I broke so many. Later, when I was old enough to be left with the young ones—my small brothers—I used to take some maize and beans, mix them together in a small pot and put it on the fire to cook the way I'd seen my mother do. All this I did with the smallest child tied to my back. Then I would go and fetch green vegetables from the garden. I would chop them, then peel potatoes, called *kahuro,* and chop them, too. After the *githeri* cooked for a while, I'd put in the potatoes, then the vegetables. While these cooked, I'd sit down and take the baby on my lap—just to train myself—and squash some food in a calabash using a *mũiko.* Then I'd chew a bit of the smashed food, spit it out onto my first finger, and feed it to the baby.[2]

Some days, I would not cook. On those days, I waited until my mother left to go to her *shamba,* then I would go into the granary and get millet and grind it on a big stone with another smaller round stone, with the baby tied onto my back. If the child started crying and stopped me from grinding, I would pinch him. After grinding the millet, I went for water, which we kept in a gourd, and mixed the millet flour with water into a paste. Then I mashed the paste and put it in a cooking pot with more water over the fire. I was told by my mother never to put the baby down when cooking because he could crawl to the fireplace and get burned, so with him on my back, I stirred the porridge until it cooked and then put it into a gourd and hid it under the bed where we slept with my mother, so it would sour. It would sour [ferment] in about three days.

During that time, we never had our own beds. Children slept with their mother until they were quite big. I was taken from my mother's bed at about the age of seven. At that time, a goat was slaughtered and a piece of its skin was put across the chest called *rũkoro* and the rest of the skin was spread on the floor after it dried to make a bed for me. The ceremony is called *mambura ma twana* and means that the parents can have sexual relations again. But I do not remember much about this because it was a long time ago.

The first important change in my life was when I pierced my ears—something my oldest brother, Maina, never wanted me to do. You see, he was a Christian by that time, and he wanted me to go to school and not pierce my ears. He was the firstborn of my older mother, and when he came back from the Italian war [World War II], he forced me and my brother to go to the missionary school. He bought me a dress and took me to sub-A, which was like today's nursery school. I never reached sub-B, which is like Standard One. When coming from school one day, I was beaten by some girls of my *riika*—age group—who were all about ten years old, because I had not had my ears pierced *mbuci* and *matũ.* During those times, anybody who did not have her ears pierced was termed still a small child, no matter how big she was. So I vowed to get my ears pierced, but my brother was against it. One day, I ran away from school and threw the dress my brother had bought away and tied on a sheet. I pierced my ears myself with an orange-tree thorn, but the holes never got so wide because anytime I went to my brother's *thingira,* he would remove the sticks and throw them away. Then I would take cow dung and smear it into the holes to prevent them from disappearing. As soon as I got home to my mother's, I'd put other sticks in. I had watched my mother pierce girls' ears, so I knew how to pierce my own. And nowadays, I pierce a girl's ears if she wants it.

* * *

[Wanoi relates two different accounts of her experience with *Irua*. When I questioned her about the discrepancy, she explained that the story of going with one friend, without the knowledge of her parents, is her own experience, whereas the other relates to the normative experience of most Agĩkũyũ girls of her generation.]

It was my grandmother who told me how one sits when she goes for circumcision and how to take care of oneself afterwards. She told me that the first thing to do after *Irua* is to check to make sure that the *ithangu* [soft leaf used as a bandage] has not been put too far back so as to cover up the hole where shit comes from. "When one is healed," she said, "you must begin to watch for blood coming from between your legs."

Before I was circumcised, I was taken to the river by many women of my clan where they washed me and threw me up in the air. Then I was carried to the big field of grass near the marketplace where we were to be circumcised. There were fourteen girls that got circumcised together. We were dressed with skirts of green colors and had hats with feathers like your hair. There were many people—men, women, and children—there that day. The women and girls were singing and dancing. The circumciser wore a cloth, and she used a knife that looked like a small axe that was very sharp called a *kienji*. After we were cut, castor oil was put on, then *ithangu*. By then the sun was going down.

[A week later, Wanoi gave the following version of what happened to her, personally. The account was so atypical, I was unsure whether to believe Wanoi or not. Her mother confirmed later that Wanoi's father was not anxious to see Wanoi circumcised and that she had not even received the uncle's permission. It seems likely that the account is fairly accurate with some exaggeration.]

When time reached for circumcision, I was a herdsgirl, looking after the goats. My friend came and told me that she would be circumcised. I did not want to be left behind. Because I was grazing the goats in a place far away from the field where the circumcision was being held, I decided not to tell anybody, but to just go, because I knew my parents would not allow it. The reason my father had refused to have me circumcised up to that time is because my body build was small and he was afraid I would be beaten by *irigũ* [uncircumcised girls].

When I saw people going toward the field, I sent the goats into the bush, then gathered *mathakwa* [leaves] because I was told by my grandmother that a girl being circumcised sits on such leaves. After collecting them, I went to the field and reached there just when the other girl—my friend—was being circumcised. I quickly put down the *mathakwa* leaves and sat down on them with my legs spread. I didn't even have a supporter! After being cut, women took me home.

I went home slowly, slowly, with women of my clan on either side of me, holding me and dancing and singing. When I got home, I found my mother had gone away somewhere to drink beer where people were celebrating the *Irua* season. But I met my father's eldest brother, whom I called *Baba.* He told me that as I had braved the ceremony without a supporter, he would give me a goat. So you see my bravery is not recent. I was brave even a long time ago.

When I entered the compound, people remembered that my father had never beaten my mother, so they went to look for her. You see, it was the custom that a mother should be beaten on the day that her first child gets circumcised if she had never been beaten before. So when my mother finally got home, my father found some *mukenia* [type of plant], and he beat my mother before I was allowed to go into the house. My mother and father were surprised to find me circumcised, but they did not show it.

I did not stay long in the house before I was taken outside behind and the clotted blood was removed from the cuts and they were washed with warm water. Then castor oil was put on *ithangu,* and it was put over the wound. I stayed for three days, and then my head was shaved, and as I was the first daughter of my mother, her head was shaved, too. It took me three months to heal.

How did I feel after going for *Irua? Irua* was like being given a degree for going from childhood to womanhood. One became mature. It was very important in those days, because when one got circumcised, one would not joke about with uncircumcised girls and they would give us respect. If I got circumcised a year earlier than you, you would not be able to abuse me. If one refused *Irua,* she was beaten by others, abused, and would not have anybody visiting her home looking for her to marry. But the minute you got circumcised no one would stand in your way—you were ready to marry.

Once circumcised, a young woman could talk and joke with young, uncircumcised men, but we did not move with them sexually until one got married. But now, my small daughter Karuana [aged ten] knows things about sex, and even Njeri [daughter, aged twenty] knows, even though she is uncircumcised.

And another thing, there are no *mariika* today. The girls who went for *Irua* stayed friends and would talk until dark, asking each other questions about the day and joking with each other. People knew which age group they belonged to and what behaviors were good for their age group. Nowadays, there is no difference between age groups. That is why children are so naughty—there is no way they know when they are grown up, because circumcision is no longer practiced among the girls. *Irua* meant becoming a member of a *riika* and learning Agĩkũyũ traditions, but after *Uhuru,* people started saying that Mary in the Bible was not circumcised, so why should we? That is when *Irua* started losing its meaning. I would not like to see girls circumcised now, but if the old people are to be believed, *Irua* would come back.

* * *

I wasn't full grown when I delivered my first child as a midwife, but I had had my ears pierced and was circumcised. I was almost Njeri's age. This is what happened.

One day, I was up on a wooden tower, frightening the birds away from the millet field when a woman came by carrying a basket and sat down near a sugarcane plant. She started calling to me. Now me, I assumed that she was a lunatic, so I came down from the ladder and started to run away from her. But she called me again, telling me that she was giving birth. I started wondering what to do and was feeling a bit scared, but a voice deep within me told me to go back and help her. So I went and saw that she was sitting with her legs apart. She told me to take the sheet she was wearing and put it on the ground to catch the baby. Then I saw the baby's umbilical cord after the baby came out but had nothing to cut it with. So the woman asked me if I took snuff and told me to take the string from my tobacco pouch and use it to tie the umbilical cord. She told me to cut a piece of sharp stem from the sugarcane plant and peel a thin thread and cut the umbilical cord with it. From then on, all my fear disappeared.

How did I first learn about being a midwife? It happened that my mother was a midwife, as I have told you. She used to circumcise girls during *Irua* and helped women give birth, even removing the afterbirth by pressing on the ribs of the mother. As I accompanied her everywhere, I saw all that she was doing.

A long time ago, there was a woman whose children used to die. The last born, the one who survived, was always carried about on the woman's back when she was going to do any work. My mother was like that woman, and as I was the only child for some time, even when I was big she used to tie me on her back, and I was able to see all that she did when she went to help a woman give birth. I would see that she did not wash her hands when she delivered a baby. She just took some *migio* string—the one that's used to tie the *igoto* [banana stem cover used for a case for carrying ground tobacco used as snuff]—and used the string to tie the umbilical cord. Then she'd wash the baby with cold water in a broken cooking pot. She would go for the fern that grows on top of the *mukoigo* tree, and when she got back the fern leaves were chewed and the liquid given to the baby so it would not get a stomachache.

Later, what happened is that any time a woman was to give birth, I would follow my mother at a distance and watch her. You know, in those days the houses had walls only on the side where the bed was. The other side walls—the ones on either side of the fireplace—were movable and were called *rigi*. One of these blocked the view from the entrance of the hut, so you could not see the fireplace and the mother's bed, where women gathered for a woman's birth. So I used to hide behind that *rigi,* just inside the doorway of the hut and peek around and see what my mother was doing. There was nothing done in that house that I didn't see, but I wasn't frightened. I would watch and then go and tell the children my age that so-and-so gave birth—the way the woman was breathing hard, pushing hard, sitting on the stool with the other women telling her to push hard. I saw my mother pushing on the woman's stomach with her fingers to get the baby out.

From watching my mother, I saw that soon after the child comes out, she told the mother to kneel down and hold the child on her lap. After the mother knelt, my mother would tie the umbilical cord and cut it with a sharp piece of sugarcane thread or razor and then take the baby and wash it. Then she would wrap it in blankets. The afterbirth was taken outside and buried away from the place. But the mother of the child never used to wash herself in my mother's time. She just wrapped herself with blankets for about eight days, then took them off and washed in the river. Right after the baby was born, I used to hear the women give the ululations —"*ariririti,*" five times if it was a boy and four times if a girl-child. So I saw all my mother did and I told myself that someday I would be doing like her.

My mother did not know I was sneaking and watching her, but she realized that I knew everything after I first helped that woman in the sugarcane field because I came and told her what I had done and how I went about it. She was surprised and asked how I knew what to do. I told her, "At so-and-so's place, I saw you give five ululations. At another place you gave four and washed the baby in a broken piece of pot." She was happy and told me not to stop what I was doing but to continue being a midwife, because now I would be able to help others. I don't know how my mother came to know midwifery—maybe from *her* mother. Knowledge is passed on that way.

My second time to deliver a baby was when I was going to Kerugoya. I met a woman in the bushes struggling very much, so I went and asked her whether she was about to give birth and she said, "Yes" and told me to call any woman who was passing by and could help her. I told her that I could help. She was surprised and asked me whether it was true. I told her, "Wait and see." So I helped her deliver and meanwhile sent a woman to borrow a razor blade from a nearby homestead and I used it to cut the umbilical cord. That woman never went to the hospital, so I took her home, and when a goat was slaughtered for her, I was given some of the meat and I carried it home to my family. So now I was a midwife.

I was delivering women when we were in the concentration camp. [Wanoi refers to the enforced villages set up by the British beginning in 1953, after the Mau Mau Rebellion a year earlier. Her depiction is accurate because the Gikuyu, who were formerly living in scattered homesteads, were now forcefully concentrated in the temporary villages.] I was newly married then. Later, just before we got *Uhuru,* I was about eight months pregnant with Njeri, when a woman and her husband came from Nairobi in the evening to visit our relatives who were from the same home village. The woman was very pregnant, too, and she happened to deliver that evening in the house of our relatives. But the afterbirth got stuck up inside her.

My brother's wife came and told me that the woman, Kabuchi, had given birth and the afterbirth refused to come out. I felt badly when I heard the news, because Kabuchi had already given birth and left me behind—still pregnant. I went to see if I could help. An old grandmother had been called who was a wise midwife, but she had not been able to get there yet, so the women encouraged me to try. I thought for a few moments, then I asked for a razor blade and cut my sharp nails and removed all the dirt and washed my hands. I asked for Sunlight soap to apply on my hands and make them slippery. The woman's stomach had swollen by now, as it had been several hours since she gave birth. I slipped my hands up inside the woman's body and pulled out the afterbirth. Everybody got astonished—even my mother when she heard about it. By the time the old midwife came, it was all over. After I removed the afterbirth, I washed my hands and went straight home, full speed without waiting, because I was feeling badly, as Kabuchi had given birth and left me still pregnant. I had helped her, but I was still pregnant.

So after that, people started talking about what I'd done and the skill that I had, and the news traveled wide. For that skill of removing the afterbirth that way, I learned it on my own—maybe it was God that gave me the knowledge, because I had never seen anybody remove stubborn afterbirth, nor had I been told how to do it. After one month, I gave birth to Njeri and the afterbirth refused to come out. My mother said it was because

I had removed Kabuchi's afterbirth while I was pregnant. That same old midwife was called and she removed the afterbirth in me.

From then on, people preferred to have me help them with a birth. I can help my own cow give birth, and if the afterbirth gets stuck, I can remove it just as I did with Kabuchi. For learning how to press on the ribs and deliver a baby, you can say that I stayed with somebody who knew something—my mother—and then copied what she did. But for removing the afterbirth, I did not copy from anybody, as I had not seen it being done at any other time. The knowledge of what to do just came from my own discovery.

Then I learned things from other midwives as I went along—like if a woman is bleeding, maize cobs are roasted and then put in a container with water and stirred. The black solution is given to the bleeding mother to drink. It stops the bleeding. But usually, mothers don't bleed.

Another thing—I was told by an old midwife that if ever I attended a woman who shits while delivering, I should tell the people nearby and hide the shit with clothes. After that I should fetch a climbing plant called *mukengeria* and take it and some *mugumo* tree leaves and hold them together with the umbilical cord, then cut them together as a sacrifice, as shitting while giving birth is a bad omen and not normal. But nowadays, there is no such thing. Even if a woman shits while delivering, nothing special is done.

When somebody comes for me to help with a delivery, I can't go without those people giving me something in return, as going has made me leave my own work. I can remember one day, two women came for me to go and remove the stubborn afterbirth from a friend of theirs. I told them to take her to the hospital, but they didn't want her to go there. So after I had removed the afterbirth, I was given 30 shillings [equivalent to 2 U.S. dollars] and then taken back home.

One day I went to Wanyuki's Maternity Clinic [a private maternity home in a nearby town], and Rebecca, the trained midwife, was not there. A pregnant woman came to the clinic and was just about to give birth, so I helped her deliver and washed the baby with Dettol [a disinfectant] and wrapped it in a blanket and laid it on the bed next to the mother. When Rebecca came, I told her that she should share her salary with me for I had done her work. She is the one who made me go to the midwifery course at Wambugu Farm in Nyeri. She knew that I could be a trained midwife and help in the clinic because I used to visit her there and watch how she did things. Sometimes, I would help her tie the baby's umbilical cord. The only thing I didn't do was to weigh the baby—I left that to her.

When we went to Wambugu Farm for midwife training, we taught the medical officers the things I'm telling you about and how, if a woman has a threatened miscarriage, we would give her honey and her pregnancy would be saved. If the honey didn't work, the woman was taken to a *mũndũ mugo* to have banana leaves and other traditional herbs applied.

It used to be that if a baby was coming out feet first, there was nothing we could do except press on the mother's ribs and try and help her give birth feet first. But many babies used to die, as the head would get stuck in the mother's womb. A child born with the umbilical cord surrounding its neck was believed to be a *mũndũ mugo* if it was a boy-child and a circumciser if a girl-child. Certain kinds of plants were collected from the forest, and before the umbilical cord was removed from the baby's neck, a goat was slaughtered and a *mũndũ mugo* splashed *tatha* [contents of a goat's intestine] on the child, because it was believed that such a child was God's work, so the child was blessed.

Occasionally a child was born still in the placental membrane such that you would not know it was a child until the membrane was removed. When this happened, people used to say that the child was born without *rugwiki* [sexual intercourse]. So a goat would be slaughtered, too. Then I would pierce the membrane, and the whole thing would come away from the baby. If a baby's head is very big, I have to cut the mother's vagina with a razor blade to make the birth easier.

A few times I have delivered twins. There is a woman who is a neighbor of mine, and I was helping her deliver. She was very big and gave birth to twins. But they were not old enough, so one stayed alive for only four days and the other for seven days and then died. Maybe if she had gone to the hospital, the twins would not have died. But the problem was that she was giving birth in the middle of the night and she was far away from any road.

Nowadays, when I am called to assist a woman, before doing anything, I put the razor blade and piece of string for the umbilical cord into a *sufuria* [aluminum cooking pot] to boil over the fire. And I use Dettol when washing. I learned these things at the training course. After the course at Wambugu Farm, the health officers are interested in our progress as midwives, and they said they might bring us the materials they promised last year—things like scissors, cotton wool, thread, and big bottles for keeping our things in.

At Wambugu Farm we went to learn more about midwifery and how to keep records for every child born in the area—with the name of the child, its mother and father, when the child was born—and then to take the record to the headman or chief. Our teachers at the course were health officers from the government and nurses from the hospital. There were even some whites with their interpreters. After learning about different types of problems during a delivery, we were taken to the hospital. We went to the maternity ward and then, four women at a time, were taken into a room for our lesson. In the room was one woman who had her baby lying crosswise in the womb, in an astride position, another with a child coming out feet first, another one with the baby's head at the vagina in a normal position. We were given rubber gloves and told to put our hands in these women's wombs and feel the positions of the babies. The first two were to show us the kind of women we would not be able to help deliver easily at home. Then a woman who did not have enough blood [anemic] was brought in, and we were told you can tell such a woman by the color of the inside of her eyes and color of the palms of her hands and nails. We were told *never* to try and deliver such a woman at home but take her to the hospital.

The problem with some private maternity clinics is that the midwife does not check the health of the mother she is assisting. I've learned now that it is important to check to see if a woman has enough blood, the position of the child in the womb, and if the woman is big enough to have a normal birth at home.

After looking at the births at the hospital, we were shown a woman who had given birth two weeks earlier. We were given gloves to feel that her womb was not completely closed and saw how one could put in a coil [I.U.D.] when the woman is ready. We saw another woman who had stayed for five weeks and saw how the womb was getting closed. We were told that a woman cannot have a coil put in until after her first menstruation has resumed. All that knowledge we got from Wambugu Farm, and I still have it here, stored in my head. You see, I did not know how to write at the time. But when I came back from there, I went to the adult education class to learn how to read and write, so after one year, when the medical officers came back to see my work, they saw that I had written the things I had learned at the course and had kept a written record of the births I had delivered in the area. Only now I have lost that book with the births recorded in it.

The difference between what I learned from my mother and what I learned at Wambugu Farm is that today I cut the umbilical cord with a clean pair of scissors and before we used to use a razor blade. At times, the razor blade would be rusty and would have been used for shaving a number of times. We did not have any cotton in those days or any Dettol to sterilize the instruments. Now it is better, because I can help somebody deliver without the danger of the baby contracting tetanus—though that never happened to me. So, you see, I have kept on learning and improving my skills.

* * *

Long ago, when I was *mũirĩtu,* we did not know about sexual matters before we were married. Even if we knew our parents were sleeping together, they would tell us later that they were "eating tortoise honey"—by that they meant that they were tasting the sweetness of sex—but we did not understand. We were told by our grandmother that if we had sexual relations with young men, we would be given a bunch of bananas to give the child we had been looking for by our husband when we got married. If a man discovered that his wife already knew about sexual intercourse, he would go and tell his parents. Then his mother would cut a bunch of bananas and give it to the wife to give the child she had looked for earlier. So we were careful about our behavior before we got married.

Even before I started menstruating or had any breasts, I used to go to dances once I was circumcised. There was one kind of dance I remember called *mweretho,* where young men and women would hit each other against the chests, then the girls were thrown up in the air by their male partners. I liked watching that dance, but I did not have many girls to participate with me. By that time, some girls were beginning to go to school, and the missionaries told them not to dance—that it was bad.

There was another dance where young men and women met called *kiruri.* A young man would hold a girl and she would twist and whirl around. Even young men from school would sneak away and spend the nights dancing, and then in the morning they would sneak back to school without having eaten anything. Then such a young man spent most of his time dozing in class—that's what we heard.

During the night, after dancing, we would sleep there in the bush next to the dancing field, each with her man, and we would not do anything under the blanket. In the morning, we would separate. I used to attract men because I knew how to crack jokes. They liked to sit near me and feel good. There was always one handsome man we called *kiumbi.* He was the one who was clean, good to talk to, and a good dancer. We girls would go to his place and all of us spend the night there. He had a very big bed. It would hold twenty girls with him alone. So we'd spend the night with him embracing each girl in turn. He would do nothing to us, as our skirts were tied to keep him from having sexual intercourse with us.

It was during that time, after *Irua,* that we put these cuts on our cheeks for beauty and others on our breasts. The ones in the cheeks were cut with a razor blade and soot from a blackened pot rubbed in, but the ones here [on the breasts] were made with a hollow bamboo stalk. We'd press and press until the upper skin came off, then smear in oil. [Wanoi describes a different technique of scarification than described by Wangeci.] We found it beautiful to make designs on the breasts, and later when one got married and was suckling a child, the breasts were decorated.

Those years after *Irua,* before I got married, were my happiest years, because I didn't have much work in the homestead then. I would wash and dress well, fix my hair, and go to a dance. I would come home and get food—I did not have all the work I have now. *Haiya,* when you are married, what kind of happiness do you feel? It is nothing but work. Like now—all the work I have in the *shamba,* worrying about the children, their school fees, where the husband is, and where I will get the money for the radio I want.

I first met Kamani at one of the dances. When we went to dances, we didn't have much chance to talk with a young man—we just danced. Talking came later, when he came to visit you at your home. A man would come to woo you, and if you liked him, you would arrange to ask your father for tobacco. Otherwise, you might tell him you are not ready for marriage. With Kamani, I wanted him. So I went and told my father that there was a young man asking for tobacco. My father told me to go and find out which clan Kamani came from and about his family. If the clans are ones that intermarry, then your father gives you the tobacco. That is what happened with us. Then Kamani's father brewed beer to take to my father. After that came the negotiations for *rũracio.* I found out that the number of cows that Kamani agreed to give my father was two cows that hadn't calved, a bull, and thirty goats. Four of the goats were to be slaughtered for me, and Kamani's relatives promised to dig up the *shamba* I would get when I moved to his place.

Kamani's relatives dug up the grass with sharp-pointed digging sticks, and women from my place were called to do the work of cultivating and planting. During this time a lot of beer was being brewed. I was still at my mother's house, and on the day the women from Kamani's place came for me singing and ululating, I found the *shamba* nearly ready for harvesting and a house almost completed. That day I did not wear anything special, just a string of beads and a white sheet tied at one shoulder. My head was shaved clean and I went with it shining. I liked the women singing, but I felt sad to be leaving my mother's house.

I lived for the first two months at the house of Kamani's mother, but during this time we did not look at each other. I could not go out at all, only stay in bed. The mother would cook food like porridge and pass it to me in bed to eat. After the harvest, Kamani announced that the house he was building was completed, and some beer was brewed. Then a *mũndũ mugo* came and took me to the river to be cleansed. He poured *tatha* from a goat's intestine over me and then in the house to bless it.

Kamani's mother went to the river and got three smooth, round rocks and came and put them in the center of the house to make a fireplace for cooking. Then she went back to the river and collected some arrowroots and put them in a pot to cook over a fire she had made. As the bride, I could now enter the house, and I cooked the arrowroots and shared them with Kamani's mother, my own mother, and the other guests who had come to watch the ceremony of me going to my own house. Now I was free to stay in my own house and cook for my husband. However, as a bride I still could not eat meat until a goat had been slaughtered. Even as girls, we would not eat when we saw men nearby, nor would we want them to catch us chewing because it did not look nice to see our teeth or us swallowing. So we used to eat away from our husbands after we cooked for them.

It was just at the time the British declared the Emergency that I went to live at my husband's home and we could not get a goat because the British would think we were going to give it to the Mau Mau freedom fighters. So it was some time before I could eat meat at my husband's home. When I moved into the house with Kamani, I started to cook for him, warm water for his bath, and even wash his body if he wanted me to. Once you are married, you are governed by somebody else, so there is a big change from when you were living with your mother.

My mother had told me that the best way to be with the husband is to be obedient. When you are told to do anything, you do it without asking questions, because if you refuse, you will be beaten by the husband. "If you try to run away from your husband's home," she said, "you will be returned, and if your husband accepts you back, you have to pay a goat and a gourd of beer to appease him." I learned that a good wife is the one who stays at home, cultivates her own food, and after selling some, buys some goats. At that time, wealth was measured by the number of goats and cows a person had. A woman who was hardworking and was able to buy many goats was called *ngatha* by people, because she had her own wealth and took care of the home. But nowadays, *ngatha* only means a wife who is not wandering about.

I used to be told by my grandmother that a wife who does not obey her husband is called *mbura matũ* [deaf-eared]. Even when dancing with the women, you would hear us singing, "Look at the sun, so you may have time to go and cook for your husband and children." Nowadays, we have songs that we sing at weddings about being a good wife. At that wedding you were at with us, you heard us singing the songs about being a good wife to the bride—to love only her husband and children, be hospitable to the people of the village, and everybody will know she is good and she will be praised.

* * *

I was lucky to get pregnant with my first child before even a few months had passed after Kamani and I moved to our new house. I did not know I was pregnant until the baby inside was about three months old and I missed menstruation. I went and told my mother that I was feeling something kicking in my womb and at times it would kick hard. She told me I was pregnant and to not tell anybody. So I waited.

Then the time came when I felt sick and my stomach was aching. I did not know what kind of disease I had, and I started screaming to my husband, telling him that I felt as if somebody had poisoned me. I was scared and was not sure what was wrong. When my husband came and saw me in pain, he went and called four women who came and stayed with me. They lit a very big, bright fire. We stayed at the fire for quite a long time with one or another of the women coming and feeling my stomach after each pain to see if the baby was coming.

When the child was ready to come out, there was not much pathway for him to pass out, so one woman took a razor blade and made a cut to make more room for him. When he came out, she tied the umbilical cord as I have described to you before. I was kneeling down, holding the baby, and the cord was cut and tied. Then some parasitic plant from the *mukoigo* tree was brought to me and I chewed it and the liquid from it was given to the baby to prevent him from having stomach upsets. The women called "*aririririti*" five times, and the child was named Wacira.

I did not move around much for about three months. During that time other women were bringing food and fetching water and firewood for me. The tradition is called *itega* and is still practiced. Nowadays, though, we go with bread and sugar and sometimes money, instead of just bananas and porridge.[3]

I felt a big change after Wacira was born because now I was a mother. I was happy because I'd jumped to the next stage. You see your *riika*mates who have not passed to motherhood, and you know, now, that they are yet to face the birth of a child. Now you are looking to your children, not just the husband. And also, now one is wide enough so that other births coming afterwards are without difficulties.

* * *

Wacira was born just before we were put into a concentration camp at the beginning of Mau Mau. What happened is that the British put Kamani and me in a village with a lot of other people from this area. Later, a big trench was built to keep Mau Mau fighters from the forest from coming down to the villages. Bamboo spikes were put inside the trench, so the freedom fighters wouldn't get access to the people in the villages who were feeding them—that way, the British thought the Mau Mau would starve.

We got food to the freedom fighters anyway. Like me, I was one of the women who used to take food into the forest for them. I would first tie the food with banana leaves, then put it up beneath my normal wearing sheet, tie a belt around myself to hold it, and go to the *shamba* outside the fenced village. I would always take a *kibanga,* a *mũkwa,* and a *kiondo* as if I were going to cultivate. Nobody asked me where I was going, and if asked, I would tell the Home Guard I was going to the *shamba.* Then I would walk idly for some time and start collecting firewood in bushes. Finally, some scout for the Mau Mau would come out of the bushes, and I would give him food. I felt more excited than scared. I wanted to help because my brother was one of the freedom fighters by then.

There were quite a few scouts for the Mau Mau—even girls and small boys like Mugo, here, who would sing, "*Itho, Ingoritho, Itho, nĩ politho*" [Father, you are met, Father, by the police]. This was to alert the Mau Mau that the police are coming. The child would sing, beating his vocal cords at his throat to distort the words being sung enough to fool the Home Guards. The Home Guards did not know what the boy was singing, but the Mau Mau knew what the words meant.

During Mau Mau, women were also fighting. Some even went into the forest to help. Women in the villages fought by singing. It was authorized by the British that each village should catch freedom fighters and hand them over to the Home Guards. When we found some, the Home Guards were very happy. Once one came in his jeep, and he seemed very happy that some Mau Mau were captured. To show him we were happy, we began singing and dancing, but then we grew mad, and as we were dancing we started cutting the tires of his vehicle with *ibanga* [machetes], still pretending we were happy. It was ironic. We were destroying the vehicle—almost him—but he still thought we were happy. Because so many older women's sons were fighting, we used to sing:

Mũka ũciaraga ihĩĩ	Women who give birth to boys
riua rĩkuuma naĩ.	the sun has risen badly.

There was a big change when we went into the villages because we could not move about without a Home Guard watching us. We could not do a lot of cultivating either. At times, we would just stay there, waiting for the authorities to let us out. One could only wait and pray to God to take care of you. What one had to do in the village was to make sure she did not meet with either the Mau Mau or the government police for fear of being killed. We took a lot of care and were obedient to the orders issued by the British, otherwise there was trouble. Sometimes we were removed from our houses in the middle of the night, even beaten like slaves. We were forced to work during the day digging the trench, even though it was not our wish to do so. When we heard the droning of aircraft coming to bomb the Mau Mau in the forest, we'd run a lot until it was over. The British planted bombs up near the forest and some are still buried near Gatwe. A few years ago, some children playing uncovered one and, thinking it was a ball, began to play with it. It exploded and killed one of them.

When I began to act as a scout for the freedom fighters, I took the Mau Mau Oath—I would not have failed. I had long hair that I could plait at the time, and it was cut with a blunt *kibanga.* Then I became the one who used to beat the girls who refused to take the Oath, and I cut their hair with a blunt *kibanga.* It was a way of making sure that people were loyal to the Agĩkũyũ traditions and to the freedom fighters who were working to liberate us from the British. I knew my brother was fighting, but I only saw him once. Then he looked very tired and hungry.

When we finally got our freedom, we had something to rejoice about. There was much happiness and singing. I can remember one of the songs we were singing that day.

Kamatimu, mũhoe Ngai	Home Guards, be praying to God
Riria nyakeru akainũka	When the British go back home
Mũgatwika nyama cia nderĩ.	You will be fed as meat to the vultures.

On the day of Independence, *Jamhuri,* I was with Njeri, a child born one week earlier. People from here had gone to watch Munyao raise the flag on Mount Kenya. There were so many fireworks the night before, and that morning the Union Jack Flag was lowered and the new Kenyan flag was raised at Kerugoya. On that day, Maina, who was in nursery school by then, broke his hand because of shaking those small flags given to them at school so hard. So I watched the celebrations at Kerugoya while taking Maina to the hospital for treatment. Yes, those times—one can never forget them.

* * *

Soon after the British declared the Emergency, I got my first child, Wacira. Then I got another who only lived for six months, and then another who died at the age of one year. So there were three children who were born before Maina, but only one was alive when he was born. Then Wacira died when Maina was only about seven months old. What happened is that he was sick with measles. He was feeling pain, and I had taken him to the hospital to be treated. The next day when we were at the garden cultivating for the short season's crops, I told Wacira to hold Maina while I cultivated. He refused, telling me that I had refused to take him to the hospital again and he was still sick.

When we came back from the garden, he said he was going to sleep outside—to rest and ease the pain. Suddenly, I heard him produce an "ah 'aaa" sound, and then he kept quiet. I got scared and took him back to the hospital. He spent three months there before he died. After he had been there awhile, wounds began to develop because of urine infection. The children were never removed from their beds or turned over, nor were their sheets and clothes changed, so Wacira would urinate and it would cause the sores.

The day I took Wacira back to the hospital, the heavy rains of 1961 started, and he died when it was still raining. It rained hard for many days. Later, I realized that Wacira died of tetanus—it had come from the measles. That boy's death changed me. If you have something and it is taken from you, you would not feel so happy. Me, I started to get thin, remembering I'd never see Wacira again or the things he used to do. I stayed a long time before I got used to his absence. That was just before *Uhuru,* and it was not long after that that I became a Catholic.

* * *

My mother became a Catholic while we were in the villages during Mau Mau. She used to tell me about going for catechism classes in order to get baptized. She advised me that being a Catholic helped one to leave bad behaviors like abusing people, singing and dancing during *Irua,* and drinking beer.

I joined the church after *Uhuru* because I wanted to continue making my name clean and to learn to leave behind bad behaviors. I decided to join the Catholic Church because it was the first denomination here on earth—it was left by Jesus. And the Catholic Church does not discriminate. Even people with clothes that have lice are found seated together with clean, smart people. What the church emphasizes is to like everybody. It wants to have unity and peace among all people.

Once, before Mau Mau, I went to church, but I did not understand what was happening. I only saw a white man preaching. I was told he was a priest. But I do remember one reading from the Bible. The priest read that "Nations will fall against nations." I asked myself, "How are they going to fall against each other?" Then one day during Mau Mau, I went to harvest millet and I met my oldest brother called Maina. The first thing he asked me was whether I knew him. I thought that strange, but answered, "Yes." He slapped me. I was surprised. He asked me again and I said, "Yes" again, and he started to beat me until I denied that I knew him. My brother was a Mau Mau, and the reason he slapped me was because he was afraid that I might reveal him to the Home Guard and he was testing me. But I didn't understand that at the time, and I thought about the prophecy of that priest and realized that it was coming true—"Nations will rise against nations;" fathers will deny their own children, and a brother will deny his sister and she will deny him.

That same day I went home and my mother asked, "Do you know me?" and I said, "Yes," and she started to beat me until I said I didn't know her, then she stopped. She explained about my brother. In fact, it happened that during Mau Mau times, a son could kill his father and vice versa.

That priest had also told us that after some time, things that fly like birds in the sky would come, and during Mau Mau I saw airplanes for the first time. Then I really believed the priest. Another time it was prophesied that *amemenyi*—destroyers—would come. Before, maize kernels stored in the granary used to be infested only by weevils. But now, if you go into a granary, you can see moths destroying the maize completely into flour. Aren't they the destroyers we were told about?

So I joined the Catholic Church and that's when I got this name Mary. I changed when I joined. Before, if I was abused by anybody, we would fight and I would never keep quiet about it. If I heard that people were gossiping about me, I would go and ask them about it. I could stand outside my house and abuse anybody hard without caring. But now, if someone came and started beating me, I would not return their beating. Even if one were to come to my homestead and start cursing me, I would just ignore her. So there is a big change. I am able to humble myself now to follow Jesus's teaching that even when he was abused, mocked, and saliva thrown at him, he only humbled himself.

When I go for the Sunday service, the reading from the Bible and the interpretations help me in straightening out my behaviors. At times, a reading can be concerned with how wives abuse their husbands and so in return are beaten. If I have abused Kamani the night before, I go and apologize and make good our relationship. My husband is like one organ of my body. We two make one body, and when hating him, I am also hating myself and vice versa. The church taught me that.

I can remember a time when I was very sick with a high fever for three months. It wasn't malaria. I had a bad stomachache as well. All those months, I never cultivated my *shamba*. The church members came and cultivated the whole *shamba*, collected firewood, fetched water, and washed the clothes. They cooked for my children and my husband every day. The members have helped on two occasions like that when I was sick. Now I'm having my renewal wedding, and the women will help me with money and cooking for the guests. So in our church, we help each other.

We have a group that teaches us to be better wives and mothers. It's called Catholic Church Women's Action Group. I have been a member for five years. Its work is to help every woman to love her husband's parents, the people of the community, and her people at home. It teaches us how to treat our husband well and bring him closer to God. At times, my husband might come home drunk. We are taught how to deal with him, touching him all over and asking him why he got drunk, so that when he sees our concern, he will not feel like beating us.

When we first started the group, we were only 20 women. Now we are 370 women. We go helping the poor—like if somebody does not have a house, we contribute money and build a house for that person. We help each other when we are sick, like I told you, and encourage women to renew their vows with a church wedding. Anytime there is a wedding, like mine next month, each member of the group gives a contribution and then they go and sing songs and dance and make the people who have come to the homestead after the wedding happy. We also visit schools, giving advice to girls about how they can be better women of tomorrow by not being loose around men and staying in school. Some of our girls now are becoming pregnant while they are in school, and then they are forced to leave and come home. It is not a good thing. Our group also goes into homesteads preaching and teaching good morals. We have found it necessary to compose songs and go singing as a part of our teaching, because that way the people listen.

It was members of our church women's group who decided to form Winyerĩĩkia Women's Group. But Winyerĩĩkia is commercial, because we make money from our projects. Like this one of weaving banana fibers—those women from Nairobi who came and taught us how to make the baskets are paying us 20 shillings for each basket. They also gave us 1,500 shillings, which we divided amongst ourselves, each woman getting 50. But we were counseled to give our husbands 20 of it, so they will know that the place we go each week is productive. Our group raises pigs, as you know, and slaughters them and sells the meat to raise money for the group.

Long ago, when I belonged to neither women's group, I always waited for that time when my husband would give me money, and when he didn't I remained poor. Now I am able to take care of myself with the money we contribute each month. Like the granary I'm adding here at this homestead, I will not ask my husband for a cent, even though he got his coffee harvest money just the other day. If I rely on him to give me money, the day he misses I will have a problem. So the women's group really helps me financially, and I'm learning how to do new things like these baskets.

Even though the women's group helps me in many ways, I still have to cultivate the coffee to raise money for school fees. We started growing coffee in the villages just before *Uhuru,* and we planted it here afterwards. At first, we were afraid the government might just take our coffee away from us, because the British had not allowed us to grow it. But when the first yield was ripe, extension workers came and paid us for the harvest. Then they came around and showed us how to plant seedlings, digging the hole, then filling them with manure and putting dirt around the seedlings. We plant coffee trees in straight rows with the help of *conti,* which is a sort of line measure. Picking has not changed since we began. What has changed is the way we take care of the coffee. We plant with less manure now. At first, agricultural extension workers did the spraying for disease, but now each farmer sprays his own coffee. Nowadays, we know how to prune back the branches of the coffee trees in such a way that there are more berries in the next year.

Coffee is only harvested twice a year, but we get more per kilo than people who plant tea. I am always learning something new to improve my *shamba*—look down there, all that maize I have planted and the tomatoes you see here. When the passion fruits and avocados are ripe, I will take them to the market and sell them. Though we don't have much land here, my *shamba* is good because I work hard.

* * *

I do not forget anything I learn. For instance, when I was at Wambugu Farm, I learned that when a male pig is made sexually inactive, it grows fat quickly. I learned how to circumcise [she means castrate] the young male piglets so they can be fattened. When I came back here, I taught the Winyerĩĩkia members how to do it. I learned that when the mother pig gives birth, we have to watch it carefully so that it doesn't eat the first piglet, which is something a sow normally does. Now we raise the pigs with the knowledge I learned when I went for the course.

I also teach the Winyerĩĩkia women new ways of weaving baskets. Another woman and I were the supervisors on decorating sisal baskets with woolen thread for designs. We taught the rest how to make the designs. And these banana-fiber baskets, mine was "number one," and I even made a big tray that was given to Vice President Kibaki when he came for the *harambee* fund-raising for the secondary schools. That is why the woman from Nairobi told me that I have my own kind of blessings, because I learn many things quickly, then I am able to teach others the same things. And I like learning new things, too. That is why after I returned from the course at Wambugu Farm, I decided to join the community adult education class so I could learn to read and write.

I first heard about the class when it was announced in church that the president was giving free adult education classes and that old people should go to school, too, and learn how to write their names and read the names of places—like that sign on the road that shows the way to Kamuiru. Before I had not known what it said, but now I know. I can read anything written in Kikuyu and written in large letters.

I first joined the class a long time ago because Mugo [last-born son, now age six] was not born yet. We used to pay 6 shillings and were taught by a man called Kamenyi. When I became pregnant with Mugo, I became lazy and stopped going until 1982 when President Moi announced that it was important for adults to go.

I joined because I wanted to know how to write and read without anybody's help. Like now, my daughter at school at Mwea, she writes a letter in Kikuyu, and after reading it I know that she is asking for cotton wool or something else. We can also talk our secrets in letters. Now if Kamani is in town working somewhere, I never tell somebody to write him. That somebody might abuse him in the letter without my knowledge, and then he would accuse me for nothing. Now, I write my husband and say what I think is important, and he writes back.

Because I know writing and some maths, I was made the clan's treasurer, and when we went to put the money in the bank, I was happy to be able to put down my signature instead of a fingerprint. And I know the amount of coffee I pick and keep a record.

Sometimes at the adult education class a community worker comes and teaches us things that are good to know. You remember the day last week when a woman from the family planning clinic came and taught the women in class about different food groups and what is the best combination to feed one's children. And she even asked the women with babies if they knew about family planning, but some of them were shy. I think family planning is a good idea, and I'm training to be a community educator so I can teach other women how to go about it.

What do I like best about the class? I like reading and would like to know how to talk in English because if I knew, we would be talking together in English. The hardest part for me to learn is maths and especially when we were having thousands. But adding smaller numbers is easy. Reading and writing Kikuyu are easiest because they are my language. Sometimes there is a newspaper printed in Kikuyu called *Githomo* ["Reading"]. I enjoy that newspaper.

I would like a newspaper in the class, but the visitors [guest speakers] give information, too—like about raising chickens and cows. A cow like this one here [she points to one of the family's cows], now that it is hot and there is not enough grass, I learned we must buy extra food in the shop for it. I also learned to boil water for drinking and to keep it in a pot. But we do not follow that practice because what I do is go to a spring that produces very clean water and fetch water there for the homestead. But some women with very many children do not have time to fetch water and then boil it. Usually we boil water when we make tea—that way it is clean.

If I had to choose between attending the adult education class and the women's group, I would attend the women's group, because it is the one that gives me financial help. The adult education classes teach good things, but it does not help us with school fees for our children or to get a new granary.

The way I learn best is by comparing myself with other people and trying to work better than them. The Agĩkũyũ says that "a woman never challenged does not give birth." We also say, "Going wide is seeing and learning much." The one who just stays in one place is a fool. When I move outside, I learn something new and when I come back I try to use new methods I've learned.

* * *

Long ago, when a woman had a son as old as Maina, she could become an elder and was made a member of the *kiama* if the woman wanted to. But these days there is no recognition when a woman's child gets circumcised. Some children are even circumcised without the knowledge of their parents. The old customs are not followed now. The only change I felt when I stopped menstruating was feeling sick with a lot of heat and sweating sometimes. That was about four years ago. Now that it's over, I'm happy. I am not very interested in wanting my husband sexually either.

Of all the changes I've told you about, the one that changed me the most was when I gave birth. That's because I knew then that I had become a woman entitled to some duties and respect. But when I stopped menstruating I was happy, because now I'm like a young girl again because I'm not always having to wait and wash clothes and cook for everybody. My daughters help with those things now. If I spend the night anywhere, nobody can ask me about it, and I do not have any small child who is crying—that makes me happy.

My biggest role is working at home in my *shamba* and in the homestead. Then next is being a mother. Third most important is going to the Women's Church Group and Winyerĩĩkia, because there I'm taught how to stay comfortably at home. Leave the work of midwifery to last—I can only do it when it is there to be done. Before that comes the wife's role, because it means that I am able to keep my home whole, as the word *mũtũmia* means "one who can mend and seal and make whole." The role of student is more important because then I learn a lot of new, good things that I did not know were there before. The role of teacher should come between the role of student and midwife.

What am I proudest of having achieved? I know I have achieved a lot of things—like making that granary there. It is me who thought how to make it. My husband never asked. I also know that I'm able to cultivate my *shamba* well and get a lot of yields from it. That is because I am a hard worker. But I use my brain a lot, too.

I always dream and pray that before I die, I may see my children grow up to support themselves, with the boys marrying and having good homes, because I see that it is me who supports them now. The boys should finish school and also the girls. Long time ago, when I was a child, parents used to say that they wouldn't take their girls to school because they might become prostitutes. But now, girls can help people at home as well as going to school. Some even go further than their brothers—look at Njeri. She has gone further than Maina, who stopped in Standard Seven.

My strongest character is loving people and never discriminating between them. Anybody who is friendly to me becomes my friend. I do not choose whom I make friends with—they choose me. My weakest character is that if anybody makes me annoyed, I feel frustrated that I can't shout back and tell that person my mind.

What does womanhood mean to me? It means taking care of the home so that where there are loopholes, I mend them, and when my husband comes home drunk and furious, I try to cool him. Agĩkũyũ means that I have gone through *mbuci* and *matũ,* then *Irua.* These things make me pure Mũgikũyũ. You can never be a pure Mũgĩkũyũ, but if you stay around us long enough, you will learn a lot about our ways, because now you are my friend.

Notes

1. Local chiefs were appointed by the British colonial government during the period to which Wanoi refers.

2. I often saw the ten-year-old daughter in the compound where I lived feeding her small sister in the same manner, using her first finger and shoving mashed food into the baby's mouth.

3. There were a number of occasions during my year and a half in the field when I participated in *itega.* It was always a joy-filled event, when women sang and danced as well as providing food, firewood, and, today, shillings for the new child and mother.

8

Nyambura: Child of Independence

Sixteen women made up the sample cohort born slightly before or after the eve of independence. Schooling had had a major impact on the lives of these women then in their twenties. The average number of years attended was 6.4. Only three had reached the secondary level and none had reached university. Though a few Mutira women do reach the tertiary level, they are the exception. The majority of young women in rural areas do not have the opportunity of attending government secondary schools, which requires a financial investment on their parents' part. Some attend *harambee* (self-help) schools, which usually are less well equipped and where teachers, often hired by the local community, are either inadequately trained or not trained at all.

Nyambura and Wanja represent two different trajectories for rural women who were in their twenties in 1984. Nyambura was formally educated through Standard 5 (fifth grade), when she dropped out of school. She represents roughly the average for her age cohort. Wanja is one of two women in the sample cohort who completed Form 4 (four years of high school). She represents an increasing number of young women who, armed with a secondary-school certificate, return home to search for wage work and a better life. She did not have an opportunity for further training after secondary school and she did not do well enough on her secondary-school leaving examination to earn a place in university.

Half of the women in the cohort were Catholic, a third were Anglican. One belonged to the Full Gospel Church, and another stated merely that she was a Christian. Nyambura is Catholic; Wanja is a member of the Anglican Church and sings in its choir.

Nyambura typifies her cohort group because she is married and has a family. At the time she became a life narrator she

Nyambura, with Kamau

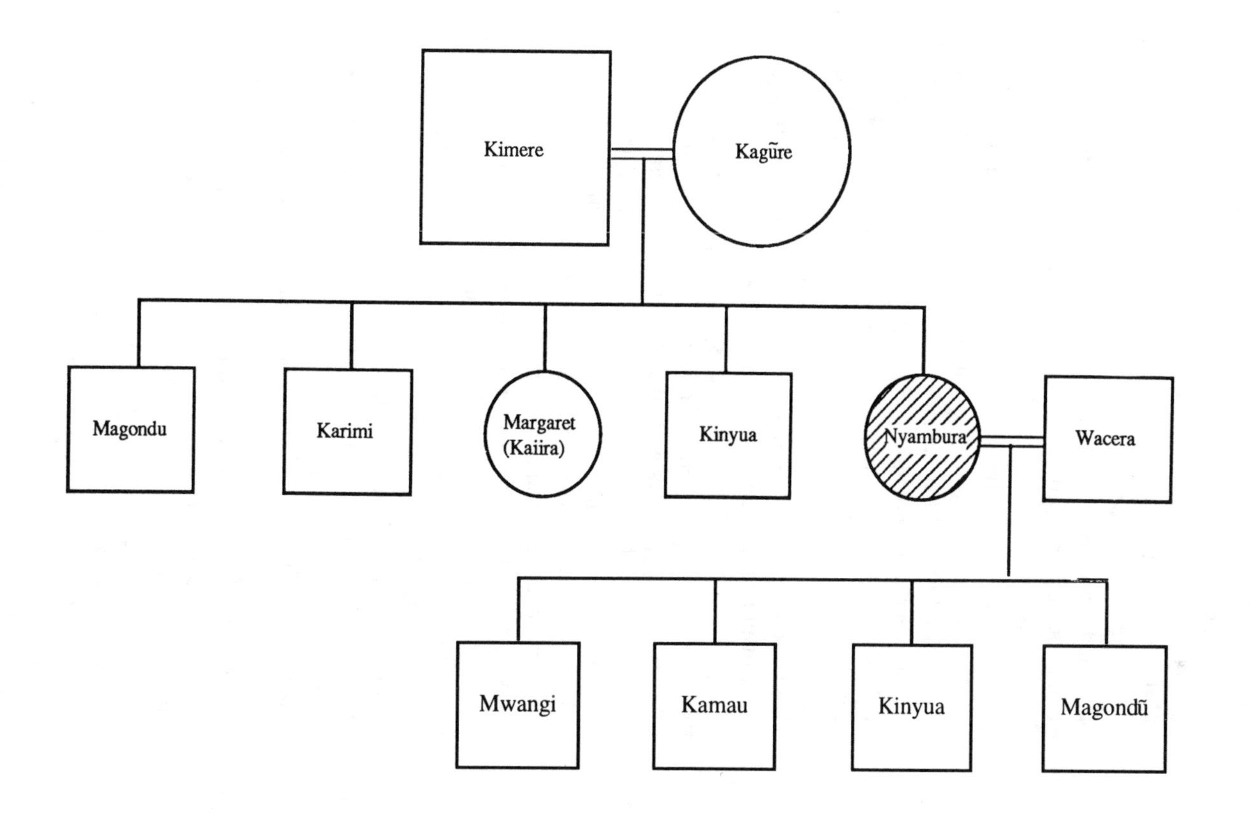
Kimere
Kagũre
Magondu
Karimi
Margaret (Kaiira)
Kinyua
Nyambura
Wacera
Mwangi
Kamau
Kinyua
Magondũ

had two small sons. Another was born in 1985 and the last one in 1987. The last-born son, Nicholas Magondũ was very large, and Nyambura experienced some problems in giving birth. As a result, Nyambura and her husband decided not to have more children. She uses the pill, a contraceptive method she refused to consider in 1984 for religious reasons. Nyambura lives at her husband's homestead. She depends economically on her husband's salary as a postal clerk and the money she earns from picking tea.

I had opportunities to spend time outside of the scheduled interviews observing Nyambura, who lived at the homestead of a family I had known previously and often visited. She has a cheerful disposition and is extremely hardworking. She delighted in teaching me the rudimentary skills associated with fetching water and cutting wood for the cooking fire. During our first few interviews she was shy. As the sessions progressed, she began to reveal her feelings and candidly talked about significant events that had occurred in her life.

At the end of 1984, her second-born son—then eleven months old—developed what was diagnosed locally as a heart problem. Both parents were distraught, fearing that they would lose the child. I offered to take them to a hospital in Nairobi for diagnosis, having been dissatisfied with a local hospital practitioner's diagnosis. Nyambura and her husband remained in Nairobi with little Kamau for four days. Their son finally received the medical attention needed. He did not have to have surgery, as they had feared. He recovered, and as a result, by the time I visited Mutira in 1989 I was being lauded as the one responsible for "saving the child." Nyambura jokingly said that I should take five-year-old Kamau back to the United States with me since I had been responsible for saving his life. She called him to her and, holding him in front of her, explained my significance as he listened solemnly with his eyes downcast but his toes in the dirt betraying his nervousness. He was much less sure of his mother's proposition. I quickly assured him that I had sons of my own and it would be best if he stayed with his mother. The tension was broken by laughter.

In 1992 when I again returned I found that Nyambura was in the hospital having surgery for an abdominal problem. Her husband appeared very worried. I visited her four days after she came home from the hospital; she was still very weak and in much pain. She tried to explain the problem she had had, a rupture between the uterus and colon, then got out X-rays the doctor had given her to illustrate to me where the problem had been. She winced, relating that the pain had been unbearable. She hoped now that she had been through surgery she would not be experiencing that kind of pain anymore. I sympathized, then reassured her that by the time I next saw her she would probably have forgotten it.

I asked her if her husband was treating her better these days. He seemed to be concerned for her health. She said, "Yes, those days are gone when he used to beat me. He has not beaten me for some years now. He had to take on more work with the children and the *mashamba* since I came to have this problem." My own reading of the situation is that Nyambura's medical problem and surgery scared her husband profoundly; he woke up to realize what a special person he had as the mother of his children. When he appeared in the doorway after having given us time to be alone, he brought cold sodas and was very solicitous of Nyambura's well-being.

Nyambura's conversations with me in 1994 about the changes in her life since 1984 appear at the end of the narrative she helped create in the early 1980s.

—J.D.

I was born at Kamuiru, the last born of Kimere and Kagũre. My father, Kimere, was a tall, slender man—slightly taller than me—and he had a quick temper like Kinyua, my brother. Kagũre, my mother, is a cheerful woman and hardworking. I was named Nyambura for my mother's mother, who was born during the Long Rains [*mbura* refers to rain]. I am of the Ũnjiru Clan, and my Christian name—the one I was baptized in the Catholic Church—is Meri. There are three brothers—Magondũ, the firstborn, then Karimi, and Kinyua, who is eight years older than me. Magondũ is talkative and polite. Karimi is also talkative, but in a different way. I really cannot remember too much about them because they were already big and were married when I was still little. Kinyua, I remember. He was a good, young boy who didn't know how to defy order, but he did have a quick temper. There was also a sister, Margaret Kaiira, who was cheerful, as I remember her when growing up. She follows Karimi and was a big girl of eighteen years when I came to understand things.

Margaret and Kinyua were the ones who took care of me, but Margaret loved me the most. I could tell she did because she would bathe me, make up my hair, wash my clothes, and give me food. At times, she would carry me around tied to her back. Because there were no other girls in the family, she used to knit nice cardigans for me.

Margaret and Kinyua were the ones who used to tell stories and riddles around the cooking fire in the evenings. I can't remember any of the stories right now, but here's a riddle:

Gwata ndai.	Catch a riddle.
Ndagwata.	I am ready.
Wathiĩ na njira wathekio nũ ?	Who smiled at you as you walked along the road?
Mwatũka wa thi.	A crack in the earth.

I was a child who liked to hear riddles and try to figure them out. I also liked to try new things. If people went to the *shamba* to cultivate, I would not like to be left behind—I wanted to go, too. I learned how to cultivate with a *kibanga,* go for water, and wash clothes from my mother. If she went to the river, I would be given a small gourd, and she would go and tie it with a *mũkwa* to my back after we had fetched the water. I learned most of the things like washing clothes with soap and scrubbing them to get them clean by watching my mother, then doing what she did.

I learned about all my relatives from both my mother and father. We would go to visit some relatives—like when my mother carried me on her back to visit my uncles and aunts. When we met them, I was told who they were and how they were related to me. It was important for us as children to know which people we were related to and who were clanmates.

How did I learn good from bad characters? My mother would advise me. If I was visiting or moving with a girl with bad characters, she would tell me never to visit that girl again. Like the girl who is lazy or does not respect the elders—that one is bad. I also taught myself, because I would know when I made a mistake and stop doing that thing and never repeat it. I can remember once I was sent somewhere by my father, but I refused to go. Then I was beaten. So I learned that it is bad to refuse when one is sent somewhere, and since that day my father has never beaten me.

When we were little girls, we used to play games like *mbiya,* where children try and hit each other with a ball made out of strings. We'd also play *ciũthi,* which is played with five stones thrown in the air. First, one throws one stone up in the air and at the same time tries to get another from the ground. Then she throws again and gets a second, third, and fourth stone. Finally, one throws all the stones on the ground and this time, she has to collect two at a go, each time, then one. The last time, one would fold the hands and throw up all the stones, meanwhile turning the hands, palms down and flat, to catch all five stones together on the backs of the hands. Then we'd throw the stones again to start over. We liked that game. We'd also sing songs and jump, using a rope. Sometimes we made toys out of maize stalks and string or bottle tops.

* * *

I can remember the first day I went to school, because it was Magondũ, my oldest brother, who took me. His children were like my age-mates, so he took all of us together. We spent the first day there trying to reach our one hand over the head, like this, to the other side of the head, and anybody who was able to reach her hand over and touch the ear with her fingers on the other side was big enough to go to Standard One. As we were chosen, we entered the classroom. We spent the day like this, then it was time to go home. On the way home, we chased each other and talked about the class and the teacher.

My home was at Kamuiru and I went to school at Mutira. We would start the journey to school at 7:00 A.M. and reach school at about ten minutes to eight. On our way, we'd go playing on the road and sometimes running instead of walking—racing with each other. We never wore shoes to school, but we had a uniform—a green tunic with a light pink blouse. The tunic had pleats with a belt behind and the blouse had a round collar. I used to hear my sister Margaret complaining about how dirty I got those uniforms while she scrubbed them in a *karai* [metal basin rounded at the bottom, used for washing clothes].

In the first year of school, we learned how to draw, make toys, and solve some math problems—like counting and subtracting maize and bean seeds. Also, we made pots out of clay. We were given homework—like making baskets—and would have to take the basket to school the next day for inspection. My sister showed me how to make the basket and prepare the threads into strings for weaving, as I wasn't able to do it yet. I was smaller than Muthoni [a niece in the compound, aged nine] when I learned how to make baskets. My sister and mother knew which plants had the best threads for weaving, so they would collect them for me. At first we used *migio,* then later we began to use sisal. It was hard to learn the patterns. My sister would show me how to weave the threads in and out of the main strings. Then I would try as I saw she had done, but sometimes I would make mistakes, and she would tell me, "No, that is not the way it's done, here watch me again." Then I would try again until I learned. About the same time, my sister was beginning to knit cardigans with knitting needles, and she could also crochet, so she used to teach me these things.

The school I went to was made of mud bricks. Only the two Standard Seven classrooms were built of stone. We used to sit on long benches, and we wrote on cut pieces of blackboard. Later on, we started writing in notebooks. If a child forgot her notebook, the teacher would punish her with a beating. By my last year of school—in Standard Five—I was going very early in the morning to sweep the classroom and then pour water on the floor to clean it [most classroom floors are polished concrete]. After cleaning the floor, I'd go for parade with the rest of the children, where the teacher on duty inspected us. Anybody who had lice on her hair was shaved over a portion of her head and sent home. Those who were dirty were pinched hard by the teacher and sent to the river to wash.

I can't exactly remember which lesson we used to start with, but we would go to class at 8:00 A.M. By the time we had reached Standard Four, we got each lesson [subject] from a different teacher who would come into our classroom. But the first three years we had only one permanent teacher for all the subjects. There was a break time at mid-morning. During that time we used to play games and chase each other around the yard, then back to the classroom. Each lesson was about thirty minutes. The break came after the fourth lesson, then there were two more hours of lessons, and we'd have a break and go home for lunch. We'd come back at 2:00 P.M.—after about an hour and a half—and have three more lessons, then a break, then back to the classroom to collect our books before going home at 4:00 P.M.

The way math was taught is that the teacher wrote numbers on the blackboard, and we copied them down into our exercise books or on our small blackboards. After solving the problems, we took the book up to the teacher who would mark the problems we'd done. When we were learning numbers or words, after the teacher wrote them on the blackboard, she would call someone's name and that student would wake up and read what was on the board with the other students repeating after her.

Sometimes we had plays, songs, and dances that were in Kikuyu or Kiswahili. We sang songs like:

Ĩi wakĩthonjo gikura.	Yes, you are noisy, making noise.
Thonjo kiratũ kiega nĩ kia mwalimu.	The best shoe is that of the Teacher.

We had plays that usually had something to teach us—like respecting the elders or working hard at our studies. Once I remember a child was beaten because he had been fighting with other children. And another child was beaten when he came late to school. I was beaten once, too. The teacher used to use a stick against a boy's back—that's the way he was beaten—but a girl was beaten on the palm of her hands.

After school, I would run home to help my sister go for water at the river or to collect maize stalks for the cows. On Saturdays, we helped in the *shamba,* weeding the vegetables, or during the harvesting of coffee we'd pick coffee berries. My sister would give me a small *kiondo* to carry to the *shamba* and I'd pick the berries on the lowest branches. We used to see who could get the most. On Sundays, nobody worked. We'd get up, bathe and get dressed in our best clothes. Then my mother took us to the Sunday School at the Catholic Church. We'd have Bible lessons and singing, and afterwards, on the way home, we'd visit our relatives and neighbors. We were always fed well on those visits.

I stopped going to school in Standard Five. What happened is that at that time, the local brew called *karabu* was on the increase, and my father used to drink so much that he was unable to take all his children to school. We used to be sent from school often because the parents had not contributed to the *harambee* fund for building another classroom or because we didn't have writing materials. I could spend the whole term without going to school. I never lacked the school fees but my father was a drunkard and never viewed education as something very important; there were so many of us children who were school age that with the drinking, my father could not afford to keep us all in school. I felt badly about leaving school, but there was nothing I could do.

* * *

Soon after leaving school, I went to live with the Mwais, who are relatives. Ever since I was little I was used to going to visit the Mwais, and I liked the place. So when they wanted me to go and stay with them, I was ready to go. [At this point in the interview, Nyambura's husband's mother entered the cooking hut where we were having the interview and, on hearing the exchange, explained, "Sometime back, people used to ask for young girls to help them in bringing up their own children. Usually, the girl was a relative. She became an *ayah*. So Mrs. Mwai went to Nyambura's mother, who was a relative, and as Nyambura was the last born and the mother did not have another child, she asked to be given Nyambura. Nyambura agreed and stayed with the Mwai family until she got married."]

I went to the Mwais' home when I was a child of about ten years. There I was taught by Mrs. Mwai things about how to care for the children, to cook, and to keep the house clean. This was a change because at my house I had never had to do much work, being the last born. There weren't any big differences between Mrs. Mwai and my mother, though, because Mrs. Mwai used to treat me just like one of her children, and we were related. Mwai is son-of-Kibuga, who is son-of-Ndegwa, who is son-of-Kimere, whom my father was named after.

The children I looked after at the Mwais—one was very small and the other was about the size of Mwangi [Nyambura's four-year old son]. The baby was put in a woven baby cot, and my work was to put the cot outside and, after some time, to bring it inside again. I remember how Mrs. Mwai used to wake earlier than me, and she would go and milk the cows. Then I would wake, and as she was preparing to go to school—she was a teacher—I would help her by putting tea into her thermos flask to take to school. After she left, I would start preparing the lunch, peeling the potatoes and carrots carefully so as not to cut myself. After preparing lunch, I would wash the baby's nappies [diapers] and other clothes—that took the rest of the morning. Then everybody would come home for lunch, and afterward I would wash up the dishes and look after the baby.

In the evening, Mrs. Mwai came home, and we would prepare supper together and then do the dishes together after dinner. Then she used to correct students' notebooks by the kerosene lamp. It was my job to keep the lamp full of kerosene and the glass clean. I remember that Mrs. Mwai and the husband never used to fight—if he said something that annoyed her, she would just keep quiet, but he knew that he had done something that made her annoyed and would apologize to her. They never argued with one another.

* * *

[An interview with Mrs. Mwai revealed the following about Nyambura's years with their family.]

When Nyambura came to live with us, she was very young. She was about ten years old. She worked for me as a maid. It is me who asked her to come because I needed somebody to take care of my children while I was teaching at the primary school. Her roles here were to take care of the children, cook, and care for the home. I taught her how to take care of the home—keeping it neat and clean—how to do the laundry, ways of cooking, and care for the children. I also taught her how to knit, toward the end of her stay, and bought her a knitting machine. She has it now and knows how to knit cardigans for sale. With the cardigans she sold while living here, she used to earn her money for clothes and other things I did not provide. No, she was not paid here. I taught her by talking to her—giving instructions—and showing her how to go about things. I was not sad when Nyambura was old enough to be married, even though I was not so happy to be left without a maid. I would have liked her to stay longer, but as her time to marry had come, I would not have denied her. A girl must one day get married. Wacera, whom as you know Nyambura eventually married, used to come here and visit. I knew him, and he did not seem a bad man for Nyambura to stay together with.

* * *

Did I go through *Irua* before I was married? *Wĩ* [you], those days are over! You know I am a Christian, and we do not believe it is a good thing. Why? Because it was a thing of the past. Going to school and learning some things helped us see the difference. We learned that we no longer needed *Irua*—that was for the old people. You know the president made it against the law. There are some who still do it, but not many. No, I didn't get my ears pierced, either. That was for our mothers. Some of those old women used to hurt each others' ears when fighting. I once saw a woman grasp another's *matũ* [hole in the earlobe] and pull it until it ripped. That woman was screaming very hard from pain. No, I would not want *matũ*.

How did I meet Wacera [her husband]? Well, while I was staying at the Mwais, I used to go to the post office down at Kutus to collect the mail for them, and that is where Wacera worked—at the post office. So we used to see each other that way. Then one day he asked me where my home was, and I told him, and he promised to pay a visit.

When Wacera first came to the Mwais to visit, I ran away from him. But then I came to like him, as he visited me. That continued for some time, until I noticed he was not coming to see me as much and maybe had found another, better girl. After he stopped coming so much, I found I was two months pregnant. I went home and told my parents what was happening. My mother was unhappy. Wacera was called by my parents, but he refused to go. I have never had such mistreatment. He didn't deny that he was responsible for the pregnancy, but he didn't say anything about marrying me either. What defeated my understanding was that although he used to visit me every day after work, now that I was pregnant, he ignored me completely, and even when I tried to approach him about the pregnancy, he showed no sign of interest. To me, it seemed that everything was over between us. I was really angry with him.

Mwangi [Nyambura's firstborn child] was born while I was staying at my parents' home, knowing that there was no relationship left between Wacera and me. Even though everybody knew about the relationship—both our parents—it seemed to have died. I felt badly that I was having a child with no hope of getting married. I decided I would just have to raise the child alone. When it came time to deliver, I went to Tumu Tumu Hospital. The pains began about one in the afternoon and lasted up until nine that night. Mwangi was born that night, and I stayed in the hospital for about eight days, then went home to my parents' place.

Things really changed for me after I had Mwangi because I suddenly became conscious that I was totally responsible for this tiny human being and what the future holds for him. I started thinking about how I would bring Mwangi up, and when he grew bigger, take him to school. I started my knitting business so I would get money to take him to school. Now I knew I was a *mũtũmia*—a full-grown woman. When you are a girl and then give birth, you find that you are changed. Your body features change, too—the breasts drop, and the features show that you are no longer a girl. And you change mentally, too, because you are always thinking about your children. So you have gone from girlhood to womanhood. Even when walking with a young girl my age who is not a mother, I would not call myself a girl anymore. The woman with a baby on her back signifies that she is a mother. When I became a mother, that was the biggest change for me.

While I was at my parents' home, my father gave me a piece of land to cultivate. My mother helped me plant maize and beans and some *skuma-wiki* [kale]. I worked hard to keep my mind off my problems and to get plenty of food for those at home. Sometimes my mother would look after Mwangi so I didn't have to work in the *shamba* with him on my back. Then I would make sure I returned to the compound in plenty of time to suckle him.

By that time, my sister was married and living down near Embu. Sometimes we would go and visit her. We would take a *matatu* [a station wagon or car, privately owned, used as a public means of fee-paying transportation] from Kagumo to Kutus and then another one to Embu. We'd stay there the afternoon, eating and even dancing with the women of her husband's homestead, then return home by dark. My sister had three children by then, and they liked to see my child. Margaret's husband is a teacher. He has planted a lot of coffee and even hired some workers to help with the harvest. He is saving some of the profits for building a stone house. Margaret is lucky to have such a good husband. When we visited her during that time I was separated from Wacera, it made me sad to think I had no husband.

At times during the period when Wacera and I were separated, he would come to my home to visit, and I'd realize that there was no love. So other times when he came, I just ignored him and continued with my work without becoming involved. During this time he married a girl, and they were staying together at Kutus—in fact, she and I were pregnant at the same time!

I tried to be happy on my own, but it was hard to find happiness because I was still young and to be a mother, without marrying—that is something I never imagined. I was feeling sick sometimes and would go to the hospital to be treated, only to be told that I was not sick. Finally, I learned to swallow the bitter pill and stay alone. Sometimes Wacera and I would meet on the way to Kutus, and he'd tell me a lot of nonsense—how he's coming for me. I ignored his words and began teaching myself how to use the knitting machine by watching a neighbor of the Mwais. Toward the end of 1982, I went to Kutus to start my knitting business there.

I set up my knitting machine in the *nduka* [shop] of one of Mr. Mwai's friends. I was making sweaters and jackets. People liked what I made, and I began to sell the sweaters. During that time, I stayed with my sister and her husband near Embu. While I was there, Wacera started visiting me. By this time he had chased his wife away and left another girlfriend. He was staying alone and wanted me to come and stay with him. I told him to go and talk to my parents. He persuaded them that he wouldn't repeat his bad behavior, so I decided to take Mwangi and go and live with him. Mwangi was about two and a half years [old] then.

We stayed in peace for a few months, then I found I was pregnant again, and the mistreatment began—he even started beating me and slapping me around until I couldn't eat anymore. I felt that I couldn't leave him, because now I was having two children by him.

Finally, I decided that I should come here to Wacera's parents' place and tell them I was leaving after all. When the parents found out about the problems, they called Wacera and talked to him about the other girls he was moving with and whether he wanted any of them for his wife. The father said to Wacera, "I have known Nyambura for some time now, and I say that she should stay here with us, and if you have anything to say, then say it." Wacera kept quiet. He was going for a course in Nairobi, so I came here to live with Mwangi. When I got here, I found the father had recently died and Wacera's mother was very sad, with nobody to fetch water for her and the cows a pathetic sight. When I came, Wacera's mother was so happy that she didn't want me to leave, so she talked to Wacera and he cooled down and vowed not to mistreat me again.

At the time, Wacera had another woman friend, and he found me to be a barrier because I was stopping him from enjoying himself with other girls. Because we are here and not in Kutus, he has his freedom to do anything he wishes down there. Now he's not so angry and acting like a lunatic. When we have a problem, I go tell his mother. Things are much better now, and I only pray to God to help me to be strong.

At the time that Mwangi and I went to live with Wacera in Kutus there was no *rũracio* given, but just recently, when Wacera decided to come and live here with us at his parents' home, he took a thousand shillings to my father. Nobody asked him for it—he just chose to take it. The tradition of *rũracio* has changed from long ago—today's men who want to take it to the girl's parents can and those who choose not to, nobody forces them. But good men, they follow the old customs by giving the number of goats or cows that were given for the girl's mother. If the *rũracio* for your mother was ten goats, that amount would be calculated in terms of money, so the young man would give the amount in shillings to the girl's parents. People here negotiate in both goats and shillings. The more schooling a girl has, the higher the rũracio asked, because the father has made a big investment in her education.

* * *

Now that I am a mother with two children, I think about how I can teach them good behavior. First, a mother should teach her children to respect elders, to have good manners, and to obey the mother and father. I have two boys, but if I had a girl I would want her to be hardworking—like farming, washing clothes, and cleanliness. Also, hospitality to visitors is important and caring for one's things. I would teach the girl how to cook, and when I go to the *shamba,* tell her to accompany me and see the way I do the cultivating. When she is young, I would tell her to make sure she goes straight to school without passing through other children's homes. And I would watch her to see which friends she moves with—whether they are good or bad and counsel her. If she went to secondary school, I would tell her that after school she should not get in the habit of sneaking away from school like some girls and going to visit boys, making endless journeys moving from place to place. After she is mature, I would tell her, as Mrs. Mwai told me, not to have sexual relations until the time she is married. I would advise her to be firm on it, for a man who is really serious and not just after sexual enjoyment will wait for her until she is ready.

I am teaching my sons to be obedient and to work hard at things like farming and taking care of goats and cows when they get older. Boys of five or six begin to care for the goats and sheep, so these sons of mine are still a bit young. Another thing—they should learn how to cultivate the tea.

You have seen me picking tea here. It is only recently that I learned—in May 1983. At home we only had coffee. It was *Cũcũ* [husband's mother] who taught me. She told me that one picks two leaves and a bud, and not to leave a big stalk but to pick close to the leaves. I used to pick very slowly, like a child. The first time I picked 5 kilos [11 lbs.]. Then I was able to pick more kilos as the days went by. Now, when I start after my morning work of the homestead, I can pick about 25 kilos [55 lbs.].

When I am not picking tea, I am working in the *shamba,* cultivating the maize and beans or sweet potatoes. We plant maize and beans together, but *waru* [European potatoes] and *ngwacĩĩ* [sweet potatoes] are planted separately in another plot. We plant kale and cabbage in one plot together with carrots and tomatoes at the border. We have maize and beans planted up here and down at the river where the soil is best. Altogether, we have about six different plots, but some are very small. Most of the land on the hillsides is planted in tea. I think there must be about 5 acres [2 ha] of tea here. Does *Cũcũ* own it? No. Now that *Mzee* is no longer alive, it belongs to Wacera and his brothers. But Wacera does not have much to do with it unless it needs pruning.

Does Wacera ever help me in the *shamba?* Yes. When the soil needs to be prepared for planting, you will find him here working. Also at harvest time. But by the time he reaches here from Kutus on Saturday afternoons, all he wants to do is rest from the week's work—so I don't count on him. But when he comes, he usually brings some meat and bread or some other thing we might be missing here. Last month, you remember, there was a shortage of sugar. Not even the shops down in Kagumo had any. But Wacera found a shop in Kutus that had sugar so he brought some home to us. The same with *unga* [maize meal]. Six months ago, during the dry season, there was a shortage of *unga.* When that happens, people start buying it up and hoarding it. Then you miss *ugali* [maize-meal porridge cooked to a hard consistency] for a few weeks. Wacera knows where to buy *unga* when there is a shortage.

During the dry season, there are no vegetables to find up here. Then potatoes mixed with green bananas and *ugali* are our main foods. But I know it is good for children to have vegetables, so on market day, I go to Kagumo or Kutus and buy vegetables we no longer have here. The old people—they are happy without vegetables like carrots and tomatoes. They prefer *githeri* or millet porridge. But we who are young like vegetables—especially carrots.

I want my children to grow up healthy. Right now I am worried about the baby. The doctor at the clinic says he has a problem in his lungs. I see him breathing hard and wonder what is to be done. I want to take him to the hospital in Nairobi, but I'm told one needs to be recommended by a doctor here. Sometimes I become fearful, wondering if this baby will survive. Then I pray to God for an answer.

I would like to have as many children as God gives me. I do not like these family planning ideas. It is not good to put chemicals into the body. My husband would not allow it either. Children are a blessing to the Agĩkũyũ.

Being a farmer and doing my work here are my most important roles, because without them I would have nothing to feed us. It's also important to keep the home clean—I learned that from Mrs. Mwai. Next most important is my role as wife to Wacera, then my role as a mother. My role as a daughter is less important, because I am now married and living at my husband's homestead. Do I ever cultivate the *shamba* at my parents' home? Sometimes I go there for a visit, but my brother is taking care of the *shamba.*

I do not belong to any women's group because I don't have time—there is too much work to do here. You have helped me fetch water—it takes many trips [I counted five on an average day] down to the stream and back again at the end of my work in the *shamba* to have enough water for cooking supper and bathing. The only day I take a rest is on Sunday or when I go down to the market.

Have I ever experienced the death of someone close to me? I have never had a child who has died, but there was an old woman who was staying near our home who died. She was a neighbor to my parents, and she liked me and Mwangi. When I was going anywhere, she would take care of Mwangi for me and she enjoyed staying with him. When I went to the market, I would bring her bread, and she would be very happy. When she died I was sad. She got sick, and as she was old we never took her to the hospital. Even though she was sick and old, I was very shocked because I liked her very much. I came to learn, then, that the body is just like a flower and will die sometime, somewhere. I know that I will die one day. I see life as just something short—"*ũtũũro nĩ kindũ kĩnini.*" A person must work hard during this life so at least she will leave those who stay behind without many problems.

* * *

The things I'm proudest of are that I'm now able to pick tea, I cultivate and cook well, and look after my children. At times I keep quiet and know that if I work harder one day I will be rich. I do not think I will die poor. My strongest character is being hospitable to people when we meet or when they come to visit me. When they come here, I cook food or tea for them—they cannot stay long without eating. But my weakest character is that I don't like moving out and going to visit other people much. I don't feel free to do it—it's just not me.

Being a woman means one who has her children and a family. Also, it means doing women's work like cultivating, feeding the cows—all those things. Being Mũgĩkũyũ means following the customs—like the things the clan does. It means going to clan meetings, attending its ceremonies, such as a marriage or burial. But today, I think of myself more as a Kenyan, because we are a nation now, not just Agĩkũyũ, or Kamba, or Maasai. Just last month we celebrated our twenty years of independence as a nation, and I was born just before independence, so we who are younger know that we are all Kenyan now. We have a new country and new ideas.

* * *

[On my return to Mutira in 1994, Nyambura continued:]

Nyina-wa-Stepheni, you have returned again [she hugs me and takes me into the sitting room of her cement house]. Last time you saw me [1992] I was still feeling terrible from the surgery I had then. When I went for that surgery I was very frightened—I was not sure if I would survive. But now you can see that I am better. I have had no pain since then, I thank God. Yes, that surgery taught me the value of my life. [I concur and then ask her about the house which is plastered on the outside and has been painted yellow since I last saw it.]

The house was built in 1991. In 1990 we bought the cement and blocks. The stones for the floor came from the other old house. We bought trees and had the timber made. Some of the iron sheets for the roof came from the old house but we had to add about ten new ones. We added two new rooms last year as our children are growing up.

Mwangi [the oldest] is in Standard 7. Soon he'll be going to secondary school. All the children are in school now and doing well. Even that one you rescued, he is doing well—fifth in his class. After Nicholas Magondũ was born in 1987, we decided not to have any more children. He was very big and I had some complications. I went to the doctor two days before he was born, feeling some pain, and was told to go home. Magondũ was born at home. *Cũcũ* helped but there were complications. So after that I started using the pill, which I still use. The husband was against my having a tubal ligation in case we wanted a daughter. I see no problem in using the pill—I have to take care of myself. I cannot keep having children one after the other.

But I haven't told you the happiest news [Nyambura was bursting with barely contained excitement]. Wacera and I are having a [church] wedding. We have been saving our money to pay for this wedding for a long time. You know it takes a lot of money to pay for a proper wedding. It will be the fourth of February. You will come, won't you? Nyina-wa-Stepheni you have to come. [I told her that I would be working in Ethiopia then but I would try and make it. If not, I would send my representative—my former research assistant. I then asked her what were the biggest changes she'd seen in her life over the past ten years.]

That's a big question. First, all our children are healthy now so there is less worry. I would say that we are more settled—Wacera and I. Otherwise we wouldn't be getting married in a church. Sometimes I used to think that Wacera would neglect me and the children. That made me feel sad and then I would talk with his mother. She would talk to him. That seemed to help—he listens to his mother. But now he has changed his ways so we have no problems.

Another change is that Wacera's brother has moved away because he wanted his own homestead. So it is just Wacera and me who are here to look after his mother and the family's land. But things are not so good between the two brothers. The older one fears that Wacera will get all their father's land because we are the only ones here. But each brother will get his share—he should not worry for nothing. No, we have not registered the plots because the Ministry of Lands and Adjudication authorities require Ksh. 7,500 from each family for a title deed. We could not raise that amount immediately so we have to wait for title deeds.

When you were last here, there was the tea strike. It bothered other people but it didn't bother me—I was in so much pain that time it was a blessing not to have to pick the tea leaves. When the strike was over Wacera helped and we hired some people to help us.

Now it is Wacera and I who cultivate the tea since his brother left. The KTDA [Kenya Tea Development Authority] pays us Ksh. 4.50 per kilo. But we have to pay the government taxes, buy fertilizer, and pay those who help us in picking the tea so eventually each farmer gets very little. [I ask how much per month and she gets a receipt for July 1993, which we read together.] After picking 213.50 kilograms, our total [gross] amount was Ksh. 960.75. But after we paid the taxes, we got only Ksh. 817.75 [US $22.50] that month. [Producers pay 15 percent of the gross amount earned in taxes.]

The KTDA is not paying people in cash as when you stayed here. Now they pay directly to our bank accounts. It is safer. There used to be problems when people got their tea money. Someone was even found murdered down near Kagumo after one of the tea bonus [paying] days. Paying through the bank is more orderly and it saves problems. Also there are more tea weighing stations so we don't have as many people queuing at the station here. Since the tea strike, things have improved. Although the tea pay is okay there is a lot of inflation.

We are lucky to be growing our vegetables, but still we have to buy some things like sugar, cooking oil, and *unga* [maize meal flour]. We are experiencing problems of food prices—they keep going up. It seems like the shilling doesn't have value these days. It takes three times as many shillings as it once did to buy sugar and other things. If we don't have the money we do without. But tea without sugar doesn't taste so nice.

What other changes have we seen in the last ten years? Well, you can see that things have changed in Kagumo. There are many new shops and buildings. That tall one painted red, near the road to Gatwe, belongs to a bottler. Wangari [a niece] works at the new chemist's—have you been to it? Kagumo never had a chemist when you were here; we used to go to Kerugoya for such things. Kagumo has been developing these last two years. But the market is still there. There is also a small clinic now across from the market. It's where the tailor's shop used to be—you know the one that was in front of where you stayed when you first came here [in 1983]. And there are two new cafes.

At Gatwe, a new secondary school has been built. This has been a big assistance to people here as it has been difficult to find a place for children in a secondary school. It was built in 1988. It has Form 1 to Form 4. People here are proud of that secondary school. It was the assistant chief who helped get the project started. It was built with *harambee* efforts. The community raised the money. Now the government is sending teachers. But it still is expensive to send a child to secondary school—Ksh. 20,000 [US $362 at 1994 exchange rate] for one term. [There are three terms in the school year, which means that for one child the cost, including board and tuition, would be US $1,086 per year.]

My main concerns now are seeing that my sons do well in school and that our wedding is a success. I worry if we will have enough food. The women from the church are helping. Margaret [her older sister] will be in charge of the ladies helping to cook. Yes, I have my dress. There are so many things to think about. I hope we will be ready. I am happy that Wacera agreed to have a wedding. It is time with our children growing big.

We don't see the brother's daughters much these days. They are the ones who should be helping *Cũcũ*. But they are always occupied with schoolwork or other activities. It would help me if they helped their grandmother more often. Yes, my mother is still there and I see her sometimes when I go down to Kagumo. Also Mrs. Mwai, the lady whom I was working for as a maid. But she is a busy lady with her women's group and their income-generating activities. Her children are big now.

What do I think about the elections that happened at the end of 1992? Well, I voted but I don't think it made much difference. Your friend, Mrs. Mithamo, was one of the monitors at the polls. People were very orderly. The monitors kept it that way. There were some foreign visitors, too, who were watching. We were told they were there for the UN. But I don't see much change after the elections.

Yes, I've heard of AIDS but we don't talk about it much. We know that it can be passed through sexual relations and people are being urged to use condoms. It is something that affects people in Nairobi more than it affects us here. People in Nairobi tend to have loose morals so they are more apt to get AIDS than we are here.

Even though my life has had its goods and bads since 1984 I would say that except for that year when I was in such pain, things are better for me. We have a better house, our children are in school and doing well, and we are having our wedding. Now we will be married in all ways. That was my goal—for us to be married in the church.

Nyambura and Wacera were married April 14, 1994, in the Catholic church in Kagumo. I was unable to be there, but Karuana, my former research assistant, represented me, presenting my gift with a speech during the formal presentation of wedding gifts.

—J.D.

9

Wanja: Forward-Looking Woman

Wanja lived a greater distance than Nyambura from the compound where I lived. She was often away teaching during the day. This made it more difficult to observe her everyday activities. Our relationship was largely confined to what we shared during interviews and seeing one another at the local Anglican church on Sundays. At the same time, I found Wanja's descriptions, particularly of her childhood, full of insight. She has a keen awareness of what it means to be Gikuyu, and at the same time her dreams and aspirations are tied to a Kenya of the future—one that recognizes educational merit and awards its citizens on the basis of ability rather than age and sex.

Wanja is a single mother with three children. She lives at her parents' homestead and depended in the early 1980s on her father for access to land for cultivation. She was earning a small salary as a part-time nursery school teacher in 1983–1984, but wanted to be fully employed. She has the advantage over Nyambura of more education, and life in a boarding school provided her with new skills and her first taste of independence from home. Because she completed secondary school, Wanja believed in 1984 that she deserved more than the tedious job of picking tea. She yearned to become a business entrepreneur, opening her own shop. At that time she viewed her position as a preschool teacher as merely a stepping-stone to the goal of becoming a shop owner.

As a single parent, Wanja expressed the hope in 1984 that one day she would be able to support her children without the help of her parents. If she were able to obtain her own land, she reasoned, it would enable her to become financially independent. At that time, land of her own and a shop were Wanja's goals.

When I returned in 1994 the first news Wanja told me was that her father had agreed in 1992 to divide his farm equally among his three sons and Wanja. In 1993 they went to register

Wanja

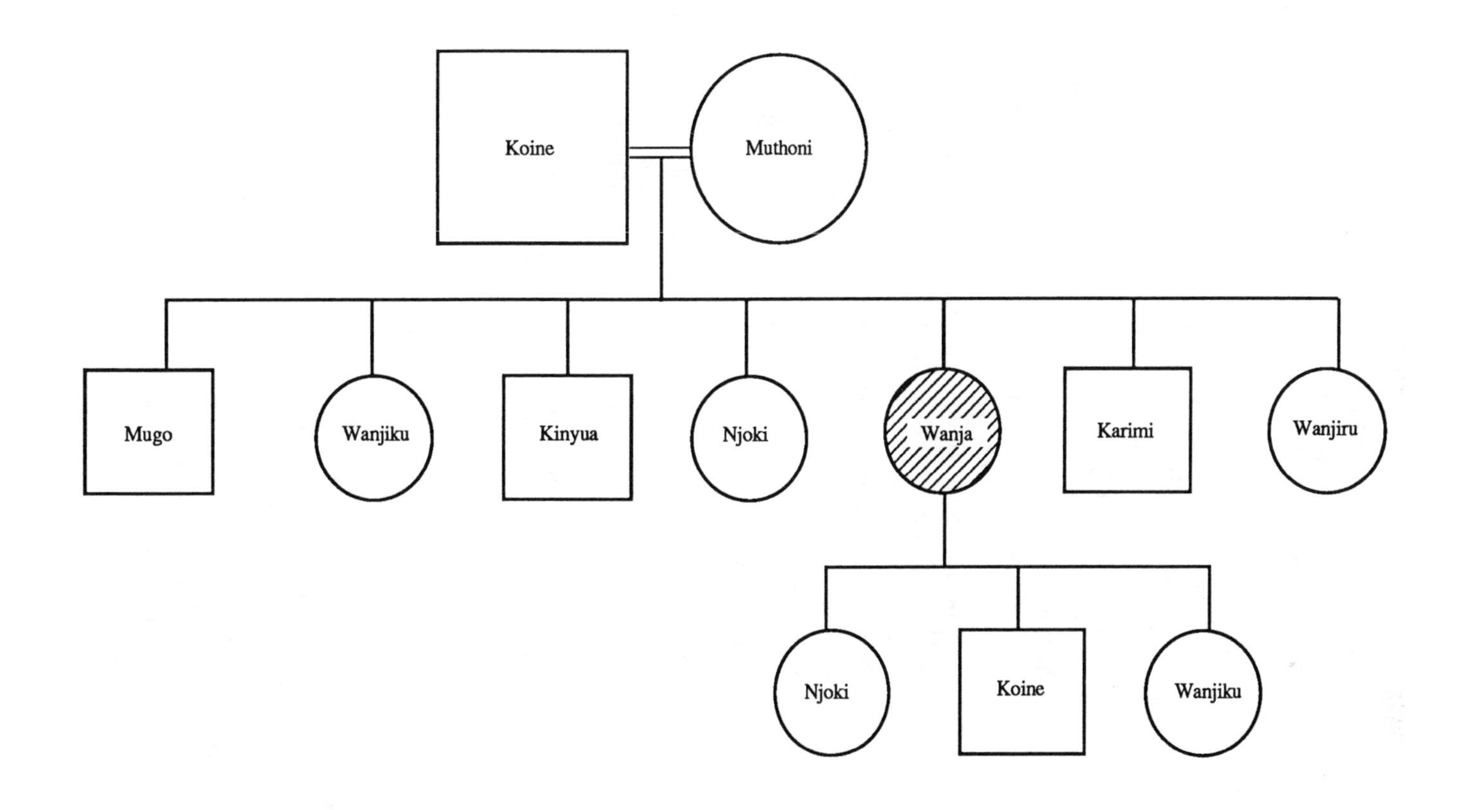
Koine
Muthoni
Mugo
Wanjiku
Kinyua
Njoki
Wanja
Karimi
Wanjiru
Njoki
Koine
Wanjiku

the parcels in their own names and were in the process of getting the title deeds in January 1994. She had built a small shop in Gatwe not far away from where she was teaching.

Wanja's goals, by 1994, had become entwined in a way she could not foresee in 1984. She was balancing full-time teaching with the management of a shop and farm. Income from vegetable and tea production enabled her to employ part-time labor to assist in picking tea and cultivating the gardens. She also hired someone to staff her shop during the hours when she was teaching. She had come to enjoy her work with small children as her own children grew up. She no longer thought of teaching as a temporary position.

Similar to other women in her age category, Wanja had difficulty in 1984 in answering the question, "What does it mean to be a woman?" She agreed with Nyambura that motherhood is a key factor. But beyond this, she was uncertain. The old Gikuyu norms were changing, and educated women like Wanja were seeking new definitions of what it meant to be a woman in the midst of rapid social change. By 1994, Wanja had a much clearer picture, as she explains at the end of her life narrative.

Wanja was much more open and forthcoming in 1994 than she had been earlier. I attribute this to two factors: (1) she had matured and become more sure of herself as a woman; (2) she had gained confidence through the process of acquiring her own parcel of land, developing it, and then building a house for her family. These achievements led to a sense of increased self-worth and empowerment in her thirties. As a competent teacher, a single mother of teenagers, a successful landowner and shopkeeper, Wanja had come of age in her middle years.

—*J.D.*

My father is Wilson Koine and my mother is Mary Muthoni. Everyone in my family has both a Christian and a Gikuyu name. I grew up going to the church at Gatwe, where I am still a member as you know. Wanja is my Gikuyu name, but Nancy is what I was baptized in the Anglican Church.

I am the fifth born. There are seven children, with Mugo the oldest, then Wanjiku, Kinyua, and Njoki just ahead of me and Wanjiru and Karimi behind me. My father has always been a good person—patient and merciful. My mother, too, is patient with her family and faithful spiritually.

She is a member of the church choir—you have seen her there singing on Sundays.

Besides my parents teaching me as I was growing up, my older brother called Kinyua was also a teacher to me. He is eight years older than me and patient like my parents. When I was old enough to go to school, it was Kinyua who helped me with schoolwork. He was employed in Nairobi at the New Stanley Hotel, but he came home every weekend and that's when he used to help me with reading and maths.

When I was young, my parents used to tell me about my clan, Ũnjiku, and our nearest relatives. According to our family, we used to celebrate certain occasions together. For example, if some relatives wanted to slaughter a sheep, they'd call all the members of the family and they would come and share the meat equally. They would slaughter when there was a birth, for a circumcision, or when a girl got married. When the relatives came together, my father would introduce me to them—"This is your aunt who is your mother's sister. This is your uncle who is her brother." The brothers to my father I called *Baba* [Father] when I was growing up, because they were like fathers to me as we lived at the same place. But my mother's brothers, I called them "uncle." I call the sisters to both my father and mother *tata* [aunt]. As for my grandmothers, I never saw them. So slowly I got to know who my relatives were.

My clan refers to where my father came from. Even my oldest sister is called Wanjiku, which means "of the Ũnjiku Clan." My sister is named for my father's clan. The clan is still important to the Agĩkũyũ, and sometimes, when something has to be decided—for example, about land or even bridewealth—the members will call a meeting.

My mother told me that when I was small I loved my oldest sister very much and I often cried anytime I saw her go somewhere, so she rarely left me behind. She would tie me on her back and do her work of gathering wood and fetching water and cooking during the Mau Mau time, when we were in the village and my father had been sent to a British prisoners' camp and my mother was away digging the trench. We were left with my sister during much of that time, because both of my parents were away.

There was no difference between the way my parents treated the boys and the girls in our family. Long ago, the boys—when they got to be about six years [old]—were sent to graze the cows or goats, but now they are fetching water and firewood just like the girls. When I was young I never wished to be a boy, but now I sometimes wish I was a man, because when I'm staying here at home with my parents, if I were a son, I would inherit some property from my father—a piece of land after he dies. But being a woman, we cannot inherit land or property.

I was shown how to do the work of the homestead by my older brothers and sisters and by my mother. If my mother wanted to go to the market, she would go and tell my sisters to go and fetch some water or go to the nearby bush and gather firewood while she was away. I would take a small *sufuria* [metal pot] and follow my sisters to the river, and when I had filled the *sufuria* with water, I would put it on my head and carry it carefully up the hill to our home. But a lot of it spilled out. When I was a small girl, I did not collect firewood until I was a bit older, when I would go with my sister to the bush and start gathering the small pieces. Then she would tie them for me with a *mũkwa* to carry back to the homestead. Sometimes, we would go to the big forest with my mother. We would see a tree that had been cut and she would tell me to gather the small branches but to stay close to her because there are animals in the forest, such as elephants, hyenas, and leopards. That used to scare me. Once, later on, when I was alone with my sister and two other girls, we went into the forest to gather wood and when we reached there, we heard the voice of an animal. We turned and ran out of the forest as fast as we could.

When I was bigger, I started cooking for my baby brother, Karimi. I would make *gitero* [soft food cooked for a baby], using a *muiko* [wooden spoon flattened at one end for mashing]. I'd mash the potatoes and bananas together for Karimi just as I'd seen my sister do, then I would take some that was stuck to the *muiko* off with my finger and put it in my mouth and chew it until it was smooth. I'd put a bit from my mouth on my first finger and push it into Karimi's mouth while he was sitting on my lap.

About 1961, when I was almost nine years [old], I began to pick tea. I can remember this because I was in Standard One at the time. I used to go with my mother to the tea fields, and I would care for my small brother while she picked tea. I would stay at the side of the field, playing with Karimi or feeding him under a tree. Then, when he fell asleep, my mother would call me to come and start picking. While she was picking, I could see that she picked two leaves and a bud. I first started picking with one hand, slowly, putting each stem I picked into the other hand to hold until I got a bunch. Then I put the bunch into my mother's large tea basket, called a *gikabu,* that she carried on her back. I continued that way, picking with one hand at a time. Then, later, I saw that people were picking with two hands, and I tried it because you can get a speed in picking that way. Each is a different way of picking, and I learned both by watching what my mother and others were doing—they didn't have to tell me how to do it. I just saw for myself. On Saturdays and during holidays—that's when I would pick tea, because during the week I was in school.

I can't remember the first day I went to school, but I know I went alone with my older sister Njoki. When we got there, we were introduced to the teacher and went out to play. We were not taught anything that first day. But later, we learned to write by practicing on the ground with our fingers what we had seen in the class. We began number work by using maize kernels, beans, and pieces of stone to count.

What was a typical day in Standard Five? Well, I went to school at Kiamaina, so we'd start for school from here at 6:00 A.M. and reach school at around 7:00. There were morning studies for one hour until 8:00, then we went for assembly. We used to sing songs during assembly, and some passages from the Bible were read to us. Then we had a prayer and went to classes at 8:15. Depending upon how the timetable was arranged, sometimes we'd start with maths and other times with English. During the morning break we would go to the field and play with balls, beanbags, or we'd play *ciũthi,* tossing stones up in the air and catching them on the backs of our hands. Another game we played was called "rounder." The children would divide into two groups. One group made a circle outside and the other group inside. Then spikes or sticks would be placed in a large circle. There was a ball and a stick shaped like a *muiko.* One person from inside the circle would throw the ball to the one outside who was holding the *muiko.* The one outside would aim and hit the ball very far and then drop the stick and run round the circle and when the ball was caught, the person running would stop at the nearest spike. Each time the ball was hit, that person would run round the spikes until he/she had completed the circle and won.

After the last class of the morning there was a time for lunch. I did not go home—I carried a packed lunch. In the afternoons, we had handywork or subjects like geography or history. The teacher used to write on the blackboard, and we children would read the lesson from there and copy it in our notebooks. We would start for home at 4:30 P.M.

Sometimes after school, we would play games when our work was done—games like *ciũthi,* rounder, and *nginyangi. Nginyangi* refers to false walking legs—a pair of poles with a support for each foot [stilts]. The person would get up on the supports and try and see how far she could walk without falling.

When I was in primary school—in Standard One—the teacher told us to make a basket and bring it to school. I didn't know how to go about it, so my mother showed me how to make one. She taught me by showing me how she made the circle weaving of strings that would later support the basket. Then she showed me how she took the threads and wove through the main strings being sure that the threads were tight. At first it seemed very hard. When she finished a basket, I took the short strings left over and made my own small *kiondo.* That was my first basket, and I took it to school. But my mother did not know how to knit, so I taught myself later how to do that by watching a friend knit.

Before there were books, children used to learn from stories, riddles, and proverbs told by the adults. Stories were given at night and sometimes riddles, too. But proverbs could be given anytime. There's one proverb I remember—"*Kahora, kahora karĩ indo*" ["Slowly, slowly gets things done."] There are two others I remember. One is "*Kaihu gacanga cangi gatigaga kwao gũgĩthĩnjo,*" which means "One who moves about and never stays at home, leaves a goat being slaughtered there but never eats it because he/she is never around." My mother would also say, "*Rurigi rũrĩ nja rutiagaga gĩakũoha*"—"A string outside does not miss anything to tie." She would use this one when one of us children had just thrown something outside that might be useful sometime.

Before our mother told us a story, she said, "*Itho a.*" This meant that a story was beginning. Those listening would reply, "*Itho.*" Then a story, like this one, would begin:

Long ago, there was an old mother bird and a young bird. The mother bird was very old and could not even go to the river. One day, she told the young bird to go for water so she could have a drink. The young bird refused, saying that it was going to dance *kibata.* The mother bird grew very thirsty and, at last, died because of thirst. But before she did, she cursed the young bird, telling it that it would never be able to take water from the river again, but only water from rain. And so, until this day, that bird takes only the water that drops on the leaves of plants.

What did I learn from the story? It taught us not to ignore our elders, to do what we are told unless we want something bad to happen to us. Even today, I remind my children that they must respect the elders and always obey what they say.

These were the kinds of things we were learning at home from our parents while we were learning other things from the teachers at school. By the time I got to Standard Seven, we had a lot more work to do, because it was the last year of primary school and we were busy reviewing and preparing for the C.P.E. [Certificate of Primary Education Examination]. It was also during that year that I got my first menstrual period. I remember the day because I was in school, and I started feeling aches along my backbone and in my lower abdomen. I came home that afternoon, but I never told anybody. I knew what had happened, because I had learned about menstruation from other girls of my age. They had taught me what to do when the time comes. My mother never told me about it.

The morning of the examination, I woke very early and took my pens and went to school. I went into the room where we were to have the examination and took the seat I was assigned. The examiners came and gave us the papers, and we worked on them the whole day. Some were difficult. During that day, our parents and relatives were saying prayers for us so we might pass. I was very tired when it was over and just prayed that I had passed. But it took a whole month before we heard the results. I was lucky and found I passed, so I could qualify for secondary school.

We found out the results in January, and I did not go to secondary school until that September, so I had some months home to pick the tea and help with my young sister. Because Wanjiku was married by then, it was my work to fetch water and to wash the clothes. This took me about three hours. Also, I had to sweep the compound and cook the lunch while my mother was working in the *shamba.* If I finished that work, then I helped pick tea leaves.

My father got a letter telling us I was accepted by a school down at Mwea—where the rice scheme is. I left home in September. In Kenya, most of our secondary schools are boarding schools, so we live at the school. When I got to the school in Mwea, I found so many girls from all over Kenya—Kiambu, Murang'a, even Kisumu. In primary school I had worn a smock with a blouse, but in secondary school we wore a uniform that was a dark blue skirt, a white blouse and a blue sweater. We also had to wear black shoes.

At first when I got there I was a bit scared, but I gradually got used to the place. During the weekdays, we'd wake up at 6:00 A.M., I'd go to the bathroom and bathe, then dress in my uniform. Breakfast was at 7:00 and was usually porridge. Then we had to go back and straighten up our bunks and clean the dorm before going to classes. The dorms were long rooms with rows of metal bunks on each side. Each girl had a box that she kept her things in at the end of the bed. We had to keep the dorm clean by washing the floors regularly. And in the dorm we were not allowed to speak Kikuyu. We were required to speak in English because that is what our lessons were in.

At 7:30, we would go in to study for half an hour, then there were morning prayers. At 8:30, we started the lessons of the day. We stayed in classes until 10 and then we broke for morning tea, which everyone liked. Then back to classes until 12:30 P.M., when we went for lunch in the dining hall. Lunch was usually *githeri* [maize and beans]. There were afternoon classes beginning at 2:30, and later, after classes were over, we'd go for general cleaning of the classrooms and compound, games like netball, and, at times, club meetings like the Young Christians Club or Young Farmers Club. I joined the Young Christians Club.

From four to six o'clock was the time for personal cleaning, like washing our clothes. At six was supper—usually *githeri* with some vegetables or *ugali.* After supper, we went for preps—preparations for the next day's classes—and were in bed by nine o'clock. I can remember one time, when I was in Form Two, during prep time, one of the girls switched off the kerosene lantern. The teacher on duty came and asked who had done it. When she found out, she wrote down the girl's name, and the following morning the girl was taken to our headmaster and was beaten. But usually when somebody did something she was disciplined by talks.

The curriculum for our lessons was to prepare us to take the O-levels (ordinary secondary school examinations] at the end of Form Four. We had English and Kiswahili, and some girls took French. We also took history and geography, and health science because we did not have a laboratory for other sciences at the school. If a person did well on the O-levels, she could go on to high school for two more years and then take the A-levels (advanced level examinations). Only those who do very well in their A-levels have a chance at the university. I finished Form Four, but I did not do well on my O-levels, so I stopped there.

I found secondary school very different from primary because we had new subjects like biology and commerce that we'd never had before. The teachers were different, too, because they gave us a lot of tests and were more educated than primary school teachers. Most of the teachers at our school were men, even though we were all girls.

After I finished Form Four, I came home here to live. By that time I was nearly twenty. It was that year I became pregnant by a man from here. When that happened, I knew that I was no longer a girl. I started to think of what course I would take or where I would be employed. When a girl has her first child, she becomes a *mũtũmia* regardless of whether she has a husband or not.

I have not gone through any of the traditional transitions like *mbuci* and *matũ* or even *Irua*. But I have heard of other girls being circumcised, though it is against the law now. I was a young girl when I saw a group of girls being circumcised, one after the other. That was sometime in the 1960s. But today one would not know if her agemates are circumcised or not—we don't talk about it. Sometimes one reads in the newspapers about a girl dying because she was circumcised badly. That is to let those who would try it know it is unsafe. Most of these old traditions I do not see as important, because they only take people backwards, not like Christianity, which came to take people forward and brought development. Even *mariika* [age groups] are not important anymore. A Form Two girl and a Form Four girl are no different because none of them is yet a mother. But if one of them has a child, then they cannot be of the same *riika*. Before, *Irua* made the difference, but now that it is no longer practiced, the only division is when a girl becomes a mother. Then she finds herself with a new kind of responsibility.

* * *

After I finished school and came home here to live, I was cultivating and picking tea. I had my first child—my daughter—in the hospital. Most younger women today prefer hospital births. Then I began living with another man down at Kerugoya who I thought would be my husband and had two more children by him. But things didn't work out and I came back home to my parents. I felt very disappointed that after completing my education I wasn't able to find a good job. I hoped to find a job as a primary school teacher, but there were no openings. Finally after staying here for awhile, I got a job teaching old people like my mother at the adult education class. It was not easy teaching there because those women didn't know how to read, but they were older than me. Also, they never came regularly. Sometimes, I was not paid on time either. I taught there for two years, and then the class stopped, so I was home here again without a job.

During that time I was helping my mother pick the tea leaves and cultivate the *shamba.* We have about one and a half acres of tea and other small plots for cultivating food crops. But the money from tea cultivation goes to my father. Then he gives some to my mother and me. My father helps prune the tea bushes, but he does not do much picking. He is usually away on some business. He is on the church committee, so he is busy.

The only food crop my father cultivates is yams—that is a man's crop. Sometimes he helps by preparing the land for maize, and he helps with the maize harvest. My mother is very clever. She saw that women in Mwea were earning good money with their pineapples, so now she has planted a small field to see if they will grow up here. She also grows a lot of garden vegetables like cabbages, tomatoes, garden peas, and carrots. Though my father has given me a piece of land, I usually plant maize and beans. I would like to have a big enough parcel of land to grow tea. Then I could make a profit.

About a year ago, I was invited to apply to the nursery school near Gathũthũma. They wanted somebody who had some teaching experience, so I was taken. I like teaching nursery school, because I am helping the young children to get knowledgeable. Because I stayed for a time at home without employment, I can only thank God for giving me this job. While I am at school, the two younger children are here with my mother, but the oldest girl goes to school now.

If I were married, would I want my husband to give *rũracio?* No. That is one of those traditions of the past. When my mother was married, my father gave so many goats and cattle, but today a man is expected to give shillings if a girl has been to school. Sometimes the relatives ask for a lot of shillings if a girl has completed Form Six or gone to university. But I think it is a stupidity. It makes it seem like a girl is nothing but an object if a man must pay a cash price to marry her. I would not want a man to pay *rũracio* for me because then he would feel he has complete control over me and can do what he wants, even beating me if he feels like it! To me, that tradition is meaningless in today's world.

Nowadays a woman has to be self-sufficient, because you can't depend on a husband. Whether a woman is married or not makes no difference, you are still responsible for your children. Of all my roles, I think the one of mother is most important. That's the one that changed me the most because now I began to think about how to get money to buy clothes for my children and, later, to take them to school.

Farming and housework are the next most important. Living with my parents, I have to help cultivate and pick tea, do the cooking, and other things. Next, I would say that my role as a teacher is important because I like children, and the job gives me the money I need to help my children. Being a member of the church group is less important, but I like going because I meet my friends and we do things together. There is one role missing—I am a member of the church choir, too, but that role is least important.

The thing I'm proudest of is being a mother to my three children—that I am able to feed and clothe them well. What do I think of family planning? It is a good idea if one has the number of children she wants. Some women my age are having too many children—like rabbits, one after the other. Also, some girls get pregnant while they are still in school and it may not be their fault. A teacher [male] can play dirty tricks with a girl and then she ends up pregnant. And there are the "sugar daddies"—those who come and seduce schoolgirls. They are the ones who offer to buy a girl things—like new shoes or a dress—if the girl will become their friend. Usually, a girl is too young to understand and then she gets pregnant. She is forced to leave school and go home to her parents. It is a problem.

About my future dreams? I would like to be a businesswoman. I want to have a shop and sell things. If I could save enough money from picking tea leaves, then I could get a shop. My strongest character is being obedient—like now I obey my parents, because I have to depend upon them. I can't think of my weakest character—I don't think I have one. Being a woman means having children and taking care of them and the home. I think of myself first as Mũgĩkũyu because I speak the language. I was born Mũgĩkũyu. I only became a Kenyan citizen when we got our independence in 1963.

How do I think schooling differs from how we learned at home? At school we had certain lessons that had to be learned and these were put on the blackboard and we learned them by copying the teacher. There are subjects we had to learn in order to pass the examinations, whether we might need them or not. But in learning things at home, like cultivating and picking tea, nobody made us learn. We just went out and learned those things on our own in the best way that suited us. The trouble with the things one learns in school is that one may not be able to use what is learned unless one is lucky enough to get a job. But going to school is important these days so one can learn how to read and write and do figures. If I did not go to school, I would not be able to teach others or think of beginning my own business. So each is important in its own way.

I met Wanja at her homestead in January 1994. The first thing I noticed was a new stone house. Wanja told me she had saved enough from the proceeds of tea production and teaching so that she was able to build a new, more permanent house for her parents and herself in 1992. She added that the tea strike had not helped her as it had threatened the progress of construction. Nonetheless, the house was completed by the end of 1992. Wanja took real pleasure in showing me the solid house she had built. She led me to the sitting room for our visit. I noticed that the old timber house where I had met her in 1983–1984 had been demolished. Wanja continues with her life reflections . . .

—J.D.

The thing that satisfies me the most now is having my own land. We were each given an acre of land. The parcel that my father gave me is down near the river. The soil is fertile there. I plant vegetables and maize that we sell in the market, and I have tea planted further up. I also rent tea plants from a neighbor so I can have them picked to earn additional income. Because I am busy teaching I pay a laborer Ksh. 1.50 per kilo to pick the tea bushes. The person responsible—usually the owner—earns Ksh. 4.50 per kilo. For the bushes I rented I get paid this money. [Wanja realizes a profit of Ksh. 3.00 per kilo but pays a third of it back in rent.] I am doing well enough to pay for my daughters' schooling and even to pay the taxes on one of my brother's parcels. Of my two brothers, two are here growing tea. The other one stays in Nairobi.

My three children are nearly grown. Njoki—do you remember her?—she completed Form 4 last year. She's away for National Youth Service [a postsecondary requirement for students that combines community service work and military training prior to further studies]. You just met Wanjiku [she had served us tea]. She is in Form 3 at Ngaru Girls School and doing very well. She helps me a lot here at home. Koine [Wanja's son] applied for Kenya Polytechnic last year but has not been admitted yet. I have no complaints about my children.

Yes, it's very expensive these days to send a child to secondary school. But I saved money from tea production and teaching and managed to pay their fees. The cost of everything has gone up. I see that when stocking my *nduka* [shop] in Gatwe. We carry small essentials that everyone needs, like Omo [powered detergent], cooking oil, sugar, and bread.

But the cost of transporting these goods to rural areas like Gatwe adds to the cost.

Where is my *nduka*? It's near the new secondary school. I got it in 1990. Now I employ a woman part-time to manage the shop while I am teaching. But after school hours I go to the shop to make sure that things are running smoothly. I also go there on weekends, especially after church on Sundays as that is when we get a lot of business as other *nduka* are often closed. That is the day that people get visitors so a *mũtũmia* will find herself having to cook but she may have forgotten some small thing. *Ĩĩ*, I work so hard between the shop, teaching, and managing the farm that I'm exhausted by nightfall. All I want to do is sleep.

The thing that has made the biggest difference to tea growers like me [in the last decade] is the new tea factory and four new tea-buying stations. One was built near the Catholic church on the road to Kagumo. Another was built at Kianduku and another at Kiambungu. Having more tea-weighing stations means that people don't have to wait so long to sort and weigh their tea before it is taken to the factory. It was taking until nightfall to complete the task before, but now people can get home in time to prepare supper. Also we are better paid for the tea leaves.

Another positive change has been the building of the new secondary school at Gatwe. It was built through *harambee* efforts in 1988. I have seen in my own life that education is very important. That is why I wanted to make sure that my daughters and son had at least a secondary school education. There was a shortage of secondary schools in Mutira Location but now things are improving. More children are able to go beyond primary school. But now it seems that there are not enough jobs in places like Kerugoya or Kagumo to employ all the children who complete their secondary level. One has to have a university degree or additional training. Njoki will go for a secretarial course once she has completed the National Youth Service. She did not get a place in university. Then hopefully she will get a position somewhere.

I have now become the major "breadwinner" in our family. My parents are too old to be of much help in the gardens. Yes, when you last saw us my mother was trying to grow pineapples to sell. But the weather gets a bit cold up here so she decided to give that up. She helps out with my brothers' children now. I saw that my parents needed someone to take care of them so when I built this house I made sure that it has a place for them. They are satisfied.

Yes, I have heard of AIDS. But up here [in Gatwe] people are not thinking too much about it. Malaria is a problem for us now. We never used to have the malaria-carrying mosquitos because it was too cold up here. We thought we were safe. But these days there is malaria here so it looks like those mosquitos got immune to the cold. Also pneumonia and TB [tuberculosis] are problems, especially in the cold season. What we need is a clinic at Gatwe. But the government is not helping us here because we did not vote for Moi.

I voted [in 1992] even though I don't see a difference. It will take some time for things to change. Did you hear that a woman was elected MP [Member of Parliament] from Kirinyaga? Yes, finally we have a woman there. I don't know if it will help though. At least women can inherit land and have a title deed. Men are not trustworthy so it's good to have one's own land and resources. Even with brothers I can say that.

Women are known for their generosity and hospitality. But actually these are not traits associated with one woman—they are attached to a household. It is the women in a particular household that together have these traits, not any single woman. For instance, in this home it is Wanjiku who served you tea that my mother had made. And I am talking with you. So together, as a household, we are showing hospitality. People living close together want to live in peace, and having a code of conduct like generosity and hospitality helps to maintain communal tranquility. If the government would use this code, maybe we wouldn't be having so many problems.

What kind of problems? Problems such as scarcity of goods and the low value of the shilling. Transportation has become a problem. Look at our roads. They are in very bad condition with too many potholes. There is no effort to fix them. And the *matatus* (vans) are the same old ones you saw. There is little difference. I have problems when I order goods for my *nduka* to get them up to Gatwe. And sometimes I have to go to Kerugoya to get shipments. But at least Kerugoya has a new post office since you were here. That's one improvement.

I have no time to join a women's group but I still sing in the church choir. I like that. Are you going to the church on Sunday? Everyone will be surprised to see you again. [I explained that I was on a tight schedule and couldn't stay through Sunday.] Next time you should spend more time here.

What do I think it means to be a woman now? It means being able to stand on one's own two feet, having one's own money to be able to send her children to school and not depend on others. It means being able to manage a clean, well-ordered home. In my case it also means being able to manage other people like the children at school, the people I hire to help me in the *nduka* and those in the gardens or picking tea. It means being able to keep the books so that one knows the budget and how much money is in the bank. Also managing my children to see that they don't wander and that they get the best education possible.

Women have many things to do at once, at the same time. It's not like we do one thing and then the next. All are occurring at the same time. So we have to be good managers. I think I have learned to be a good manager. Yes, and people respect me. They see I have helped develop my home. Someday maybe I will have enough money to buy some more land and develop it the way I have developed my land here. I know now that such things are possible. Ten years ago I wouldn't have dreamed of such a thing; women change, too, even though we think we don't. In the future my daughters may have more opportunities than I did. One might even be a big person in a company—a manager. That could happen. No one can tell about another person's life, even your own children's.

10

The Life Histories in Retrospect

Time is an illusion that, like an accordion, gets stretched or compressed depending on the way we perceive the melody of our lives. In this collection seven women's lives are caught like slivers of glass in the kaleidoscope of a constantly changing twentieth century. Historical incidents, defying distance, cast shadows larger than reality and shape future options. Cultural responses mediate history, creating new formations among old patterns. Individual experiences and personal talents mark each woman's life with bold brushstrokes, capturing her uniqueness, shaping her development.

In the process of creating and re-creating her life, each woman uses a variety of skills learned through daily living. Observation and imitation from earliest childhood provide the cultural scaffolding for future competence as adults. Listening to elders opens the way to a rich network of relationships extending back in time to Mumbi and Gikuyu. Stories become models for future behavior. Ritual events form arenas in which youth test their readiness for the next life stage and learn the secrets of their elders. Discovering new talents under adverse conditions as an adult leads to changed perceptions of self. Recalling old events, long forgotten, makes possible a perspective from which to view change and one's place in social history.

The Impact of Sociocultural Change

Changing Rites of Passage

When asked in the second session to list all the major changes in their lives, the older informants named *mbuci* and *matũ*, *Irua* and *ũhiki* (marriage). It was only later that idiosyncratic events were acknowledged as having brought changes. At one time ethnographies gave us the impression that *rites de passage* are traditions impervious to change. We now know that these rituals, like the people who perform them, change according to new circumstances and needs, just as other facets of culture change. I analyze in this section transformations in Gikuyu cultural rites of passage between 1914 and 1994 as perceived by the life narrators.

Mambura ma twana. Even though some of the narrators had participated in *mambura ma twana* (the children's ceremony that removes a child from her mother's bed), it was not mentioned as an important rite perhaps because it is least remembered. The women in their fifties in 1984 slid over the event, acknowledging that it may have occurred but not supplying much information. Neither of the younger women knew of it. Only Wanjiku, the oldest woman, remembered it in some detail. It appears that *mambura ma twana*, although it is mentioned in the early colonial anthropological literature (e.g., Routledge and Routledge 1910; Hobley 1910), may have died out in Mutira by the second third of the twentieth century. It may be that missionization (the conversion of Gikuyu to Christianity with the draw of health and education services) had an impact on this rite of passage. First, the Christian ceremony that occurs in a child's infancy, baptism, was perceived as a cleansing ceremony, a purification rite performed with the sprinkling of water. It was identified with the washing away of original sin and entrance into a church community. On the other hand, the purification identified with *mambura ma twana* entailed the slaughtering of a goat, with a strip of the goat's skin being tied across a baby's chest to signify a physical break between the child and her mother to allow the latter to resume sexual relations with her husband. Such a ritual, if witnessed by Christian missionaries, could only have been judged "primitive" and "unhealthy" given their propensity for cleanliness. Additionally the explicit acknowledgement of the resumption of sexual relations after weaning may have further alienated Christian sensibilities. It is likely that *mambura ma twana* is a ritual that the missionaries discouraged early on.

Mbuci and matũ—the ear piercings. The older women who had had their ears pierced—*mbuci* and *matũ*—did remember this rite of passage. By the time a girl went through *mbuci* and *matũ* at the age of eleven or twelve, she was old enough to understand that it marked the first stage of separation from childhood in the life of a Gikuyu girl. Moreover, ear piercing was a prerequisite for *Irua*—that most important of all rites.

The narrative details of *mbuci* and *matũ* vary from one woman to the next, depending upon personality and family circumstances. Thus, Wamutira went with a sister to have her ears pierced at her mother's urging, whereas Wanoi had to pierce her own ears in secret because her oldest brother opposed *matũ*. In almost all cases, permission for *mbuci* and *matũ* was secured from the uncle, the mother's oldest brother. Wamutira admits that *matũ* was painful, and Watoro relates that *mbuci* became infected. Both piercings seem to be visual symbols of a historic past and are rarely seen in women below the age of thirty-five. In fact, a number of older women have had *matũ* stitched up to prevent the holes from being caught on something.

Irua—the transition to adulthood. It is *Irua* that marked the real transition in social status from girl to woman. Mũriũki, the Gikuyu historian, says of *Irua:*

> In the absence of any formal centre of instruction, initiation served as one of the main educational channels in Kikuyu society. This education was both practical and theoretical and covered such fields as tribal traditions, religion, folklore, modes of behaviour and the duties of adults, taboos and sex. Also, the initiates were invested with important roles, responsibilities and privileges in the social system [1974:119].

Although Mũriũki mentions religion and folklore, there is very little evidence of these in the life history accounts of *Irua.* My guess is that the reason lies in gender-specific spheres of knowledge—spiritual knowledge, in particular, was linked with males. Male, rather than female, elders acted as intermediaries with Ngai and offered prayers on behalf of the community. It is for this reason that one finds no female *mũndũ mugo*—shamanism belonged to the realm of men.

What Gikuyu women learned from female relatives concerning expectations of adult behavior and sexuality during *Irua* prepared them for accompanying responsibilities. *Irua,* as a ritual transition, created a disequilibrium that Vizedom (1976) compares to the transitions that occur between developmental stages of growth. For the Gikuyu, *Irua* was characterized by disequilibrium—a liminal state in which the norms of behavior were suspended in the act of transmitting a new set of adult, gender-specific norms that served to reorient a girl's status to that of a woman. For girls, as for boys, circumcision was part of the ritual process that enabled the initiate to assume a new sexual and a new social status. Turner's (1969:53) observation that "powerful drives and emotions associated with human physiology, especially the physiology of reproduction, are divested in the ritual process of their antisocial quality and attached to components of the moral order" is applicable to *Irua* as it historically was practiced.

Older women describe the process by which gender role expectations were transmitted by women elders through ritualized dance and songs during the ceremony. At the same time, a girl's biological sex was dramatized, with its accompanying potential for reproduction. The physical act of removing *rong'otho* (the clitoris) freed a Gikuyu female from categorical ambiguity, while it signaled her readiness to assume sexual relations upon marriage. But each woman's experience of *Irua* differed. Some went as part of a group, others with only one other girl. Wanoi was circumcized against her family's wishes.

Not only status and gender became crystalized, but relations between age groups were delineated with membership in a particular *riika.* *Irua* had an integrative role in enabling a girl to gain access to an age set that had both historical and social significance. Historically, the attachment of a *riika* name provided a means of keeping track of events, as each age group was identified with an event that occurred concurrently with *Irua.* Socially, *riika* meant identification with a "sisterhood" that provided solidarity and mutual aid throughout the life span. Finally, *Irua* was an enabling process that allowed the mother and father of the initiate to assume new role statuses as elders in the community. Formerly, such a transition included eligibility for the *kiama* (council of elders), as we learn from Wanjiku's narrative.

At the individual level, each woman describes how she felt personally transformed by the experience. States Wamutira, "After I had gone through *Irua,* I felt different. I felt like I was a grown-up girl now, ready for dances. And everybody termed us as adults. . . . Nowadays, you wouldn't know who is mature and who isn't."

Irua marked the transition to adulthood for older women, but the two women in their twenties did not go through the ritual. All of the older women were intensely interested in talking about the social changes that have occurred surrounding *Irua,* as the discussion between Wamutira and her co-wives illustrates. Though none of the women believes the operation itself is beneficial, most feel that the end of *Irua* in terms of its symbolic meaning for the age-grade system is detrimental to the Gikuyu way of life. Wangeci even goes so far as to suggest that young women today are *outside* the culture: "*Irua* has no meaning to Agĩkũyũ girls today because now they have become people of a different culture. The only important thing to them is schooling—to pass or fail."

By the time Wanja and Nyambura were eligible for *Irua* in the late 1970s, female circumcision no longer stood as a nationalist symbol for the Gikuyu, and both girls' parents had converted to Christianity. The Gikuyu, now in power, had embraced "modernization." Though Wanja indicates that "female circumcision" was still prevalent in Mutira when she was a girl in the 1960s, by the mid-1970s educated Christian women were questioning the relevance of clitoridectomy.

Brought to the forefront of discussions at the UN Decade of Women Conference in Copenhagen in 1980, "female circumcision" in its various forms became an issue between African and Euro-American women, with the latter assuming a feminist stance that African women were unprepared for. All forms of female circumcison were labeled "genital mutilation" by Western feminists who set out to abolish practices of infibulation, excision, and clitoridectomy. The essentializing of various practices under one rubric—genital mutiliation—for political purposes alienated many African women, including Kenyans, who saw Western feminists as gynocentric and ethnocentric, to the point of being hegemonic in their attitudes. At the same time, media coverage in Kenya of the medical dangers involved in clitoridectomizing young women under often-unsterile conditions began to appear. International opinion condemning the operation added fuel to the fire. Urban, educated women joined the debate. Under such pressure, a ban on female circumcision was initiated by President Moi in 1982.

All of the life history informants, except the oldest, Wanjiku, were aware of the ban and supported its intent—at least to me. Though one woman in her fifties confidentially told me that her oldest daughter had been circumcised, none of the other women with daughters desired to have her daughters go through the same kind of pain she had experienced. What accounts for the change in attitudes over the twenty-year period?

First, although clitoridectomy was viewed as a symbol of cultural loyalty (and as a symbol of defiance against European colonialism) during the Mau Mau struggle, it no longer had the same significance once independence was gained. Second, the postindependence conversion of many Gikuyu women to Christianity, with its accompanying lessons—Wanoi cites the fact that the Biblical Mary was uncircumcised as a basis for her changed attitudes—made clitoridectomy less meaningful. Finally, the impact of formal schooling, which acts as a modernizing agent, including the transmission of Western values, contributed to a social climate in which a cultural tradition slowly gave way to health considerations and progress. The rationale currently given by Gikuyu women for no longer practicing clitoridectomy is based not on sexual rights or sexuality (except among educated urban feminists), but on health dangers—cited by Wamutira—and cultural asynchronicity, illustrated by Wanja and Nyambura's comments that *Irua* no longer has meaning.

If *Irua*, in fact, no longer takes place, how then do younger women know when they have made the transition to adult status? Nyambura has an answer: "When you are a girl and then give birth, you find that you are changed. Your body features change . . . and shows that you are no longer a girl. And you change mentally, too, because you are always thinking about your children. So you have gone from girlhood to womanhood." Wanja concurs: "Before, *Irua* made the difference (between girls and women), but now that it is no longer practiced, the only division is when a girl becomes a mother."

Today's young Gikuyu women lack the ritually marked social transition from girlhood to womanhood that their mothers and grandmothers experienced. At the same time, there seems to be a felt need on their parts to validate their transition to adult female status. In place of a socially recognized event they seek a biologically recognized event to mark the transition. Motherhood, with or without marriage, has taken the place of *Irua* as the validating event. Such a change in attitude, has, in part, led an increasing number of young women to have children outside marriage.

This phenomenon concerns both young women like Nyambura and Wanja and older women like Wanjiku and Wangeci who often find themselves responsible for the child care of their daughters' children.

Ũhiki—marriage as a sequential rite. In addition to *Irua*, the five older women refer to *ũhiki* as being a significant change in their lives, one that marked a geographical, physical separation from their families. Marriage is a transition not only in social status but in location. Even in 1994, a girl leaves her father's homestead and travels with her husband to his homestead to live if they are not already cohabitating. Attending several Christian weddings while in Mutira where women escorted the bride to her husband's compound once the Christian ceremony was completed confirmed this practice. A bride's attitudes toward relocation vary depending on the historical period of time in which she was married and on her relationship to the man she is marrying.

All the older women expressed sadness at leaving their natal homes when they married, and some even resisted on the way, as we learn from Wamutira: "I went slowly with Murage, sometimes sitting down because I did not want to go. Sometimes I wondered whether I could escape and go back home, but then I was threatened with a beating and I would start walking again."

When a woman marries, she becomes a part of her husband's extended family. Though she will see members of her own family and clan during ceremonies and visits, her affiliation is now with her husband's people, and any children she bears will be members of his clan.[1] For the older women, the first month was often spent isolated in the sleeping quarters of the husband's mother's house as a sign of respect for the older woman. The bride was being symbolically reborn as the daughter of her husband's mother, according to Wangeci: "She [sister-in-law] took me to Ngiricĩĩ's mother's house. Ngiricĩĩ's mother lit a fire but I went into the room where the bed was . . . to show that now I had become her child."

Fear and loneliness were not uncommon feelings at such a time, as Wamutira and Watoro testify. The young bride was, and still is, very much at the beck and call of her mother-in-law. The isolation period constituted a form of marital apprenticeship, when the new wife learned from the older woman the normative behavior expected of married women. Wanjiku (the oldest woman) relates: "When I first came here, I stayed in Wamai's mother's house. . . . During the time when I was staying with the mother, I was observing how she was cooking food and taking care of her house. She also gave me *kirira*." *Kirira* consisted of the secret knowledge and moral codes that only older people knew and had the power to share with younger ones. Watoro relates that her husband's mother warned her not to wander, or stray, from the husband. Wangeci learned that she should not sleep with her husband if she were having her menstrual period.

If a newly married woman was a second or third wife, she had to adjust to co-wives and their personalities, as Watoro and Muthoni, Wamutira's younger co-wife, explain. Watoro, upon arriving at her husband's compound, suddenly realized that the eldest wife was angry with her husband for taking a second wife. "Wangui, the first wife, was there, and I could tell she was not happy to see me. That scared me. Right away she started screaming and abusing me. She had known me before, but now she had different feelings because she didn't want the husband to marry another wife. He insisted. . . . I learned that she had had no say in the marriage. So she and I stayed that way, abusing one another."

Being a young wife in the husband's compound was not always a pleasant experience. Homesickness and feelings of inadequacy might plague a woman for the first time. LeVine and Pfeifer (1982:66) point out that among Gusii women in Western Kenya, a new wife relocated to her husband's home tends to idealize her natal home. "From a distance her parents appear generous and wise, her siblings and grandparents are remembered as loving, and the family farm seems bountiful, in contrast to the ambivalence, coldness and depriving circumstances of her new home."

At the same time, a young woman knows that once *rũracio* has been exchanged, she has a commitment to make her marriage work. She must obey her husband now, as she obeyed her parents in the past. Wanjiku explains the advice she got prior to marriage: "My mother warned me that if people (at the husband's place) discovered I had *ng'aa* and did not care for other people there, the *rũracio* might be taken back because it showed that I was one who could not be ruled. . . . 'Now that you are going to your husband's place,' she said, 'you are no longer in my hands, but under your husband's care and rule. Respect him and do what he wants.'"

From the life histories, we learn that marriage was actually a sequentially arranged series of rituals. First came formal exchanges of tobacco and beer. Second were the negotiations for *rũracio*, followed by *gũthokia*—the period during which a young woman shared beer or porridge with the young man's friends. The third event was *gũthinjiro*, a blood sacrifice that bound the two extended families together. Finally, the bride went to her husband's homestead, where she served an apprenticeship in the house of her husband's mother that could last anywhere from a month to three years. The last ritual was *kumanda*, when a bride was officially welcomed by her parents-in-law into her own house and could start residing with her husband. The last ritual was a significant moment for the bride, because it symbolized her mother-in-law's willingness to allow her to cook for her son and to sleep with him. It also meant that the young wife had to do more things for herself, as Watoro explains: "When I moved there, I found a big change because now I was required to fetch my own firewood. . . . I was fetching my own water and washing my own utensils and keeping the house clean all by myself."

In 1995, most steps described by the older women have disappeared, with the exception of *rũracio*. Bridewealth is still an accepted practice, though it has become capitalized, with the transfer of shillings as well as herd animals. The amount of shillings is dependent upon the bride's level of education, with university-educated women's families' receiving the highest amounts. It is for this reason that young women like Wanja (and my research assistant) rejected the idea of *rũracio*. They felt that attaching a monetary value to bridewealth commoditizes the wife and gives too much power to the husband. However, not all young women agree. Nyambura, for example, views *rũracio* as a validating aspect of marriage, one that she supports as a sign of respect for the bride's parents.

Typically, a young woman moves into her future husband's home once she discovers she is pregnant by him. Sometime later, when the couple have saved enough money for a ceremony and feasting, they will legalize their marriage through a civil or church wedding with all the trimmings, as Nyambura and Wacera did in 1994. Several middle-aged women who earlier had had customary weddings, prior to the enactment of post-independence marriage laws, were "renewing their vows" with church weddings during the year and a half I was in Mutira Location.

Marriage, for Gikuyu women, has always meant children. Formerly, it was not long after a woman began living with her husband in the same house that she discovered she was pregnant. If she did not become pregnant, she sought the advice of a *mundũ mugo*, as in Wamutira's case. Though most women were ill-informed about pregnancy and relied on older women to guide them, the news that a woman was going to bear a child was greeted with joy, because motherhood validated a woman's marriage. It was not until the birth of a woman's first child that she achieved full status among the other women in her husband's compound (Mathu 1971). Motherhood affirmed a woman's position in her husband's home and brought security in the marital relationship. Given such circumstances, it is not hard to understand why Wamutira became so anxious when she did not become pregnant in the first year of her marriage. The transition to marriage implied a transition to motherhood. The woman who did not bear children, for one reason or another, was in danger of being returned to her natal home. Marriage, then, resulted in intrapsychic tension, a tension that was not resolved until a woman proved her ability to bear children.

Childbirth. Whereas formerly women gave birth at home with the assistance of a midwife, increasingly women are seeking hospital births. Wanja and Nyambura gave birth to their children in hospitals. This means that midwives like Wanoi are less often called upon to help with births in the community. However, *itega*—the custom of women taking offerings of food, firewood, and, now, baby items to the new mother and her baby—is still very much a part of Gikuyu culture. It gives women in rural areas a chance to get together and celebrate with singing, dancing, and feasting.

The birth of a first child was, and still is, a critical event. Wanoi views it as the most significant change in her life. "Of all the changes I've told you about, the one that changed me the most was when I gave birth. That's because I knew then that I had become a woman, entitled to some duties and respect." Nyambura, twenty years younger, concurs. "When I became a mother—that was the biggest change for me." When women in Mutira were asked what constitutes womanhood for the *Agĩkũyũ,* the majority responded that, next to agricultural production, motherhood is the most important aspect of being a woman. Nevertheless, a woman's functional role as a mother (reproducer) does not supersede her role as a cultivator or wage earner (producer).

From Nyambura and Wanja's accounts, we learn that the relationship between marriage and motherhood is undergoing change. If a woman became a *mũkoma ndi* (unmarried pregnant woman) in Wangeci's time, she did not have the chance of becoming a man's first wife, and she felt shame. Today, threats of becoming a *mũkoma ndi* seem to have little effect. The younger women's narratives illustrate that childbirth may precede marriage—a phenomenon I observed to be increasing in the years between 1975 (when I first visited Kenya) and on subsequent visits up through 1994. Males with whom I have discussed this changing pattern argue that having a child before marriage assures a man that the woman he plans to marry is fertile before he begins bridewealth negotiations. Younger women hope that once they become pregnant a man will feel compelled to marry them—a scenario that does not always work out, as we learn from Wanja's account.

Nyumithio—transition to elder status. The narratives of older women reveal that, by the time they reached an age when their first child was circumcised, *nyumithio,* which formerly initiated a woman into elder status, was no longer practiced. Wanjiku had become a Christian by the time her oldest son was circumcised in the 1950s and no longer adhered to the old ways. Women in their fifties related that the custom had disappeared.

Changes in Mariika

Of all the cultural changes that have occurred during the older women's lives, the slow dissolution of *mariika* seems to have had the most significance. Women gained access to an age set with participation in *Irua.* With the demise of *Irua,* the network of ties to one's cohort initiated with *Irua* can no longer be depended on. Says Wangeci regretfully, "*Mariika* have no importance to younger women." Older women hold school—an institution they cannot imagine and have never experienced—responsible. Somehow in the process of being educated their children and grandchildren have come to accept a different set of social principles that structure their behavior. Whereas distance between age sets historically shaped Gikuyu society, social distance is giving way to cross-age groupings and intergender groupings. Boys play and talk with girls in a way their elders find offensive.

Changes in Sexuality, Fertility, and Demand for Contraception

According to Wangeci, young girls in 1984 were acting and dressing in ways that she deemed provocative. She related this to the breakdown of strict age grading and gender separation. Especially, increased social intercourse between youth of the opposite sex was leading to promiscuity. "Look at young men nowadays," she argued, "they are tiring easily and growing old fast because they think all the time they are enjoying sex, but they are not. The girls, too, are growing old very fast, using up a lot of sexual energy for nothing." By this Wangeci meant that sexual relations were not leading to procreation, the primary reason for sexual intercourse in her day.

Along with a change in social mores, according to older life narrators, has come the problem of increased fecundity. "A young girl marries today and gets a child year after year, and after five or six years she looks older than her mother and dies early because she is wearing out," Wangeci argues. She observed that Gikuyu formerly had their own forms of family planning, which involved postnatal abstinence for up to four or five years while a mother nursed her child and regained her strength.

For Wangeci, technological contraceptive devices are not the answer to child spacing; sexual abstinence is the solution. However, Wanoi supports the idea of contraception. As a midwife, she has learned through a training course how various contraceptive methods work and has even learned how to insert IUDs (intrauterine devices). Of the two youngest women, Nyambura, who was resisting the use of contraceptive methods in 1984 as being against her religion, had by 1989 begun to use the pill. Wanja continues to support the use of contraceptives.

The attitudes of the youngest women in 1984 were indicative of the debate that prevailed over contraception in the early 1980s. Although they were not part of my original sample, several women in their late thirties and forties, who had had all the children they desired, initiated conversations with me about pregnancy prevention. They wanted to know how I had managed to have only three children. I also had a chance, on several occasions, to accompany a Gikuyu woman who is a family planning community educator—and a mother of seven—on her visits to local homesteads. During such visits I learned that an increasing number of women are seeking tubal ligations once they have had the number of children desired. However, such a procedure does require the written permission of a husband, and several women expressed concern that their husbands would never give consent. Nonetheless, a demographer with an international family planning agency in Nairobi at the time confirmed that tubal ligation was the fastest-growing form of pregnancy prevention in Kenya (Merritt 1984, personal communication).

In the last decade (1984–1994) an increasing number of women of childbearing age in Kirinyaga have adopted family planning methods—over 50 percent of the women in their childbearing years. Outreach by Family Planning Association of Kenya's Community Distributors—including men who educate males to various methods—and the escalating costs of schooling together have had a significant impact. It may be that the fear of HIV/AIDS motivates some people who otherwise would not use contraceptives to use condoms. However, Nyambura and Wanja, the two women who are still sexually active, view HIV/AIDS as largely an urban problem. Neither acknowledges that rural women are increasingly vulnerable to infection; rural women generally have been neglected in campaigns to educate Africans about HIV/AIDS (Mwale and Burnard 1992).

Mutira couples on average appear to desire fewer children in 1994 than in 1984. For example, Nyambura and Wacera have limited their family to four children. My former research assistant, who is a secondary-school chemistry teacher, and her husband agreed to limit their family to two children. Younger men and women I spoke with were aware of the escalating costs of education. The financial burden of educating children was given as a major reason for having fewer children.

Changes in Women's Lives as Producers

Mutira women's lives as reproducers are changing. What about their roles and circumstances as producers? Wanjiku, the oldest informant, notes that women were allotted several plots of land in different ecological niches when she was growing up. As a woman in her husband's father's homestead, she was granted sufficient *migũnda* (gardens) to cultivate. Likewise, women had a variety of *migũnda* when the women in their fifties in 1984 were children. But in the post-independence years, the situation had changed.

A major change seems to have occurred during the 1950s when all the women were relocated, either to Nairobi or to internment villages, during Mau Mau. First of all, the women's families were forced from their homes and gardens. Some families lost land, or it was reduced. Wamutira relates that, during her absence in Nairobi, the goats and cows were *gũtaho*—commandeered by British soldiers to feed the colonial army. It is likely that the fields were also plundered. Trying to feed their families (and members of the Land and Freedom Army) during the Emergency strained the capacities of girls and women. The social dislocation meant that their gardens could not be cultivated, and in many instances they were reduced to collecting edible greens and tubers along rivers.

Mau Mau fighters depended on women and children to provide them with food and, in some cases, clothing during the struggle for liberation. Without women and children's support it is unlikely that the guerrilla armies would have been able to sustain themselves as long as they did (Barrett and Njama 1966; Wachanga 1975; Likimani 1985; Presley 1992). Kenyan women are not alone in providing a crucial productive role connected with a nationalist struggle. More recently Zimbabwean mothers during that country's war for liberation in the 1970s played a similar productive role. Without the food and clothing women supplied the ZANU and ZAPU guerrillas, Zimbabwe's liberation would have foundered (Staunton 1992).

In Mutira one of the dramatic changes since independence has been the introduction of cash-value crops such as coffee and tea that bring a variable income depending on world market prices. At the same time, increased cash crop production leaves less land and fewer diverse ecological niches for growing food crops. The amount of land that Gikuyu farmers cultivate in Mutira over time has decreased except in cases where a farmer has had the financial resources to increase his or her holdings—a rare occurrence. As a family head divides his holdings among sons, and now daughters, the size of each parcel must necessarily be smaller than what he held. Yet smallholders have continued to set aside half or more of their land for the production of cash-value crops that do not have food value but earn income. In 1985, for instance, those families in Mutira with the most land (seven to eight acres) devoted a greater proportion of that land to cash-value crops (72 percent), but even families with minimal acres (between one and three) set aside over half their land—nearly 56 percent—for the production of tea or coffee (Davison 1988b:167). Setting aside so much land for cash-value crops compromises women's production of food crops. Crop rotation is less possible and soil depletion means lower yields unless fertilizer is regularly applied. It is particularly painful to women in years when the cash-value crops earn less, as they did in the latter part of the 1980s. That people were neglecting their coffee in the late 1980s because the financial returns were not worth the labor expended in production, as Watoro observed, is not surprising.

Wanoi is the major agricultural producer in her family. She produces most of the food her family eats, selling harvested fruits such as avocados, mangos, and passion fruits in the market to buy commodities such as tea and sugar. She also harvests coffee berries, largely with the help of her children. However, it is her husband who receives the proceeds, which he may or may not share with Wanoi. Her husband was employed intermittently in a town some distance from Mutira in 1984. By 1994 he was retired and contributing more of his time to agricultural production. Notwithstanding, Wanoi has learned to be self-reliant over the years, counting only on income she makes to develop her homestead. "Like the granary I'm adding here at the homestead," she stated, "I will not ask my husband for a cent, even though he got his coffee harvest money just the other day. If I rely on him to give me money, the day he misses I will have a problem." This remained the case in 1994—Wanoi was depending on her own monetary resources for self-provisioning and for maintaining her home.

In a study of rural Gikuyu women's perceptions of themselves and their roles, sociologist Priscilla Kariuki (1985:224) reports the observation of one woman that "most women do not rely on their husbands today. They try to get money for themselves selling vegetables, clothes, or making handicrafts and selling them. They have an obligation to make sure that children do not sleep hungry or go without clothes."

For Watoro, Wangeci, and Wanjiku, husbands are not an issue. They were single women in 1984, totally dependent on their own resources, or in the case of Wanjiku, dependent on sons and daughters-in-law. Watoro, as indicated earlier, lost her access to cropland when she left her husband. She was dependent on cultivating *migũnda* that had belonged to her recently deceased father and producing coffee that belongs to her brother. After her father's death she learned that he had sold his remaining parcel—much to her disappointment. During the drought in 1984, she was in desperate need of cash to buy *unga* (maize meal) to feed her children and grandchildren. Had she lived thirty years earlier, she might have had several *migũnda* in different ecological niches. But as it was, she had only three gardens amounting to less than an acre located in the same area. She dreamed of coming to the coffee *shamba* and finding abundant food crops growing, or waking up to find herself holding a fistful of money. She yearned for success and a way to feed her family that was less onerous. Like many other single women around the world, Wanoi is among the poorest of the poor (Deere and Leon de Leal 1981; Clark 1984; Davison 1988a; Bassett and Crummey 1993).

Of the seven women, those living on the high, moisture-laden ridges were less affected by changes in land consolidation than those living at lower elevations. Women's husbands in the lowlands found themselves with less land than they had before the Emergency, as some land around Kagumo had been set aside for returning landless veterans of the war. Thus women living at lower elevations tended to have less land than those who live in the highlands near Gatwe and Gathuthuma where their families had access to more land for production at the time of independence.

Wanja is a special case. She completed secondary school and has a job that brings a regular income. This allows her to imagine more than just farming. Owning her own land and opening a shop were her goals. Wanja has been able to do both. In 1990 Kenya's inheritance laws were legally changed to allow daughters, wives, and widows to inherit property. In 1992 her father responded by dividing his property equally among siblings. However, whereas Wanja has the financial resources to pay for the title deed she covets, Nyambura's family lacks the money to pay for a title deed. For Nyambura, putting financial resources into a wedding is more important than gaining a title deed to land that she takes for granted as her husband's wife. Wanja, on the other hand, must balance the allocation of her resources among her family's needs, agricultural production, and her shop. As her financial resources are less constrained than those of the other narrators, she has more choice in how she will spend her income.

Historical Changes Affecting Mutira Women

The three most significant historical changes with consequences for Mutira women in the twentieth century were missionization, the struggle for liberation, and independence.

Missionization

The impact of missionary activities profoundly affected Gikuyu rituals from rites of passage such as *mambura ma twana* and *Irua* to the custom of *ngwiko*, which allowed young people a safe social context in which to practice premarital sex short of intercourse. Waciuma, who was raised in a Christian mission, relates in *Daughter of Mumbi* (1969) that by the 1940s a division had developed between Gikuyu girls who practiced *mbuci* and *matũ* and girls such as herself whose Christian parents had forbidden the radical ear piercings. Wanoi tells us that her Christian brother did not want her to have her ears pierced so she pierced them herself. Similarly, Ngugi wa Thiong'o's novel *The River Between* (1965) spells out the dilemma for adolescent Gikuyu girls caught between those who had embraced Christian ethics, which prohibited *Irua* because it was associated with female circumcision, and those whose families and friends insisted on its cultural worth. (See also Murray 1974.) Among the life narrators, Wanoi was caught in such a dilemma. She solved the problem by sneaking off with a friend to be circumcised.

Chapter 2 outlines the impact of "mission messages" on indigenous Gikuyu practices from *Irua* to *ũhiki*. Watoro tells us that "some missionaries tried to stop traditions like" girls decorating their breasts with cicatures. Dances and songs referred to by the older women in connection with *Irua* and other events that had taught them about their sexuality and sexual responsibility were banned by the 1950s and had largely disappeared by the 1970s.

In the postindependence period, the missionary campaign to stamp out certain Gikuyu customs was given a boost by a new, Christian, educated elite anxious to cast its lot with "modernization." "Traditional" practices viewed as primitive by Western standards were discouraged. Neither of the younger women had participated in Gikuyu rites of passage that the older women describe. Only two "traditions" historically associated with affluent Gikuyu remained—bridewealth and polygyny. In both cases Gikuyu males had a vested interest in retaining such practices.[2] The campaigns to Christianize the Gikuyu begun by the missionaries in the early part of the twentieth century had largely succeeded.

Women's Responses to the Liberation Struggle

More than any other single factor, the liberation struggle in the last decade of British colonial occupation discontinued the pattern of Gikuyu rural life as the life history narrators had known it. Forced off their land into internment villages, or in some cases forced to flee to urban Nairobi to join their absentee husbands who were working for the opposition, Mutira women's lives were disrupted so completely that it was difficult for them to return to the kind of agrarian existence they had once taken for granted.

Mutira women could not help but be aware of the pervasiveness of British colonial patriarchy, a patriarchy that extended to Africans of both sexes but particularly disadvantaged women and girls in terms of access to training and education, agricultural inputs, and land reforms (see Nasimiyu 1985; Davison 1988b). A Mutira woman who had been a Mau Mau guerrilla fighter, whom I interviewed in 1994, told me that because land was such an issue in the liberation struggle she was sure that, once Kenya won its independence, she and other women who had fought as freedom fighters would be rewarded for their part in the struggle with parcels of land, as were their male counterparts. She was bitterly disappointed to find after Uhuru that only male veterans were being awarded such plots.

For some women, such as Wanoi, the liberation struggle as it unfolded in Mutira provided an opportunity for achieving individual and collective empowerment. "During Mau Mau, women were also fighting," she relates. "Some even went into the forest to help. Women in the 'villages' fought by singing." She describes how a group of women sang and danced while cutting the tires of a Home Guard's vehicle. Wanoi became a scout for Mau Mau fighters, transferring messages related to British military positions. Another woman I interviewed in 1994, Karua, was a child of nine years when she became a scout for Mau Mau. She related that it gave her a sense of importance and responsibility to be entrusted with secret information. She never thought about the dangers involved, only that she was helping her uncle who was a guerrilla leader in the forest. Active participation in the struggle gave women such as Wanoi and Karua a sense of empowerment that contributed to their later development.

In some cases Mutira women found their family lives caught between opposing sides as a husband or father made the decision to become a loyalist Home Guard for the colonials. Watoro's disgust over her husband's brutality as a Home Guard fed her growing disillusion with her marital situation; severance of the relationship became her primary goal once people were released from the villages. In a sense, being freed from internment marked the beginning of Watoro's personal freedom.

Wanjiku, at the time of the Mau Mau rebellion a mother of three growing boys, was separated from her husband for the duration of the war. He was working in Voi, and it was unsafe for him to return to Mutira during the Emergency. Wanjiku was interned with others in Mutira. For her, the war was not an opportunity. Rather, it was a means of testing her survival instincts and keeping her family intact to the end.

Wamutira, whose husband was involved in the Mau Mau struggle in Nairobi, also was concerned about sustaining and protecting her growing family. For support in her husband's absence, she agreed to the idea of securing a second wife so that she would not have to remain alone in the marital household. A sisterhood developed between the two wives that proved to be a threat to their husband's patriarchal power once he returned to his household in Mutira. In Wamutira's case, the war served to strengthen bonds between two women who shared the same man. The marital household would never be the same.

In sum, the war for liberation in the 1950s affected all of the older life narrators, disrupting their lives and in some cases separating husbands and wives. Each woman responded to the traumatic changes in different ways depending on her age, marital circumstances, and individual proclivities toward the war. Some women survived by keeping a low profile. Others embraced the struggle, taking an active part in it. Those who were active learned lessons about themselves that over the long haul contributed to their future growth as women.

Independence

The liberation of Kenya from colonial rule was viewed by Mutira women as a peak experience that symbolized their freedom from imperialistic "slavery" and returned Kenya's land to its rightful owners. It made their suffering in the previous decade worth the struggle. Once they left the restrictive, restless confines of an interment village, they returned home. Being able to go home and watching Munyao raise the new Kenyan flag on Mount Kenya—these were the immediate benefits of freedom.

In the long term, though, women found that fewer opportunities were opening to them than they had anticipated. With the introduction of tea and coffee, they had smaller gardens in which to grow food crops, and their time was now divided between production of cash-value crops and food. New technological inputs designed to improve production were directed to their husbands or sons rather than to them. And the increasing dependency on the Kenya shilling rather than local trade meant that women had to seek ways of earning cash income to meet expanded needs.

The escalation of school construction in rural Mutira, as elsewhere in Kenya in the postcolonial decade, brought more educational opportunities to Gikuyu children—and education was viewed as the road to a better life. Girls (and boys in even greater numbers) who had missed school during the Mau Mau years now enrolled with increasing frequency regardless of age. Several women I knew in their thirties had been forced to drop out of school during the Mau Mau struggle as the Gikuyu's independent schools were attacked and destroyed by British loyalists and mission schools came under Mau Mau attack. Wanja's enrollment in school was delayed until after the close of the war.

Wanja was fortunate to complete primary school and continue to a secondary school. But others were not so lucky. Financial constraints and family problems led them to drop out. Nyambura is among the majority who were unable to complete the primary cycle. Her father, similar to other rural Kenyan fathers in the 1970s and 1980s, did not consider education as important for girls as for boys (Davison 1984). For girls like Nyambura the options were few. She was apprenticed to an aunt who taught her the finer points of being a domestic servant in this era of national liberation. Girls continued to trail boys in school participation at all levels through the 1980s. Not until forty years after independence, in 1992, were they finally able to achieve parity with boys at the primary level (Davison 1993).

For Mutira's older women, independence has become a mixed blessing. On the one hand they celebrate the opportunities that their children have for education, travel, and employment. On the other hand, their own chances for improving their lot appear transitory. Improved technological inputs increase the production of export crops, but food crops lag far behind. They attempt to improve the quality of their own lives through collaborative income-generating efforts. At the same time few efforts by the government or nongovernmental organizations are made to assist them with labor-saving equipment that will reduce their overall labor burden.

Nor is their access to land secure. Gikuyu women helped win the war but the benefits of freedom appear lopsided; men have gained the lion's share from independence.

Changes in Women's Personal Lives

The Challenge of Life Crises

In contrast to historical and sociocultural changes, at times individuals experience events unique to their lives that may alter their behavior (Neugarten and Datan 1973; Riegel 1975; Gergen 1980). What kinds of events have had the most impact on the lives of the narrators? How does each woman go about explaining their significance? What shifts do they imply in a woman's life span development? I limit the discussion to life crises that precipitated changes in behavior patterns.

Widowhood and separation. In the case of widowhood or separation, Gikuyu women in this collection describe a change in status that often has negative repercussions in a society that structures women's adult life through marriage. Wanjiku, Wangeci, and Watoro perceive their changed status through different lenses.

Wanjiku, widowed as a young mother, found herself in a quandary because she was left with a baby to raise alone. When the baby died, she wanted to return to her natal home. However, her husband's parents had grown fond of her and wished her to remain. The younger brother revealed his affection for her and assumed the position of her husband—a normative solution in many African societies. Wanjiku's period of feeling asynchronous lasted only a short time before her remarriage to Kamau. For her the period of widowhood meant a temporary transition.

The scenario was different for Wangeci, who was left a widow in her late thirties. Wangeci's adjustment to widowhood, while difficult, led to a transformation in her pattern of living. After the shock of her husband's sudden death, Wangeci realized that she no longer fit into the norm of her age group—she felt alone and cut off from her peers. "I just decided, there and then, to stand on my own. . . . The hardest change for me was to refrain from moving with women who had their husbands, and learning to stay alone with my work. . . . So I decided to keep to myself and be self-reliant."

Wangeci had been advised by her husband not to count on outside advisers, and she took his advice. She learned not to move with married women who might be jealous, but to stay home, learning to master the tasks that she formerly took for granted as her husband's responsibilities. Part of the change she experienced as a widow was the discovery that she could do things that before she assumed she could not—trapping moles, for example.

At the same time, Wangeci perceived her asynchronous status within a larger historical framework. "Nowadays, in our society widows do not get help. They say each has his mother. It means that even the father's [deceased man's] brothers can't help as they are interested only in their [own] children. . . . But long ago in Agĩkũyũ society, if there was a feast somewhere, a share of meat would be brought to the widow, and the father's brother took over the father's role." Whereas Wanjiku is not sure she likes the levirate arrangement, Wangeci wished it were still intact.

Wangeci felt isolated by her changed status. "Even in the community, people say that you, a widow, are rich with all the things left to you by your husband. So they never think to help someone like me." But Wangeci compensated for her isolation by working hard to gain the respect of the community; hard work became her therapy.

Wangeci's attitudes and her pattern of behavior changed with widowhood. She felt isolated. She had to assume responsibilities that were formerly shared. And she could not depend on her husband's brothers or the community for help. Necessarily, she grew in her ability to be self-sufficient. She also gained self-confidence as she learned new skills. Widowhood became a catalyst for change.

Watoro likewise experienced a changed status when she decided to leave her husband and return to her father's home. She had to depend on her father's hospitality for access to land and her own resources with her children's assistance to make a new and independent life. Although her life was precarious economically, she left behind the dissension that marked her troubled marriage. It was the crisis of her only daughter's death and her husband's unsupportive reaction that motivated Watoro to separate from him. It was her daughter's death, rather than the separation, that had the greatest impact on Watoro.

The impact of a child's death. The death of a woman's child is a particularly painful crisis in that it breaks the maternal bond between mother and child that began with giving birth. The way that a mother responds to that death can alter the rest of her life. The death of Watoro's only daughter taught her that she could never depend on her husband for emotional support; his lack of sensitivity to her psychological needs at the time of the crisis amplified other shortcomings. Watoro realized that if she wanted to make a life for herself and her remaining children, she would have to do it on her own.

Wamutira also experienced the death of a nine-year-old daughter, Kanugu. That death had a lasting effect on her life. "I changed very much after that child's death," she states solemnly. "I started fearing that I might never be given others. The ones I had later after Kanugu's death, I took very much care of so they might not die—like making sure they were clean, had good food, and went for clinic. . . . There are none of my children that I take for granted."

Kanugu's death raised certain philosophical questions that Wamutira found herself struggling with intellectually. "At times I would keep quiet and think, 'I have had very strong children who have died compared to ones I have now.' . . . When the two-year-old boy died, I prayed, asking, 'Why has God taken the bigger one and left this tiny one [Wamutira's newborn infant]?'"

The death of Wamutira's daughter prompted three changes in her life: (1) it altered her knowledge of death in relation to life; (2) it brought about a personal change in attitudes toward herself as a mother and toward her children, who became more valuable; (3) it motivated her to take better care of her children. For Wamutira, then, the death became a learning experience.

Wanoi also experienced the death of a child. She related that she felt very much changed by Wacera's death—and perhaps may even have felt some guilt because she refused at first to take him to the hospital. Nonetheless, she did not name Wacera's death as one of the greatest changes in her life.

Health crises. For six of the seven women narrators, health crises have marked their lives over the past decade. Wanjiku's arthritis has left her incapacitated, and increasing blindness has forced her to depend completely on her family. Watoro and Wamutira have suffered chronic "stomach problems," and Wanoi has developed an ulcer. In the case of Wangeci, illness led to hospitalization and death. Of the two younger women, Nyambura suffered a painful uterine malfunction that resulted in surgery. The crisis acted as a wake-up call for her husband and brought the couple closer together. Of the life narrators, only Wanja has escaped major health problems in the last decade.

From the women's comments in 1994 it is clear that the health problems punctuating their lives have sapped their energies and taken away something from the quality of their lives. Health problems largely have been unexpected and therefore demand an adjustment. This is particularly true of the older women as they come to grips with their physical disabilities, limitations, and chronic disorders that medical practitioners seem unable to treat. It means narrowing the aperture of possibilities in their lives. They do not adjust easily; it is an ongoing struggle.

Idiosyncratic experiences. Occasionally a person comes face to face with what can only be referred to as a life-altering experience. Sometimes a near-death experience or an intense religious experience will be a catalyst. Wanoi mentions her conversion to Christianity as one turning point.

Having to assist a woman giving birth in a sugarcane field when Wanoi was sixteen inspired her to become a midwife.

Wanoi related that when she first heard the pregnant woman calling to her for help, her impulse was to run away. "I started wondering what to do and was feeling a bit scared, but a voice deep within me told me to go back and help her." With that decision, Wanoi changed the course of her life. She learned, despite her initial fear, that she could deliver a baby. The knowledge gained from this first experience was reinforced when she had to make another emergency delivery some time later. She then perceived herself to be a midwife. She began to deliver other women's babies, discovering in the process that she was able to devise creative solutions when the need arose—as in the case of a stubborn afterbirth.

Wanoi's curiosity and her professional involvement led her to other learning experiences: an in-service training course for midwives and eventually an adult education course. The "voice deep within"—her conscience—provoked a turning point in her lifelong development.

Conversion to Christianity

What causes a woman who has her own indigenous belief system to convert to another form of religion, especially one that originally was intertwined with colonialism? My assumption at the early stages of research was that most Mutira women were forced into conversion. I was dead wrong. All except the two youngest narrators converted to Christianity as adults, most in the postcolonial period. The youngest two women were born into Christianity. What motivated each of the older narrators to become a Christian? Had conversion in any instance been life-altering? For Wanoi and Wanjiku it had been a transformative experience in terms of their behavioral responses. For other women, such as Watoro and Wamutira, it was merely an event brought on by the pressure to conform to a movement that was gaining popularity.

Wanoi fits the normative pattern of her sample age group—she joined the church after independence, as an adult. Conversion was transformative, in my opinion, because it changed her perceptions of herself in relationship to her family and community, as she explains. "So there is a big change [since becoming a Christian]. I am able to humble myself now and follow Jesus's teaching that even when he was abused, mocked, and saliva thrown at him, he only humbled himself. . . . If I have abused Kamani [husband] the night before, I go and apologize and so make good our relationship." For Wanoi, assuming responsibility for her own behavior is crucial to change in her life.

Wangeci, as a widow in her fifties, describes her conversion to Christianity as life-altering. "Becoming a Christian changed my life—even my soul—because in the days before I became a Christian I used to cook and drink liquor. . . . But after becoming a Christian, I stopped. . . . Before, I would abuse anyone who tried to abuse me. . . . But now, even if somebody comes and abuses me or tries to fight with me, I will not fight back." Formerly, Wangeci operated on a Gikuyu belief system that linked responsibility for people's actions with external forces that included the corporate group made up of the living and the dead (ancestors). In contrast, Christian ethics place responsibility for actions on the individual rather than on external forces—for example, witchcraft, curses, or love potions. Wangeci believed that it was God's wish that she entrust her life history to another person. In so doing, she was acting as an individual to ensure her place in posterity.

Similar to Wanoi and Wangeci, the oldest informant, Wanjiku, believed that becoming 'saved' as a Christian was a transformative life experience. The circumstances of her being saved are related to the wound on her face that a local healer could not heal. The failure of the *mũndũ mugo* shook Wanjiku's faith in indigenous healing practices. She attributed the curing of her wound to her faith in God's healing powers. As a result, she became a committed Christian.

In contrast to the other women, neither Watoro nor Wamutira described their conversion to Christianity as transformative. Rather, conversion appeared to be a response to social pressure within the Kagumo community—"becoming Christian" was identified with "being modern" in the 1960s and 1970s and neither woman wanted to be left behind.

Other Life-Altering Changes

For some people, a transformative experience may occur early in life, while for others it occurs in later life. For Wanja's sister, the crisis in her family initiated by the liberation struggle forced her at the age of seven to take on responsibilities far beyond her age. She was the major care giver for younger siblings, including Wanja. It made her "grow up over night," she said. As a result of learning that she could be resourceful in the face of extreme adversity, she adjusted her image of herself—she could take on anything. Part of this image building rubbed off on Wanja. Edelman's study, *Motherless Daughters* (1994), points to a similar phenomenon; forced in some cases to take on family responsibilities at an early age because of their mother's death or abandonment, the girls in her study learned to become self-reliant and gained confidence in the process. As a result they were more likely to be "self-starters" as adults, achieving life goals they set for themselves.

For Nyambura, a life-altering experience occurred later in her life when she was forced to have surgery. At that time she was not sure she would survive. She felt vulnerable as she confronted her own mortality.

Having survived, she was left with a new appreciation for life and saw that her husband newly valued her. The positive change in his behavior contributed to Nyambura's well-being. The shift in their relationship led to a church wedding.

Idiosyncratic changes affect women's lives differently. What constitutes change is totally dependent on the way a person perceives a particular event in her life; it is the significance of meaning that an individual attaches to the change, retrospectively, that is important (Cohler 1982; Aptheker 1993; Edelman 1994). Each woman in this collection approached a crisis or transition differently depending on her marital status, religious orientation, and the family support that she had available to her.

Mediating Change over the Life Span

How do Gikuyu women in this collection mediate changes in their lives? What coping mechanisms or strategies are used? Based on the evidence of the narratives, three types of mediating responses emerge. One is rationalization, a second is resistance, and the third is transformation. In this section, I describe each response with reference to particular life narrators.

Rationalization

Rationalization enables a person to make sense of a change in her or his life, especially if it appears irrational or is unavoidable. Watoro, for instance, rationalized the transition from married to single status by initially anticipating that her new, single status would be problem-free. The problem—her husband—had been left behind. She was returning to her natal home where she would be embraced by her parents. Later she realized that, although she was given access to gardens by her father, she had little real economic security. Raising her children without a husband turned out to be financially more difficult than she had anticipated. She had to depend on access to her brother's coffee to earn income for her children's schooling and even this source of income was precarious. Being a single mother did not turn out to be the problem-free existence she once envisioned.

Wamutira similarly rationalized changes in her marital circumstances. At first when she realized that her new husband would not return from Nairobi for some time, she decided to join him. Unhappy in Nairobi, after giving birth to a first child, she returned to her husband's father's home in Mutira. Left alone with two quarrelsome mothers-in-law and an infant son, Wamutira found her life more difficult. Murage came home for a visit and suggested a solution—a co-wife. Wamutira concurred with the decision, provided she had some choice in the new wife. She justified the decision by convincing herself that an additional wife would provide her with a companion in Murage's absence, a conviction that turned out to be accurate. Later she rationalized the addition of a third wife by acknowledging that Murage was the one who "pushes the pedals"—had the final say in the family.

Resistance to Change

Wanjiku became a widow only a few years after she had married her husband. Her in-laws were eager to have her marry his younger brother. She resisted; she wanted to return to her own family after her child's death. It was only after several months of persuasion that she changed her mind and decided to remain in her husband's home.

None of the older women expected the kinds of changes in their health that have occurred in the last decade with the aging process. Wanoi complains about her ulcer but does not change her diet or life-style to accommodate the problem. Likewise Watoro and Wamutira complain about stomach problems but do not seem to see the connection between their eating habits and health maintenance. All three women realize that old age is catching up with them and they rebel against the physical liabilities that go with it.

Change as Opportunity

A third response to change is to view the change—either positive or negative—as an opportunity for personal growth. The saying, "If you get handed a lemon, turn it into lemonade" captures the spirit of a person who is able to take a life change and turn it into a learning experience or an opportunity. Wamutira, for example, was devastated by her daughter's death but she used the experience as an opportunity to learn new skills that would ensure her other children's survival.

Wanoi, when faced with the crisis of a woman delivering a baby, reacted quickly and was coached by the woman in the successful delivery of the infant. In retrospect, Wanoi realized that she was given an opportunity to learn new skills that prepared her for her new profession. She perceived herself to be a midwife once she had proved to herself that she could deliver a baby. From then on she actively sought new ways to educate herself.

Wangeci's widowhood forced her to withdraw from social situations, especially with other women. This was a tragedy for such an extrovert. But in retreating to her own homestead, she realized that she had an opportunity to become more self-sufficient than when her husband was alive. She also mastered new skills previously considered men's work.

In summary, the life histories illustrate that Gikuyu women view themselves either as a part of their culture or as separate individuals in varying degrees. Social variations and personal life experience influence each woman's ability to see herself as a distinct individual mediating change as well as being shaped by it. Thus, the life histories demonstrate a range of possibilities among Gikuyu women in an age of rapid change.

Women's Voices: Similarities and Differences

I began this study of women's lives by asking how Gikuyu women in one location in Kenya are mediating change and to what extent their experiences may be compared with women in other parts of the globe. In examining their life histories, I find that Mutira women are "like all other women, like some other women, and yet are like no other women." Similarities and contrasting differences make up the fabric of their lives. With one voice and with separate voices, the women of Mutira continue to speak. Their sonorous narratives, like their bare footprints firmly embedded in the dusty path to Kirinyaga, link the past with the future in a single century. And their voices echo those of other rural women throughout the world who struggle for a daily existence and fall into bed exhausted every night. They are born, they give birth, and they often live to see one or two of their children die. They outlabor and outlive their husbands but never attain commensurate economic power. All in all, life's ironies amuse them and they laugh; its injustices anger them and they shout to be heard. We must listen.

Notes

1. In Malawi, parts of Zambia, parts of southern Tanzania, and northern Mozambique, where the majority of people are matrilineal, the practice is the opposite. Children take their mother's clan affiliation and name. In groups where matrilocal or uxorilocal residence is practiced, a husband moves to his wife's village on marriage.

2. In 1980 a bill was introduced in the Kenya Parliament to outlaw polygyny. It was overwhelmingly defeated.

Appendix

Table 1 Sample Population by Age Group

Age Group	Number of Women	% of Total Sample
20–29	16	15.8[b]
30–39	20	19.8
40–49	18	17.8
50–55[a]	18	17.8
56–69	14	13.8
70–79	15	14.8
Totals:	101	99.8%

[a] Target sample for four life-history informants in their early fifties.
[b] Rounded to nearest tenth.

Table 2 Marital Status by Age Group

Age Group	Total per Group	Monogamous	Polygynous	Separated	Widowed	Single
20–29	16	13	0	0	0	3
30–39	20	15	5	0	0	0
40–49	18	8	9	0	1	0
50–55[a]	18	6	5	2	4	1
56–69	14	6	4	1	3	0
70–79	15	4	4	0	7	0
Totals:	101	52	27	3	15	4

[a] Target sample for four life-history informants in their early fifties.

Table 3 Child Mortality Among Mutira Women

Age Group	Total per Group	No. Who Had Lost Children	No. Who Had Lost None	Never Had Children
20–29	16	1	15	0
30–39	20	5	15	0
40–49	18	9	9	0
50–55[a]	18	11	6	1
56–69	14	11	3	0
70–79	15	9	5	1
Totals:	101	46	53	2

[a] Represents target sample of women in their early fifties.

Table 4 Religion

Age Group	No. per Group	Anglican	Catholic	Full Gospel	African Holy Ghost	Christian	Non-Christian
20–29	16	5	8	1	0	1	0
30–39	20	10	8	1	1	0	0
40–49	18	11	5	0	1	1	1
50–55[a]	18	8	10	0	0	0	0
56–69	14	7	4	2	0	1	0
70–79	15	6	7	0	0	1	1
Totals:	101	47	42	4	2	4	2

[a] Represents target sample of women in their early fifties.

Table 5 Participation in Formal Education

Age Group	Total per Group	Ever Attended School			Ever Attended Adult Ed. Classes	
		No.	percent	Mean no. years	No.	percent
20–29	16	14	87.5	6.4	3	18.8
30–39	20	9	45.0	4.7	6	30.0
40–49	18	7	38.8	5.8	7	38.8
50–59	20	5	25.0	3.6	5	25.0
60–69	12	3	25.0	1.0	2	16.6
70–79	15	4	26.7	0.6	6	40.0
Totals:	101	41	40.5	3.7	29	28.7

Table 6 Participation in Women's Groups

Age Group	No. per Group	No. in Self-Help Groups	No. in Church Groups	Total % Both Types
20–29	16	5	1	37.5
30–39	20	8	5	65.0
40–49	18	7	4	61.0
50–55[a]	18	6	5	61.0
56–69	14	5	6	78.6
70–79	15	5	4	60.0
Totals:	101	36	27	62.4

[a] Represents target sample of women in their early fifties.

Glossary

Note: In Kikuyu ũ is pronounced as a soft 'o' and ĩ as soft 'a.'

Agĩkũyũ (Mũgĩkũyũ, s.)	Gikuyu
anake	young man
andũ akũrũ	old people
athoni (mũthoni, s.)	in-laws
ariririti	trill of women when child is born
baraza (Kiswahili)	outdoor public meeting
ciũthi	children's game similar to jacks
cũcũ	grandmother
cuka	piece of material worn around waist to cover lower half of body
gakenge	newborn child
gikabu	large, woven basket used for hauling tea leaves
githeri	maize kernels and kidney beans boiled together for several hours
gũtura matũ	piercing of earlobes
gũtaho	commandeered
gũthinjiro	blood sacrifice to seal betrothal
gũthokia	giving of beer during betrothal
gwokotha	process of binding together plant fibers into string for weaving baskets
haiya	expression of exclamation somewhere between "wow" and "brother"
harambee	self-help

ĩĩ (pronounced "aye")	yes
irio	general term for food
Irua	initiation-circumcision ceremony
itega	custom of bringing gifts to new mother
ithangu (mathangu, pl.)	leaf
ithitu (githitu, s.)	containers for medicine
itumbi (matumbi, pl.)	literally means egg, but used to refer to egg-shaped items such as gourds
jembe (Kiswahili)	hoe
kaana	infant
kahiĩ	small uncircumcised boy
kanini	small one
karathiro	blessing preceding a ceremony
karigũ	small girl
kiama	council of elders
kibanga (Kiswahili is panga)	machete
kienji	broad-bladed knife used in circumcision ceremonies
kiondo	woven basket
kirigũ (irigũ, pl.)	a big, uncircumcised girl
kirira	secret knowledge
kiumbi	handsome, talkative
kithunu	bachelor's hut
kubibo	blood sucking ritual
kumanda	when bride brings vegetables from her shamba to cook for her mother-in-law
mabati (Kiswahili)	corrugated iron roofing
mambura	ceremony (also menstruation)
mambura ma twana	ceremony of the children
mariika (riika, s.)	age-sets (those circumcised at the same time)
matatu	van, public transportation
mathaga	women's dress
matũ	earlobe that is pierced
mathakwa (ithakwa, s.)	velvet-like leaves used during Irua
mathangu (ithangu, s.)	leaves
mbari	landholding patrilineage
mbuci	upper rim of the ear that is pierced
mbũgũ	objects such as bones, stones used in the mũndũ mugo's healing ceremony

migio	native plant with suitable fibers for weaving
mikwa	large ear plugs
miti dawa	tree medicine
mũcii (micii, pl.)	compound with several dwellings
mũgũnda (migũnda, pl.)	garden
mũhiki	bride with young child
muiko	long handled wooden spoon, flattened on one side and used for mashing food
mũirĩtu	adult "circumcised" girl
mũkoma ndi	"loose," unmarried woman
mũkwa	sisal or leather tumpline
mũndũ mugo	medicine man
mũongia	old woman past menopause
muratina	beanpod from native tree used as a fermenting agent (also refers to the brew made with muratina beanpod)
muthaiga	white medicinal powder
mũthuri (athuri, pl.)	man
mũthuru	skirt with slits
mũtũmia (atũmia, pl.)	woman with several children
muzungu	European/white
mwanake (anake, pl.)	young, circumcised man
mwanake kiumbi	handsome, talkative young man
mwengu	goatskin skirt with flaps for girls
mweretho	dance for young people in which young men would toss their female partners high in the air while the girls shook their bodies
mzee	respected male elder
ndebe	type of earplug, also a storage tin
ndigi	string
ndũma	arrowroots
nduka	shop
ng'aa	false talk, empty feelings
Ngai	Creator, God
ngatha	industrious, self-reliant, stays at home
ngoni	type of earplug
ngunga	type of herb used to cause an abortion
ngutwii	stinging nettle
ngwatio	women's work group
nja	pounded earth yard in a compound

njohi	homemade sugarcane beer
nyumithio	ceremony to advance to elderhood
retho	pieces of cloth tied around shoulders
rigi	wooden movable walls (screens)
riiko	central fireplace for cooking
rũkoro	strip of goat skin worn around wrist
rũracio	bridewealth
shamba (Kiswahili; mashamba, pl.)	tilled field
skuma-wiki (Kiswahili)	kale
sufuria (Kiswahili)	metal pot
tatha	insides of intestines of a goat or sheep used to smear the body during ritual
thegi	place where goats are kept indoors
thingira	man's house
thira	reed and bead skirt worn during Irua
thiri	secret
twana (mwana, s.)	children
ugali (Kiswahili)	maize-meal porridge cooked to a hard consistency
ũgo	healing ceremony of the mũndũ mugo
ũhiki	marriage
ũma	short-handled garden fork
unga (Kiswahili)	maize meal
wamũng'ei	woman with several children, one of whom is circumcised

References

Abbott, Susan. 1974. "Full Time Farmers and Weekend Wives: Change and Stress Among Rural Kikuyu Women." Ph.D. dissertation, University of North Carolina.

Abu-Lughod, Lila. 1993. *Writing Women's Worlds: Bedouin Stories.* Berkeley & Los Angeles: University of California Press.

Afonja, Simi. 1980. "Current Expectation of Sex Roles and Inequality: A Reconsideration." *The Nigerian Journal of Economic and Social Studies,* 22(1): 85–105.

———. 1986. "Changing Modes of Production and the Changing Social Order Among the Yoruba." In *Women's Work,* edited by E. Leacock and H.I. Safa. South Hadley, Mass.: Bergin & Garvey.

Ahlberg, Beth Maina. 1991. *Women, Sexuality and the Changing Social Order.* Philadelphia & Reading: Gordon & Breach.

Ajulu, Rok. 1993. "The 1992 Kenya Elections: A Preliminary Assessment," *Review of African Political Economy,* 59:98–102.

Akeroyd, Anne V. 1994. "HIV/AIDS in Eastern and Southern Africa," *Review of African Political Economy,* 60:173–184.

Amadiume, Ifi. 1987. *Male Daughters, Female Husbands: Gender and Sex in an African Society.* London: Zed Press.

Ambler, Charles. 1988. *Kenyan Communities in the Age of Imperialism.* New Haven: Yale University Press.

American Association. for the Advancement of Science. 1977. *Village Women: Their Changing Lives and Fertility—Kenya, Mexico and the Philippines.* Washington, D.C.: AAAS.

Andreski, Iris. 1970. *Old Wives Tales: Life Stories From Ibibioland.* New York: Schocken Books.

Aptheker, Bettina. 1993. "Tapestries of Life." In *Feminist Frameworks,* 3d ed., edited by A. M. Jaggar and P. S. Rothenberg. New York: McGraw-Hill.

Barnes, Carolyn. 1983. "Differentiation by Sex among Small Scale Farming Households in Kenya," *Rural Africana,* 15/16:41–63.

Barnes, Teresia, and Everjoyce Win. 1992. *To Live a Better Life: An Oral History of Women in the City of Harare, 1930–1970.* Harare: Baobab Books.

Barrett, Donald, and Karigo Muchai. 1973. *The Hardcore.* Richmond, B.C.: LMB Press.

Barrett, Donald, and Karani Njama. 1966. *Mau Mau from Within: An Analysis of Kenya's Peasant Revolt.* New York: Modern Reader Paperbacks.

Bassett, T., and D. Crummey, eds. 1993. *Land in African Agrarian Systems.* Madison: University of Wisconsin Press.

Berry, Sara. 1993. *No Condition Is Permanent: The Social Dynamics of Agrarian Change in Sub-Saharan Africa.* Madison: University of Wisconsin Press.

Bledsoe, Caroline H. 1980. *Women and Marriage in Kpelle Society.* Stanford: Stanford University Press.

Bolande, Awe. 1977. "The Iyalode in the Traditional Yoruba Political System." In *Sexual Stratification: A Cross- Cultural View,* edited by Alice Schlege. New York: Columbia University Press.

Boserup, Ester. 1970. *Woman's Role in Economic Development.* New York: St. Martin's Press.

Buvinic, Mayra. 1983. "Women's Issues in Third World Poverty: A Policy Analysis." In *Women and Poverty in the Third World,* edited by M. Buvinic, M. Lycette, and W. McGreevy. Baltimore: Johns Hopkins University Press.

Cagnolo, C. 1933. *The Agikuyu: Their Customs, Traditions, and Folklore.* Nyeri: The Mission Printing School.

Caplan, Anne P. 1975. *Choice and Constraint in a Swahili Community.* Oxford: Oxford University Press.

Castro, Alfonso P. 1983. "Tree Planting and Fuel Use in Kirinyaga District." In *Fuelwood Use in Rural Kenya: Impacts of Deforestation,* edited by D. Brokensha, B. Riley, and A. Castro. New York: Institute for Development Anthropology.

Chieza, Mary. 1983. "Participation of Women in National Development: A Case Study from Nyachuru Women's Group." Unpublished M.A. thesis. Harare: University of Zimbabwe.

Chodorow, Nancy. 1978. *The Reproduction of Mothering: Psychoanalysis and the Sociology of Gender.* Berkeley: University of California Press.

Clark, Carolyn. 1971. *Conflict in Kikuyu Kinship.* Nairobi: Institute of African Studies.

Clark, Mari. 1984. "Women-headed Households and Poverty," *SIGNS,* 10:19–26.

Clough, Marshall S. 1990. *Fighting Two Sides: Kenyan Chiefs and Politicians, 1918–1940.* Niwot, Colo.: University Press of Colorado.

Cohler, B.J. 1982. "Personal Narrative and the Life Course." In *Life-span Development and Behavior,* Vol. 4, edited by P.B. Baltes and O.G. Brim, Jr. New York: Academic Press.

Collins, Patricia H. 1993. "Towards an Afrocentric Feminist Epistomology." In *Feminist Frameworks,* 3d ed., edited by A.M. Jaggar and P.S. Rothenberg. New York: McGraw-Hill.

Conaway, Mary E. 1986. "The Pretense of the Neutral Researcher." In *Self, Sex, and Gender in Cross-cultural Fieldwork,* edited by T.L. Whitehead and M.E. Conaway. Urbana & Chicago: University of Illinois Press.

Crapanzano, Vincent. 1980. *Tuhami: Portrait of a Morroccan.* Chicago: Chicago University Press.

Cropley, Arthur. 1981. "Lifelong Learning and Higher Education," *New Education* 3(2):39–45.

Davison, Jean. 1980. "Women in Three Societies: The Quechua of Peru, the Kikuyu of Kenya and the Maori of New Zealand." Unpublished M.A. thesis. Moraga: St. Mary's College.

———. 1984. "Myths and Realities: A Study of Parental Attitudes Toward Education for Females in Kenya." Paper presented at the Educational Foundations Seminar Series. Nairobi: Kenyatta University.

———. 1985. "Achievements and Constraints Among Rural Kenyan Women: A Case Study." In *Women and Development in Africa,* edited by G.S. Were. Nairobi: Gideon Were Press.

———. 1986. "Issues of Self: Collecting the Autobiographies of Non-literate African Women." Paper presented at the Conference on Autobiography and Biography: Gender, Text and Context, Stanford University, April 1986.

———. 1988a. "Land and Women's Agricultural Production: The Context." In *Agriculture, Women and Land: The African Experience*, edited by J. Davison. Boulder & London: Westview Press.

———. 1988b. "Who Owns What? Land Registration and Tensions in Gender Relations of Production in Kenya." In *Agriculture, Women and Land: The African Experience*, edited by J. Davison. Boulder and London: Westview Press.

———. 1993. "School Attainment and Gender: Attitudes of Kenyan and Malawian Parents Toward Educating Girls," *International Journal of Educational Development*, 13(4): 331–338.

Deere, Carmen, and Magdalena Leon de Leal. 1981. "Peasant Production, Proletarianization, and the Sexual Division of Labor in the Andes," *SIGNS* 7(2): 338–360.

Due, Jean. 1985. *Women Made Visible: Their Contributions to Farming Systems and Household Incomes in Zambia and Tanzania.* Champaign: University of Illinois, Department of Agricultural Economy.

Edelman, Hope. 1994. *Motherless Daughters.* New York: Dell.

"Family Planning Makes Headway," *Daily Nation* 6 September 1990:4.

Feldman, Reyah. 1984. "Women's Groups and Women's Subordination: An Analysis of Policies Toward Rural Women in Kenya." *Review of African Political Economy*, 27/28:57–85.

Fisher, Jeanne. 1954. *The Anatomy of Kikuyu Domesticity and Husbandry.* Nairobi: Kenya Ministry of Agriculture, Department of Technical Cooperation.

Flax, Jane. 1992. "Women Do Theory." In *Destabilizing Theory: Contemporary Feminist Debates*, edited by M. Barrett and A. Phillips. Stanford: Stanford University Press.

Gaidzanwa, Rudo B. 1985. *Images of Women in Zimbabwean Literaure.* Harare: The College Press.

———. 1988. *Women's Land Rights in Zimbabwe: An Overview.* Harare: Department of Rural and Urban Planning, University of Zimbabwe. Occasional Paper no. 13.

Geiger, Susan. 1986. "Women's Life Histories: Methods and Context—Review Essay," *SIGNS* 11(2):334–351.

Gergen, Kenneth. 1980. "The Emerging Crisis in Life-Span Developmental Theory." In *Life-Span Development and Behavior*, edited by P. Baltes and O.G. Brim. New York: Academic Press.

Gluck, Sherna B., and Daphne Patai, eds. 1991. *Women's Words: the Feminist Practice of Oral History.* New York: Routledge.

Godfrey, Martin. 1987. "Stabilization and Structural Adjustment of the Kenyan Economy, 1975–1985: An Assessment of Performance," *Development and Change* 18(4):595–624.

Gollock, Georgina A. 1928. *Lives of Eminent Africans.* New York: Longmans.

Guyer, Jane. 1984. *Family and Farm in Southern Cameroon.* Boston: Boston University Press.

Hartmann, Heidi, and Ann Markusen. 1980. "Contemporary Marxist Theory and Practice: A Feminist Critique," *Review of Political Economy*, 12:87–94.

Hawkesworth, Mary E. 1989. "Knowers, Knowing, Known: Feminist Theory and Claims of Truth," *SIGNS* 14(3):533–557.

Heilbrun, Carolyn. 1988. *Writing a Woman's Life.* London: The Women's Press.

Herzog, A. 1971. "Fertility and Cultural Values: Kikuyu Naming Customs and the Preference for Four or More Children." Nairobi: Bureau of Educational Research, Kenyatta University.
Hobley, Charles W. 1910. "Kikuyu Customs and Beliefs," *Journal of the Royal Anthropological Institute,* 40:428–445.
———. 1938. *Bantu Beliefs and Magic.* London: H.F. & G. Witherby.
Hoorweg, Jan, and Rudo Niemeyer. 1980. "Preliminary Studies on Some Aspects of Kikuyu Food Habits," *Ecology of Food and Nutrition,* 9:139–150.
Inter-Parliamentary Union (IPU). 1991. *Distribution of Seats Between Men and Women in National Parliaments.* Geneva: IPU.
Jackson, Jean. 1986. "On Trying to Be an Amazon." In *Self, Sex, and Gender in Cross-cultural Fieldwork,* edited by T.L. Whitehead and M.E. Conaway. Urbana & Chicago: University of Illinois Press.
Jaggar, Alison. 1983. *Feminist Politics and Human Nature.* Totowa, N.J.: Rowman and Allenheld.
Jaggar, Alison, and Paula S. Rothenberg. 1993. "Introduction" to *Feminist Frameworks,* 3d ed. New York: McGraw-Hill.
Kaberry, Priscilla. 1952. *Women of the Grassfields: A Study of the Economic Position of Women in Bamenda, British Cameroons.* London: Her Majesty's Stationary Office.
Kalindile, Rebeka, and Marjorie Mbilinyi. 1991. *I've Been a Man!* Dar es Salaam: University of Dar es Salaam Press.
Kanogo, T. 1987. *Squatters and the Roots of Mau Mau, 1905–1963.* London: James Currey.
Kariuki, Priscilla. 1985. "Women's Aspirations and Self-perceptions of Their Own Situation in Society." In *Women and Development in Africa,* edited by G.S. Were. Nairobi: Gideon Were Press.
Karoki, Flora. 1977. Interview. Gatwe, August 23, 1977.
———. 1984. Interview. Gatwe, March 30, 1984.
———. 1992. Interview. Gatwe, August 9, 1992.
———. 1994. Interview. Gatwe, January 11, 1994.
Kaufulu, Febbie, and Jean Davison. 1992. "Mothers' Child Spacing Attitudes, Nutrition Practices and Treatment of Children's Illnesses in the Thyolo Tea Estate Compounds" (mimeo). Lilongwe, Malawi: Project Hope.
Kenya, Central Bureau of Statistics. 1984. *Agricultural Census of Large Farms, 1981–82.* Nairobi: CBS.
———. 1991. *Kenya Statistical Abstracts—1991.* Nairobi: CBS.
Kenya National Archives (KNA). 1927a. *Resolution of Ft. Hall Local Native Council* (9/27).
———. 1927b. *Report of Nyeri Native Council* (9/3/27) DC/PC 9/3/27.
———. 1930. *Correspondence from District Commissioner, Ft. Hall To Provincial Commissioner, Nyeri* (4/3/30). DC/PC 4/3/30, Central Province.
———. 1934. *Provincial Commissioner's Report, Central Province* (9/9/34). PC/DC 9/9/34.
———. 1938. *Annual Report on Native Affairs.*
———. 1951. *District Commissioner's Report, Embu District.* DC/PC 10/51.
———. 1953. *The Emergency Regulation: Evacuation 1953.* Government Notice No. 976. Nairobi.
———. 1954. *Handing Over Report: Embu District,* R.A. Wilkinson, D.C. (11/54) DC/PC, Embu District.
Kenyatta, Jomo. 1968 (1938). *Facing Mt. Kenya.* London: Secker & Warburg.

Kershaw, Greet. 1975/1976. "The Changing Roles of Men and Women in the Kikuyu Family by Socioeconomic Strata," *Rural Africana*, 29:173–194.

Kinoti, H.W. 1983. "Aspects of Gikuyu Traditional Morality." Unpublished Ph.D. dissertation. Nairobi: University of Nairobi.

Kinyatti, Maina. 1987. *Kenya's Freedom Struggle: The Dedan Kimathi Papers*. London: Zed Press.

Kirinyaga District. 1982. *Annual Report—1982*. Kerugoya: Government Printers.

Kluckhohn, Clyde. 1945. "Personal Document in Anthropological Science." In *The Use of Personal Document in History, Anthropology, and Sociology*, edited by L. Gottschalk, C. Kluckhohn, and R. Angell. New York: Social Science Research Council, Bulletin No. 53.

Kuper, Hilda. 1978. *Sobhuza II, Ngwenyama and King of Swaziland: The Story of an Hereditary Ruler and His Country*. New York: Africana Publishing.

Lambert, H.E. 1956. *Kikuyu Social and Political Institutions*. London: Oxford University Press.

Langness, L.L., and Geyla Frank. 1981. *Lives: An Anthropological Approach to Biography*. Novato, Calif.: Chandler & Sharp.

Laurentin, Anne. 1963. "Nzakara Women (Central African Republic)." In *Women in Tropical Africa*, edited by D. Paulme. London: Routledge & Kegan Paul.

Leakey, L.S.B. 1977. *The Southern Kikuyu Before 1903*. London & New York: Academic Press.

Leo, Christopher. 1984. *Land and Class in Kenya*. Toronto: University of Toronto Press.

LeVine, Sarah. 1979. *Mothers and Wives: Gusii Women of East Africa*. Chicago: University of Chicago Press.

LeVine, Sarah, and Gary Pfeifer. 1982. "Separation and Individuation in an African Society: The Developmental Tasks of the Gusii Married Woman," *Psychiatry* 45:61–75.

Leys, Colin. 1975. *Underdevelopment in Kenya*. London: Heinemann.

Likimani, Muthoni. 1974. *They Shall Be Chastised*. Nairobi: East Africa Literature Bureau.

———. 1985. *Passbook Number F.47927: Women and Mau Mau in Kenya*. Houndsmills & London: MacMillan Publishers.

Mathu, George. 1971. *Gikuyu Marriage: Beliefs and Practices*. Nairobi: Institute of African Studies.

Mbilinyi, Marjorie. 1985. "Struggles Concerning Sexuality Among Female Youth." In *Women and Development in Africa*, edited by G.S. Were. Nairobi: Gideon Were Press.

———. 1992. "Research Methodologies in Gender Issues." In *Gender in Southern Africa*, edited by Ruth Meena. Harare: SAPES Trust.

Merritt, Gary. 1984. Interview. Nairobi, October 8.

Middleton, John. 1953. *The Central Tribes of the North-Eastern Bantu*. London: International African Institute.

Mirza, Sarah, and Margaret Strobel, eds. 1989. *Three Swahili Women: Life Histories from Mombasa, Kenya*. Bloomington & Indianapolis: Indiana University Press.

Moock, Joyce, ed. 1986. *Understanding Africa's Rural Households and Farming Systems*. Boulder: Westview Press.

Moore, Henrietta L. 1986. *Space, Text and Gender: An Anthropological Study of the Marakwet of Kenya*. Cambridge: Cambridge University Press.

Muchena, O. 1979. "The Changing Position of African Women in Rural Zimbabwe," *Zimbabwe Journal of Economics* 1(1):50–56.

Mullings, Leith. 1976. "Women and Economic Change in Africa." In *Women in Africa*, edited by N. Hafkin and E. Bay. Stanford: Stanford University Press.
Muriuki, Godfrey. 1974. *A History of the Kikuyu: 1500–1900.* Nairobi: Oxford University Press.
Murray, Jocelyn. 1974. "The Kikuyu Female Circumcision Controversy." Unpublished Ph.D. dissertation. Los Angeles: University of California at Los Angeles.
Mutemba, Maud. 1977. "Thwarted Development: A Case Study of Economic Change in Kabwe Rural District of Zambia, 1902–70." In *The Roots of Poverty in Central and Southern Africa*, edited by R.H. Palmer and N. Parsons. London: Heinemann Books.
Mwale, G., and P. Burnard. 1992. *Women and AIDS in Rural Africa: Rural Women's Views of AIDS in Zambia.* Aldershot: Avebury.
Nasimiyu, Ruth. 1985. "Women in the Colonial Economy of Bungoma: Role of Women in Agriculture: 1902–1960." In *Women and Development in Africa*, edited by G.S. Were. Nairobi: Gideon Were Press.
Neugarten, Beatrice, and Nancy Datan. 1973. "Sociological Perspectives on the Life Cycle." In *Life-Span Developmental Psychology*, edited by P. Baltes and K.W. Schaie. New York: Academic Press.
Ngaiza, M., and B. Koda. 1991. *Unsung Heroines.* Dar es Salaam: WRDP, University of Dar Salaam.
Nicholson, Linda. 1994. "Integrating Gender," *SIGNS* 20(1):79–105.
Obbo, Christine. 1980. *African Women: Their Struggle for Economic Independence.* London: Zed Press.
———. 1982. "The Effects of Land Tenure Change upon Women in East African Smallholder Agriculture." Paper presented at the Colloquium on Issues in African Land Tenure. Land Tenure Center, University of Wisconsin at Madison.
Oboler, Regina S. 1985. *Women, Power and Economic Change: The Nandi of Kenya.* Stanford: Stanford University Press.
Okali, Christine. 1983. *Cocoa and Kinship in Ghana: The Matrilineal Akan of Ghana.* London & Boston: Kegan Paul.
Opie, Anne. 1993. "Qualitative Research, Appropriation of the 'Other' and Empowerment," *Feminist Review* 19(1):52–69.
Oppong, Christine. 1983. *Male and Female in West Africa.* London: George Allen & Unwin.
O'Tuathail, G., and J. Agnew. 1992. "Geopolitics and Discourse," *Political Geography* 11:190–204.
Pala, Achola. 1976. *African Women in Rural Development: Research Trends and Priorities.* Washington, D.C.: Overseas Liaison Committee, Paper No. 12, American Council on Education.
———. 1978. *Women's Access to Land and Their Role in Agriculture and Decision-making on the Farm: Experiences of the Joluo of Kenya.* Nairobi: Institute for Development Studies, University of Nairobi.
Perham, Marjorie, ed. 1936. *Ten Africans.* London: Faber & Faber.
Personal Narratives Group. 1989. *Interpreting Women's Lives: Feminist Theory and Personal Narratives.* Bloomington: Indiana University Press.
Phillips, Anne. 1992. "Universal Pretensions in Political Thought." In *Destabilizing Theory: Contemporary Feminist Debates.* Stanford: Stanford University Press.
Plummer, Ken. 1983. *Documents of Life.* London: George Allen & Unwin.
Poewe, Karla. 1981. *Matrilineal Ideology.* New York: Academic Press.

Presley, Cora A. 1992. *Kikuyu Women, the Mau Mau Rebellion, and Social Change in Kenya.* Boulder: Westview Press.

Riegel, Klaus F. 1975. "Adult Life Crises: A Dialectic Interpretation of Development." In *Life Span Development: Normative Life Crises*, edited by N. Datan and L. Ginsberg. New York: Academic Press.

Romero, Patricia W., ed. 1988. *Life Histories of African Women.* London: The Ashfield Press.

Rosaldo, Michelle Z. 1974. "Women, Culture, and Society: A Theoretical Overview." In *Women, Culture and Society*, edited by M. Rosaldo and L. Lamphere. Stanford: Stanford University Press.

Rosaldo, Renato. 1976. "The Story of Tukbaw: 'They Listen as He Orates.'" In *The Biographical Process*, edited by F. Reynolds and D. Crapps. The Hague: Mouton.

Rosberg, Carl, and J. Nottingham. 1966. *The Myth of Mau Mau: Nationalism in Kenya.* New York: Meridian Books.

Routledge, William S., and Katherine Routledge. 1910. *With a Prehistoric People: The Agikuyu of East Africa.* London: Edward Arnold.

Sachs, Wulf. 1937. *Black Hamlet: The Mind of an African Negro Revealed by Psychoanalysis.* London: Geoffrey Books.

Said, Edward. 1989. "Representing the Colonized: Anthropology's Interlocutors," *Critical Inquiry*, 15:205–225.

Salmond, Anne. 1975. *Amiria: The Life Story of a Maori Woman.* Wellington, N.Z.: A.H. & A.W. Reed.

Sanday, Peggy R. 1974. "Female Status In the Public Domain." In *Women, Culture and Society*, edited by M. Rosaldo & L. Lamphere. Stanford: Stanford University Press.

Sangren, David P. 1982. "Twentieth Century Religious and Political Divisions Among the Kikuyu of Kenya," *African Studies Review*, 25(2/3):195–207.

Shostak, Marjorie. 1981. *Nisa: The Life and Words of a !Kung Woman.* Cambridge, Mass.: Harvard University Press.

Skjønsberg, Else. 1989. *Change in an African Village: Kefa Speaks.* West Hartford, Conn.: Kumarian Press.

Smith, Mary F. 1954. *Baba of Karo: A Woman of the Muslim Hausa.* London: Faber & Faber.

Stamp, Patricia. 1986. "Kikuyu Women's Self-help Groups." In *Women and Class in Africa*, edited by C. Robertson and I. Berger. New York: Holmes & Meier.

Stanley, Liz. 1992. *The Auto/Biographical I: The Theory and Practice of Feminist Auto/Biography.* Manchester & New York: Manchester University Press.

———. 1994. "The Knowing Because Experiencing Subject: Narratives, Lives and Autobiography." In *Knowing the Difference: Feminist Perspectives in Epistemology*, edited by K. Lennon and M. Whitford. New York & London: Routledge.

Staunton, Irene. 1992. *Mothers of the Revolution: The War Experiences of Thirty Zimbabwean Women.* Harare: Baobab Books.

Strichter, Sharon. 1975/76. "Women and the Labor Force in Kenya 1875–1964." *Rural Africana* 29:56–61.

Sudarkasa, Niara. 1976. "Female Employment and Family Organization in West Africa." In *New Research on Women and Sex Roles*, edited by D. McGuigan. Ann Arbor: University of Michigan Center for Continuing Education on Women.

Tignor, Robert L. 1976. *The Colonial Transformation of Kenya.* Princeton: Princeton University Press.

Turnbull, Colin M. 1986. "Sex and Gender: The Role of Subjectivity in Field Research." In *Self, Sex, and Gender in Cross-cultural Fieldwork*, edited by T.L. Whitehead and M. Conaway. Urbana & Chicago: University of Illinois Press.
Turner, Victor. 1969. *The Ritual Process*. Ithaca: Cornell University Press.
UNDP. 1994. *Human Development Report—1994*. New York & Oxford: Oxford University Press.
UNICEF. 1990. *Status of the World's Children—1990*. New York: UNICEF.
———. 1994. *Status of the World's Children—1994*. New York: UNICEF.
Van Gennep, Arnold. 1960 (1908). *Rites of Passage*. New York: Vintage Press.
Vizedom, Monika. 1976. *Rites and Relationships: Rites of Passage and Contemporary Anthropology*. Beverly Hills: Sage Publications.
Wachanga, H.K. 1975. *The Swords of Kirinyaga: The Fight for Land and Freedom*. Nairobi: East Africa Publishing House.
Waciuma, Charity. 1969. *Daughter of Mumbi*. Nairobi: East Africa Publishing House.
wa Thiong'o, Ngugi. 1965. *The River Between*. London: Heinemann.
———. 1967. *A Grain of Wheat*. London: Heinemann.
———. 1977. *Petals of Blood*. London: Heinemann.
Whipper, Audrey. 1975/76. "The Maendeleo ya Wanawake Movement in the Colonial Period." *Rural Africana* 29:195–213.
White, Luise. 1990. *The Comforts of Home: Prostitution in Colonial Nairobi*. Chicago: Chicago University Press.
Whitehead, Tony L., and Mary E. Conaway. 1986. "Introduction." In *Self, Sex and Gender in Crosscultural Fieldwork*, edited by T.L. Whitehead and M. Conaway. Urbana & Chicago: University of Chicago Press.
Winter, Edward H. 1965. *Beyond the Mountains of the Moon: The Lives of Four Africans*. Urbana: University of Illinois Press.
World Bank. 1994. *Trends in Developing Economies*. Washington, D.C.: World Bank.
Worthman, Carol M. 1985. "Social Management of Developmental Differences: Kikuyu Adolescents." Paper presented at the American Anthropological Association meeting, Washington, D.C., December 5, 1985.
Worthman, Carol, and John Whiting. 1987. "Social Change in Adolescent Sexual Behaviour, Mate Selection and Premarital Pregnancy Rates in a Kikuyu Community," *Ethnos* 15(2):145–165.

About the Book

To update this rich, informative collection of life histories, Davison returned to Mutira in 1989, 1992, and 1994, documenting the changes occurring since her 1984 study. Six of the seven life histories in the first edition have been expanded to reflect the events of the last decade. Two new introductory chapters frame the life histories within the context both of the significant macrolevel transitions in Kenya and the current thinking about gender and the development process.

The seven women who are the focus of the book describe, with dignity, candor, and often humor, their own views of the often turbulent historical and sociocultural forces influencing their individual and collective lives. They discuss—from differing points of view—such feminist issues as female circumcision, polygyny, family violence, and experiences of mothering. And spanning nearly a century, their histories illuminate critical moments in Kenya's past.

Jean Davison is a consultant for the Education Development Center in Washington, D.C., and was formerly coordinator of the Gender and Development Graduate Program at the University of Malawi, and a visiting scholar at Stanford University. She is the author of *Agriculture, Women, and Land: The African Experience* (1988), and *Gender, Ethnicity and Lineage in Southern Africa* (forthcoming).